BRITISH CANOE UNION

GUIDE
TO THE WATERWAYS
OF THE
BRITISH ISLES

1966

(Copyright)

Printed by Pullingers Ltd., 56 High Street, Epsom, Surrey—4133

British Canoe Union

Headquarters :
26-29 Park Crescent, London, W.1

FIRST EDITION 1936

SECOND EDITION 1951

THIRD EDITION 1961

reprinted 1964

Partially revised and reprinted 1966

FOREWORD

SINCE THE PUBLICATION of the 1951 edition of the Guide to Waterways of the British Isles the membership of the British Canoe Union has greatly increased, and there are a great many canoeists who do not belong to a club. The majority are interested in touring. Consequently the demand for the Guide has increased every year and a new printing is now required.

The Union have always regarded the provision of touring information as being one of their most important services to their members and it is a great pleasure to me to commend this revised edition both to them and other canoeists who seek information about the waterways of the British Isles.

In doing so I should like to emphasise again, both to members of the Union, and to others who may read or use this book, as both my predecessors have done, the importance of upholding the good reputation of the sport through their behaviour and by avoiding all foolhardy actions. Like them, too, I would appeal to all canoeists to help to create and increase the goodwill of the Union by respecting land and water rights and other people's property at all times, also their feelings by courtesy and appropriate dress, and emphasise the importance for canoeists to become good swimmers, not only for their own sake, but for the sake of others who may have to risk their lives in trying to rescue them.

JOHN W. DUDDERIDGE
President

ACKNOWLEDGMENTS

The British Canoe Union gratefully acknow-
ledges the help given by various public and
private bodies who have furnished information
on various subjects : the Scottish Canoe
Association, who have been responsible for
the Scottish section: and many members of
clubs affiliated to the Union and to the Scottish
Canoe Association, who have supplied the
bulk of the matter now included in this Guide

CONTENTS

PREFACE

It has always been the British Canoe Union's aim to offer its members complete and accurate information about *all* the canoeable waterways of the British Isles. The 1936 edition set a high standard and was necessarily incomplete, being, as stated in its preface "the result of actual canoeing experience." A revised and much enlarged edition based, so far as was possible, on reports from canoeists who had canoed on the waters in question, was published in 1951. In order to be as comprehensive as possible descriptions were included of some that were not known to have been canoed in recent years, and also of a number of canals and estuaries which offer promising canoeing ground.

The 1951 edition was amended in 1961 and has again been partially revised from reports that have been received in the past six years, and many corrections of detail have been included.

On slow-moving rivers, weirs, sluices and locks decay, are repaired or rebuilt, but if the information given turns out to be out of date, little risk to the canoeist results. With rapid rivers it is otherwise. Here again wherever information has been received every effort has been made to correct the old itineraries. Where details are lacking there is a note in the text, and the description has been confined to a mileage table or general information on the character of the river without attempting to introduce details of particular hazards.

It is believed that this process has not led to any lowering of the standards adopted in the 1936 edition, but it must be made clear that the Union does not claim that the result is free from errors. Every guide book starts to get out of date from the day it is published, and canoeists must therefore be prepared to find that conditions have changed and in particular should not blindly push on down a hazard on the strength of the description in the Guide without seeing for themselves and making up their own minds after inspection.

The Union urges that *all* errors and omissions found by canoeists using the Guide (whether members of the Union or not) should immediately be reported to the Touring Secretary, c/o B.C.U. Headquarters, 26-29 Park Crescent, London, W.1.

GENERAL INTRODUCTION

Maps. In the sections covering England, Wales and Scotland, "O.S." followed by a number is the sheet number of the Ordnance Survey 1-inch Seventh Edition with the National Grid. In Ireland "O.S." refers to the ½-inch layered edition. "Barth" refers to Bartholomew's Half-Inch Coloured series covering England, Wales and Scotland. Irish O.S. maps are obtainable from Stanford's, Long Acre, London, W.C.2, or from The Map House, 67 St. James's Street, London, S.W.1.

Charts. For estuary canoeing it is valuable to have a chart as well as a 1-inch O.S. map. References are given in the text to the special yachtsmen's chart as follows :

> "St. 6" — Stanford's Coloured Charts for Coastal Navigators No. 6, edited by Capt. O. M. Watts, F.R.A.S., A.I.N.A. Obtainable from Stanford's, Long Acre, London, W.C.2, or from Capt. O. M. Watts, Ltd., 49 Albemarle Street, London, W.1, or from any good map shop.
>
> "Y.20" or "C.23" — charts of the "Y" and "C" series, published by Imray and Wilson (Yachting) Ltd., 143 Cannon Street, London, E.C.4, or any good map shop.

Both series can be recommended, as they are of manageable size, brightly coloured to indicate low-water line, shallow and deep water, and include much information of value to the canoeist that is not on the larger Admiralty Charts used by the Merchant Navy. They also give times of High Water by reference to Dover, the rise of tides at springs and neaps, and the direction and speed of tidal streams from hour to hour.

Tidal Constants. To obtain the London Bridge constant from the Dover constants given in the Guide, remember that High Water London Bridge is 2 hours 39 minutes *later* than Dover. Therefore, if using Tide Tables for London Bridge instead of for Dover, *decrease* a + Dover constant and *increase* a — Dover constant by 2 hours 39 minutes.

Tide Tables. Times of high water at Dover or London Bridge, or both, are published every day in most national newspapers. Times of high water at Dover and the mean range of the tide for every day in the year are published by the Admiralty about the end of November each year. They can be obtained on a single sheet of gummed paper, which can be stuck into one or more of the blank pages in the Guide, from Messrs. J. D. Potter, 145 The Minories, London, E.C.3, price 2d. (without postage), or on a small folding card from Arthur Beale Ltd., Yacht Chandlers, 194 Shaftesbury Avenue, London, W.C.2, and from other yacht chandlers. In making calculations, do not forget to allow for Summer Time.

Closure of railway stations. In the itineraries railway stations have been omitted where there are no passenger services. Some of those still mentioned may be closed during the currency of the present edition of the Guide. Inquiry should therefore be made beforehand.

Terms used

Aegre, Bore. The tidal wave on the Trent and Welland, or the Severn, Parret and Welsh Dee, respectively.

Backlash. A wave rising against the sweep of the current, e.g. where fast water meets still water, as at the foot of a weir; sometimes also where fast water runs against fixed obstacles; a "stopper."

Broken Water. Water breaking on rocks, reefs or rocky shelves; as with backlash, the boat's speed is checked; the force, direction and buoyancy of the water are difficult to judge.

Cataract. A stepped fall in level with obstacles such as boulders and ledges and accompanied by "broken water."

Eddy. Slack water moving round in a circle when the main stream flows past a bay, or a bend, or a large rock. Current fastest at the outside; centre slack, and the water hardly changes. Often provide the best landings on really fast, heavy rivers. Opposite of "whirlpool."

Lifting over. Bringing the boat up against the obstacle, e.g. the top of a weir, and carrying *over*.

Lining down. Climbing out of the boat and floating it over or down the obstacle, e.g. a weir, or shallows, by means of the painter.

Portage. Landing before an obstacle and carrying the boat *round*.

Rapid. May refer to anything from a slight quickening of the current to a really heavy succession of waves, but in most cases minor rapids in the former sense are not mentioned.

Raft Channel (on the Continent). An inclined plane at the side of a weir over which the water can be made to flow so that lumber rafts can pass downstream.

Staff Gauge. A post erected against the bank of a river or a bridge, and calibrated to show the water level.

Whirlpool. A pillar of water turning on a well marked axis; fastest at the centre, with a continual change of water. The opposite of "eddy."

Grading of Rivers according to Difficulty (international system)
Rough Water (RW or WW)

    I. *Easy.* Occasional small rapids, waves regular and low. Correct course easy to find, but care is needed with obstacles like pebble banks, protective works, fallen trees, etc., especially on narrow rivers.

II.   *Medium*. Fairly frequent rapids, usually with regular waves, easy eddies, or whirlpools. Course generally easy to recognise. (On the Continent : easy and medium raft channels.)

III.   *Difficult*. Rapids numerous, and with fairly high, irregular waves, broken water, eddies and whirlpools. Course not always easily recognisable. (Difficult raft channels.)

IV.   *Very Difficult*. Long and extended stretches of rapids with high irregular waves, difficult broken water, eddies and whirlpools. Course often difficult to recognise. Inspection from the bank nearly always necessary. (Very difficult raft channels.)

V.   *Exceedingly Difficult*. Long unbroken stretches of rapids with difficult and completely irregular broken water, submerged rocks, very difficult whirlpools and very fast eddies. Previous inspection absolutely essential.

VI.   *The absolute limit of difficulty*. All previously mentioned difficulties increased to the limit of practicability. Cannot be attempted without risk to life.

Notes on Grading

1.   If a particular length of river falls between two of the above grades, or alternates between a lower and a higher grade, and portaging round the more difficult parts would not make a continuation of the trip worth while, two numbers are used, e.g. II-III.

2.   If a length of river offers at one or two individual points (where a portage is easy) difficulties beyond its average grading, the higher grade of difficulty is shown as an index figure, e.g. II_4.

3.   A rise or fall in water level always alters a river's appearance and the rating of the stretch in question, and may make it easier or quite impracticable in difficulty. The grading given is as far as possible that for "favourable" water conditions.

"Rough water" trips should not be undertaken unless the canoeist can swim well, has a craft in sound order, and good technique and boat control ; there should always be at least one other boat.

Newcomers to "rough water" rivers should not attempt anything beyond R.W.III, and there should be an experienced leader and an appropriate number of boats. R.W.IV is a real testing, even for experienced canoeists. Rough Water V and VI should not be touched except by the most experienced wild water canoeists ; itineraries and maps can only give very general directions, and there may be a real danger of loss of life.

A WORD ABOUT SAFETY

DON'T canoe if you cannot swim.

    DO provide buoyancy : always have air-bags in your boat, and a life-jacket for yourself where a capsize would be dangerous—in the sea, heavy rapids, floods and cold water.

    DO ask about local conditions : tides, currents, rapids and weather changes can all be dangerous.

DON'T go out alone without having told someone where you are going and how long you think you will be.

DON'T put more people in a canoe than it is designed to carry.

DON'T wear wellingtons—you cannot swim in heavy boots.

DON'T change places.

    DO keep clear of other craft.

    DO keep away from weirs—they are often dangerous.

DON'T right a capsized canoe—hang on to it. It will float and you may not.

DON'T be put off by this list—it is all common-sense really.

    DO remember—better safe than sorry.

B.C.U. CANOEING PROFICIENCY TESTS

Three levels of test : novice, proficiency and advanced proficiency tests (inland) open to non-members as well as members of the Union have been established by the British Canoe Union for both Kayaks and Canadian canoes. Sea proficiency and advanced sea tests have also been established for kayaks only. The inland proficiency test is intended to show whether the candidate has sufficient knowledge of boat management and watermanship to meet minor hazards of normal easy canoe-touring without becoming a burden or a risk to his companions. The advanced test requires the attainment of general all-round competence in the use of the type of canoe concerned and ability to lead a tour.

Certificates and badges are awarded to successful candidates. For proficiency in the advanced test with one type of canoe the colour is silver ; for proficiency with both types, gold.

Enquiries about the tests and the fees for taking them should be addressed to the Coaching Secretary, c/o B.C.U., 26-29 Park Crescent, London, W.1. The details of the tests are subject to revision and alteration at any time.

INLAND PROFICIENCY TEST
(Kayak or Canadian)
(1965)

If possible the test will be taken on a river flowing smoothly at a speed of not less than 3 m.p.h., not in a swimming bath. Candidates must have a working knowledge of some appropriate knots.

1. The candidate will swim 50 yards in light clothing (e.g. shirt, shorts and gym shoes without a life-jacket). He will swim under a canoe and come up on the other side.

2. The candidate will present his canoe and certain specified items of equipment for inspection when they are ready for use.

3. The candidate will pack the canoe as if in preparation for a journey of two or three days.

4. The candidate will handle his canoe into the water, and the canoe will be made fast to the bank and left.

5. The candidate will get into his canoe from the bank, and will put out into midstream.

6. The candidate will paddle his canoe upstream a distance of about 50 yards. He will then turn and paddle back to his starting point. In a Canadian canoe he must not at any time change the paddle over from one side to the other.

13

7. (*Kayaks*). He will carry out two Ferry Glides, one facing downstream, and one facing upstream.

8. (*Kayaks*). He will demonstrate the following paddling strokes : sweep, draw, recovery of balance by slap support, sculling for support, sculling draw.
(*Canadians*). On reaching his starting point the candidate will stop the way of the canoe and propel it sideways to the bank.

9. He will capsize his loaded canoe in midstream, come to the bank with the canoe, and empty out the water.

10. He will re-embark, standing in water not less than knee-deep. He will then return to the bank, disembark and take the canoe out of the water.

Note. In items Nos. 2, 4, 9 and 10, the candidate may have assistance if he so desires.

INLAND ADVANCED CANOEING TEST
(Kayak and Canadian)
(1965)

Syllabus

1. The candidate wishing to take the Advanced Test in either Kayak or Canadian Canoe must have previously passed the Proficiency Test in the same type of canoe.

2. He must have a good working knowledge of safety measures on the water, have a working knowledge of knots, and their proper uses.

3. He must know and be able to demonstrate all the strokes normally used in the canoe that he is using (Kayak or Canadian).

4. The candidate must be able to carry out a practical canoeing test as the examiner requires. He must also, in the case of the Kayak, be able to do an Eskimo roll.

5. He must be able to carry out repairs to his canoe. He must be able to carry out proper routine maintenance of his canoe.

6. He must know the international grading system for rapid rivers and be familiar with rapid river techniques needed on rivers up to Grade III. He must be competent to take his canoe on canals and estuaries.

7. He must have a general knowledge of matters appertaining to the practice of the sport of canoeing, including the principles of slalom and racing.

8. He must be able to give a good demonstration of pairs technique with a competent partner.

9. He must have a good general knowledge of the types of canoe in use, essential equipment, and should have made canoe expeditions of an advanced nature.

Details of the Novice, Sea Proficiency and Advanced Sea Tests can be obtained from the Coaching Secretary.

THE LEGAL RIGHTS OF CANOEISTS ON INLAND WATERS

By a Solicitor

To the question whether a person has a right to take a canoe or any other boat on a river or lake, the answer is generally simple. If the place where he wishes to go is tidal, *i.e.*, affected by the ebb and flow of the ordinary tides, he has a right ; if not, he has no right.

To the first (positive) proposition there are probably no exceptions. Tidal waters are public highways, and the rights of the public cannot be taken away or abridged by anything short of an Act of Parliament.

To the second (negative) proposition there are, fortunately, some exceptions. In principle non-tidal rivers and lakes are the private property of the owners of the bed, and canoeing on them without permission is trespass. But just as a public right of way can exist, and can still be acquired, over a private field, so it can exist or be acquired over a private river or lake. Legally the pedestrian and the canoeist are in the same position. The practical difference arises from the fact that, while there are thousands of footpaths, there are only a few rivers over which the public have acquired the right of passage.

In some non-tidal rivers the right of navigation has been given by Act of Parliament. The most notable examples are the Thames below Cricklade, the Severn and the Wye. But such cases are rare, and where there is no Act of Parliament, it must be proved, in order to establish a public right of way, that the owner of the river or lake has dedicated it, or must be presumed to have dedicated it to the public. This had been done in a few cases, such as certain of the Norfolk Broads, the Severn, and Ullswater ; in other cases the public right is not disputed, though it has never been tested in a Court of Law. The task of proving dedication, always difficult, was made a little less difficult by the Rights of Way Act, 1932, which provided that proof of 20 years' uninterrupted use of a way as of right by the public shall be conclusive evidence of its dedication unless there is sufficient evidence on the other side that there was no intention to dedicate. This applies to waterways as well as land ways. This provision is now included in Section 34 of the Highways Act 1959.

When all is said and done there are many rivers and lakes of interest to canoeists, where there is no public right of way. In these cases the proper course is to obtain permission from the owner.

For the purpose of ownership of the bed, non-tidal rivers must be thought of as divided into two halves by a line down the centre. Originally the ownership of each half went with the ownership of the land on that side, and this is still so in most cases. But the ownership of either half of the bed may have become separated from the ownership of the adjoining land, and in such cases it will be presumed, unless the contrary is proved, to belong to the owner of the fishing rights. In the upper waters of rivers it is quite usual to find both banks belonging to the same owner, who is also the owner of the fishing rights. In other places the fishing rights over both halves of the river may be in the same ownership, although the banks belong to different owners. In either of these events only one person's permission will be required for taking a canoe down the part of the river in question. Elsewhere two persons' consent will be required.

In non-tidal lakes the position is similar except that the centre line will be more difficult to fix.

ADVICE ABOUT PARTICULAR WATERS

From time to time the Union learns of landowners and owners of fishing rights who object to canoeing altogether or who will permit it only at certain times of the year. On many rivers where the legal position is doubtful canoeists are in practice not challenged.

If challenged, remember that you are likely to be in the wrong—or at least unable to prove a right of passage. There is no justification for indignation or bluster. Argument is out of place, and you must be prepared to move off if the owner or his agent asks you to do so. Discourtesy will probably prejudice even friendly landowners against canoeing and cause them to refuse permission later on to others. If you ask and are refused permission for a stretch, do not try to canoe it without—it will be treated as gross discourtesy or even open defiance, and can only do harm to the reputation of the sport.

16

Experience shows that canoeing is challenged most often on rivers and lakes where salmon or trout fishing is an important item in the income of the estate. Some fly-fishermen pay a lot to fish a stretch of river and believe that the passage of a canoe will ruin the fishing for hours ; whether this is so or not, it is clearly good manners on a river where a narrow channel or pool is being fished to ask the fisherman whether he is ready for you to pass—whether there is a right of navigation, or you have the owner's permission, or not. If you have no permission where there is no clear right of navigation, you should be even more considerate.

On rivers where passage is challenged, permission is most likely to be given and difficulty avoided if the trip is arranged during the close fishing season. For fly-fishing this is approximately October to the end of February. For coarse fishing it is March to mid-June. On salmon and trout streams Easter and Whitsuntide are best avoided altogether, because they are at the height of the fishing season.

The Union invites canoeists, both members and non-members, to inform them of objections to canoeing. The B.C.U. Touring Committee has appointed a number of "River Advisers", each responsible for an area of England and Wales, to collate such information and advise members about attempting certain rivers where objection has been especially frequent or where the owners have made it known that they wish always to be approached beforehand for permission. The chief ones are—Eden, Lune, Ribble, Dee, Wharfe, Teme, Usk, Wye above Glasbury, Monnow, Salisbury Avon. Others are noted in the description in the Guide. The River Advisers' addresses are given each year in the March issue of *Canoeing in Britain*.

Before planning a trip on any of these rivers members and non-members who are using this book are asked to write to the appropriate River Adviser, or, if there is none for the area in question, to the Home Touring Adviser, B.C.U., 26-29 Park Crescent, London, W.1 (enclosing a stamped addressed envelope). They will advise whether a trip at the time proposed is advisable, and who should be approached for permission. Please abide by the advice given. It is the Union's hope that by seeking and maintaining the goodwill of owners and fishermen it will be possible to build up the feeling that canoeing and fishing are not incompatible sports.

MISCELLANEOUS

TRANSPORT OF CANOES BY RAIL & RAILWAY STEAMERS

Folding canoes packed in their bags and detached from the boat-trolley and weighing up to 60 lb. (27 kg.) are accepted by British Railways within the ordinary passenger's free personal luggage allowance of 100 lb. (45 kg.) on a 2nd-class ticket ; camping gear is also accepted within this free allowance. This applies also to the railway-owned steamer services on the West Coast of Scotland (including MacBrayne's), to Ireland and the Continent, but not in Ireland, on Continental railways or on the London Underground. Like ordinary luggage they can also be sent "Passenger Luggage in Advance," at the usual rates.

Rigid canoes and folding canoes when erected are conveyed in the ordinary luggage vans (if long enough) on passenger trains and charged for at the "Exceptional Owner's Risk Rate" (G.2 Ex) for parcels by passenger train ; charges vary according to weight and distance. Higher rates may be charged for boats over about 14 feet and may vary from Region to Region.

Canoes can also be sent by Goods Train if there is plenty of time.

Passenger fares by rail in England, Wales and Scotland are (1965) about 3d. a mile (approx.) 2nd-class.

CROSS-CHANNEL TRANSPORT TO THE CONTINENT

Folding canoes in their bags are accepted at London and the ports as ordinary baggage for registration by railway steamer services to Continental destinations. Within certain weight limits they are subject only to the registration charge as far as the Continental port of arrival. Charges for the Continental railway section of a journey vary from nothing to appreciable sums based on weight and distance. It is always advisable to inquire at Victoria or Liverpool Street stations, London, whether it is more advantageous to register the baggage through to the frontier station of the country of destination, where Customs clearance has usually to take place in any case. If registering through to a destination in France beyond Paris allow an extra 48 hours, because of transport across Paris, to make sure the baggage is waiting at destination when you arrive.

CAR FERRIES

Rigid canoes on car roofs and boat trailers are accepted on the car ferries run by the British, French and Belgian railways and on the B.R. car ferries to Ireland. The usual car and trailer rates apply, but the charge depends on the overall length of the longest boat if it is longer than the car or trailer concerned.

On private company ferries and steamers the basis of charge is not uniform, and enquiries should be made before reserving car space.

CANAL CHARGES (1966)

Canoes are classified as "Unpowered Vessels Class D" and "Powered Vessels under 25 feet Class C" if driven by outboard motor. Licences are given for fixed periods and cover all parts of the canals and navigations under the control of British Waterways, including the Gloucester and Sharpness Canal, the Crinan and Caledonian Canals, and other Scottish Canals.

Period			Unpowered Class D (without locks) £ s. d.			Unpowered Class D (with locks) £ s. d.			Powered Class C (under 25ft.) £ s. d.		
12 months	...	...	2	10	0	5	0	0	12	0	0
9 months	...	...	2	5	0	4	10	0	11	0	0
6 months	...	...	2	0	0	4	0	0	10	0	0
3 months	...	...	1	15	0	3	0	0	7	0	0
1 month	...	...		15	0	1	10	0	3	0	0
1 week	...	...		7	6		15	0	1	10	0

Licences for unpowered craft do not cover passage through tunnels unless special permission has been given. Licences will not be issued to persons under 16 years of age.

Application should be made on the printed form BW/C80, obtainable from British Waterways, Willow Grange, Church Road, Watford, Herts.

Class D period licences covering the use of locks are valid for the locks on river navigations under the control of British Waterways (Severn, Trent, Foss Dike and Witham, Lea and Stort), but canoeists without such licences can pay lock fees (given under the appropriate section in the itinerary) if they use the locks on these navigations.

Special rates *may* be granted for special purposes or for groups of canoes, e.g. youth groups, according to merits of the case. Application should be made to British Waterways.

Charges for navigations and canals *not* under British Waterways are given in the text of the guide, where known.

WORKING LOCKS

The usual way of working single locks is as follows :

To fill an empty lock (the paddles in the top gates and any ground paddles at the head of the lock will be closed):

1. Close bottom gates.
2. See that bottom gate paddles are closed.
3. Open ground paddle (if there is one).
4. Open top gate paddles (if the ground paddle has been opened, wait till the gate paddles are submerged before opening them).
5. When full, open top gates.

To empty a full lock :

1. Close top gates.
2. See that top gate paddles and ground paddle (if there is one) are closed.
3. Open bottom gate paddles.
4. When lock has emptied, open bottom gates.

Close paddles when leaving locks.

Staircase locks are more complicated to operate. Full directions are given in the British Waterways Cruising booklets.

Locks take up a good deal of time ; usually it is much quicker to portage them.

CANAL GUIDES

Illustrated Inland Cruising Booklets are published by British Waterways, Melbury House, Melbury Terrace, London, N.W.1, price 3s. 6d., for most of the canals and navigations under their control. They contain detailed diagrams with landmarks, mileages, locks, etc., and a description of the country traversed.

No.
1. Llangollen Canal.
2. Trent Waterway (Shardlow to Gainsborough).
3. Lee and Stort Navigations.
4. Staffs. and Worcs. Canal (past Autherley Jn. to Stourport— see No. 13).
5. Shropshire Union Canal.
6. Oxford Canal (Napton Jn. to Oxford).
7. Foss Dike and Witham Navigations.
8. Grand Union Canal (London to Braunston Jn.).
9. Grand Union Canal (Braunston Jn. to Birmingham); Birmingham and Fazeley Canal ; and parts of the Coventry and Oxford Canals.
10. Grand Union Canal (Norton Jn. to Trent Lock, including the Soar Navigation).
11. Macclesfield Canal.

12. Trent and Mersey Canal (Trent Lock to Great Haywood Jn.); and part of Coventry Canal (from Fradley Jn. to Fazeley Jn.).

13. Trent and Mersey Canal (Preston Brook to Gt. Haywood Jn.); and part of Staffs and Worcs Canal (from Gt. Haywood Jn. to Autherley Jn.—see No. 4).

14. Severn Waterway (Sharpness to Stourport) and Worcester and Birmingham Canal and part of Stratford-on-Avon Canal.

KILOMETRE CONVERSION TABLE

⅝ mile	=	1	km.	4 miles	=	6·4	km.
¼ ,,	=	0·4	,,	5 ,	=	8·0	,,
½ ,.	=	0·8	,,	6 ,	=	9·7	,,
¾ ,,	=	1·2	,,	7 ,,	=	11·3	,,
1 ,	=	1·6	,	8 ,	=	12·9	,,
2 ,,	=	3·2	,,	9 ,,	=	14·5	,,
3 ,,	=	4·8	.,	10 ,.	=	16·1	,,

FILMS ON CANOEING—(the B.C.U. film library)—available on hire (16mm. and 8mm.) from the Booking Manager, Distribution Department, British Film Institute, 81 Dean Street, London W.1. List on request.

FILM LOOPS—half or quarter speed—16mm., or 8mm., from C. M. Rothwell, c/o B.C.U., 26-29 Park Crescent, London, W.1. Mark envelopes "Film loops". Send stamp for full list.
Slalom Technique : 4 loops showing different strokes.
Eskimo Rolling : 3 loops showing different methods.
Racing Technique : 16 loops showing various exponents.

FILM STRIP—with notes—35mm.: Canoe Building, £1. 0s. 0d., from C. M. Rothwell, c/o B.C.U., 26-29 Park Crescent, London, W.1. Mark envelopes "Film Strip".

CANOE MAGAZINES

Canoeing in Britain : the B.C.U. Bulletin, normally quarterly. Sent free to Full and Youth Members of the Union.

Canoeing—monthly. 1s. 3d. per copy, 15s. per annum, post free, from Canoeing Publications, 6 The Mall, Brentford, Middlesex.

Canoe-Camper—quarterly magazine of the Canoe-Camping Club ; available to non-members for 7s. 6d. per annum, post free, from the Editor, Canoe-Camper, c/o Camping Club of Great Britain and Ireland, 11 Lower Grosvenor Place, London, S.W.1.

White Water : white water touring and slalom ; quarterly, 10s. per annum, post free, from C. M. Rothwell, 21 Windsor Road, Clayton Bridge, Manchester, 10.

THE BRITISH CANOE UNION AND MEMBERSHIP

The Union

The B.C.U. is the governing body of the sport of canoeing in Great Britain and Northern Ireland. There are two Divisions (i.e. national associations of canoe clubs outside England) which organise canoeing on the Union's behalf, namely the Scottish Canoe Association and the Canoe Association of Northern Ireland.

The B.C.U. is affiliated to the International Canoe Federation and represents the interests of British canoeists in International canoeing affairs.

The B.C.U. represents the needs of canoeists to the Sports Council, Government Departments and local authorities. Clubs can made representations to their Regional Sports Council through the B.C.U. Regional or County Representative.

The B.C.U. is actively campaigning for improved facilities for recreational use of water by canoeists and for extended access to inland water.

The B.C.U. works to further the interests of the cruising canoeist and negotiates with river authorities, local authorities and land-owners regarding the use of water and scales of charges when applicable.

The B.C.U. maintains an advisory service for the benefit of its members who wish for information regarding canoe touring at home and abroad. It has published a comprehensive Guide to Waterways of the British Isles and maintains stocks of British and European maps and guides for the benefit of its members.

The B.C.U. has a Coaching Scheme which is available to anyone who wants to learn to canoe properly and safely. Help may be obtained from Area Coaching panels which have been established throughout the country. The B.C.U. publishes a series of pamphlets on canoeing techniques.

The B.C.U. has a scheme of Proficiency Tests at all grades from novice to fully qualified coach.

The B.C.U. Committees organise the four types of competitive canoeing : Sprint Racing, Long Distance Racing, Slalom and Wild Water Racing and Canoe Sailing.

The B.C.U. teams selected by these Committees represent Britain in international competitions and the B.C.U. represents canoeing on the British Olympic Committee.

The B.C.U. has founded a Corps of Canoe Lifeguards to give canoeists an opportunity to use their skills in service to the community. These services may include beach patrols and rescue work, flood reconnaisance, expedition leadership and any other form which offers itself.

The B.C.U. has built up a library of canoeing films which is managed by the British Film Institute and has a stock of film strips illustrating various paddling techniques.

The **Members** of the Union are its affiliated clubs and its Individual Members (Full, Family and Youth).

You need not join a club but the BCU believes that canoeists benefit from membership of a canoe club.

Membership of an affiliated club does not by itself bring full privileges. For these you must be an Individual Member of the BCU.

Privileges of B.C.U. Members

BCU members have the right to manage its affairs ; to wear its badges and tie and to fly its pennant ; to purchase BCU publications and BCU film loops and take BCU proficiency tests at preferential rates. In addition members have the right to seek advice on canoeing matters and take part in BCU organised, sponsored or recognised events. BCU Adult and Youth Members receive the Bulletin of canoeing news *Canoeing in Britain* at regular intervals during the year. The BCU has negotiated a members' Canoe Insurance and can offer cover at very low rates.

Classes of Membership

Full Members have full privileges of membership.

If you are under 19 there is a reduced subscription. Youth Members have all rights except voting rights.

Provided that at least one member of a family joins as an Adult Member the others in the family living at the same address may join for a nominal subscription regardless of age. Family Members enjoy all rights except voting rights, but do not receive a separate copy of the bulletin *Canoeing in Britain*.

How to become a Member of the B.C.U.

Complete the Enquiry Form at the end of this book and send it to the Membership Secretary, British Canoe Union, 26-29 Park Crescent, London, W.1.

B C U Supplies

BCU Guide to Waterways
of the British Isles

BCU Canoeing Pamphlets
CANOEING
No. 1   CHOOSING A CANOE AND ITS EQUIPMENT
No. 2   CANOE HANDLING AND MANAGEMENT
No. 3   CANOE CAMPING
No. 4   THE ESKIMO ROLL
No. 5   CANADIAN CANOEING
No. 6   LONG-DISTANCE RACING

(Others in preparation)

BCU members ordering direct from the Union and quoting their current year's Membership number can obtain the above publications at reduced prices

Other Publications, Badges, etc.

The BCU sells canoeing books and river maps of a large number of rivers in this country and on the Continent.
Also (to current members only) BCU and ICF lapel badges, BCU blazer badges, ties, pennants, transfers, etc.

Canoe Insurance

The BCU arranges for insurance against loss or damage to canoes, canoeing gear and equipment, camping gear, etc., at favourable rates.

BCU   SUPPLIES   DEPT.
26 - 29 Park Crescent
London, W.1

Please send 4d. stamp for price list and order form or for canoe insurance prospectus.

ARRANGEMENT OF THE SECTIONS

Rivers, lakes and estuaries are grouped by river basins, tributaries following the main river. The river basins are taken in a clockwise order from the Pennine Rivers round the east and south coasts of England and finishing with Wales. Except for the canals in the Midlands, which overlap many river basins, and are placed at the end, canals are included in the appropriate river basin.

Key Maps — *pages 26 to 29*

Alphabetical Index — *page 265 onwards*

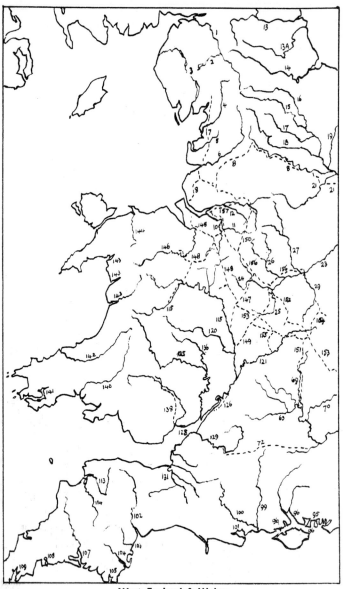

West England & Wales

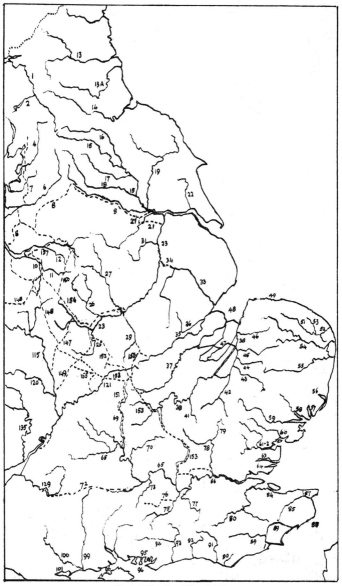

East & South of England

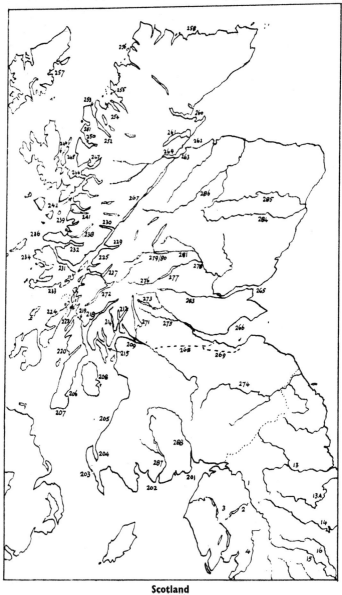

Scotland

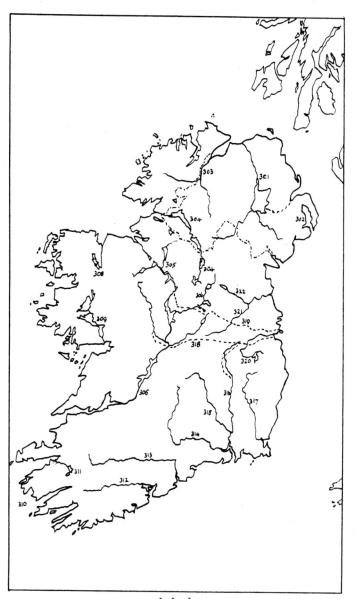

Ireland

ENGLAND AND WALES

PENNINE RIVERS (GENERAL)

All these rivers need favourable water levels for an enjoyable trip, except, of course, the Yorkshire ones where they run slow and deep across the Plain of York. Where they come down from the hills they are subject to sudden spates after rain with a fairly rapid fall in water level afterwards. For that reason it is laborious to attempt them in a dry summer, owing to the numerous boulder-strewn shallows, and the best times are usually spring and autumn after rainy spells when the water levels are medium.

RIVERS FLOWING WEST

1. EDEN

With plenty of water, canoeing on the Eden may begin at Kirkby Stephen, otherwise at Great Musgrave. A fall of 470 feet in 60 miles indicates that rough water may be expected; it is mainly concentrated in the 4 miles of the Nunnery Rapids. Conditions vary with the state of the water but the descent is invariably rocky and few clear channels are to be found.

If not in spate the water of the Eden is exceptionally clear, landings are clean and easy, and mud non-existent. Some wading is to be expected in a dry season. No towns are touched until Carlisle, and the river is unpolluted and unspoiled. The scenery is very fine, especially in the Wetheral gorge. Up to four days should be allowed for the run.

Permission should be sought beforehand for parts of the Eden—advice from B.C.U.

Rail access from several stations on the main Leeds—Carlisle line.

Camp sites easy to find all the way down.

Grading : Kirkby Stephen—Kirkoswald : Rough Water II.
Kirkoswald—Armathwaite (Nunnery Rapids): Rough Water III.
Armathwaite—Confl. of Irthing : Rough Water II.
Irthing—Carlisle : Rough Water I.

O.S. 83, 76 ; Barth. 34, 35, 38

Miles
0	*Kirkby Stephen Br.* Village, shops, etc. Stn. 1½ mls. Launch below the last mill.
3¾	*Great Musgrave Br.* Inn.
5½	*Warcop Br.* Village and inn R.
6	Boom across river. Remove lower bar and float under.
6¾	*Sandford.* Inn R.
8	Confl. of Helm Beck L. Little Ormside L.
9½	Rly. bridge. Great Ormside L.
12	*Appleby Br.* Weir ; let down on R. Town and Castle R. Stn. Shallows and deep pools alternate.
13	Small fall under overhanging bushes.
14	*Colby stepping stones.* May be necessary to get out and ease canoe through.
14½	*Crackenthorpe Weir.* Let down either side. Shootable in flood.
17	Site of Bolton Weir ; now demolished.
17½	*Bolton Br.* Inn L.
19	Confl. of Trout Beck L. Kirkby Thore R.
20	Road bridge. Shallows.
21	Rly. br. Just below is the Scaur, a striking wooded cliff on the R. bank.
22½	*Edenbridge.* Temple Sowerby ¾ ml. R. Rapid under bridge.

Miles
25½   Confl. of *Eamont* L. This greatly enlarges the Eden. At confl.
       is a deep pool followed by a rapid close to L bank.
27   *Edenhall* L.
28   *Langwathby Br.* Village and inn R. Stn. (M.R.).
31   Lane to Little Salkeld R. Stn. (M.R.).
32½   Rly. viaduct, followed by—
       Eden Lacy Falls ("weir" on O.S. map). Rough high fall, which
          can be shot on extreme R.; but better pass into millstream
          L and carry through trees. Careful approach is necessary.
34½   *Lazonby Br.* Village, inn and Stn. (M.R.) L. Staff gauge on
          bridge shows 1 foot at normal levels.
34¾   *Kirkoswald.* R. Junction of Raven Beck R.
       The Nunnery Rapids begin below here—a stretch of very
          broken water extending for about 4 miles. Prior permission
          is necessary for this stretch. Clear channels are few. Lining
          down may be possible but, like portaging, is very difficult
          owing to the steep, wooded and bracken-covered rocky
          slopes and cliffs. The whole stretch can be avoided by taking
          the canoe on the train from Lazonby stn. to Armathwaite.
36½   Confl. of Croglin R, half way through. Below here the rapids
          follow one another in quick succession except for a big pool
          about half way down. There are about 8 or 9 in this stretch.
40   *Armathwaite Weir.* The weir has recently been partially demo-
          lished and there are 2 or 3 passages. Passage on L is easy at
          moderate to high water but can be rough on the canoe.
          Passage on R should be avoided. It needs plenty of water,
          and there is submerged rock at the foot and a strong under-
          tow. There is also a narrow passage somewhat R of centre
          practicable with plenty of water. There is a strong pull to
          the right but no undertow and is not so rough on the canoe
          as the others. Keep left, into mill feeder L for portage over
          sluice by small bridge.
40¼   *Armathwaite Br.* Village and stn. (M.R.) L.
42½   *Holmwrangle Island.* Pass on left.
43½   *Frodelle Crook.* Rough broken rapid from ledges across river.
          Channel close to L bank. Prospect before shooting.
46½   *Coat House Island.* Pass on right.
47¼   *Wetheral Tower.* Ledge opposite tower ; pass middle R. River
          divided by a wall ; take L channel for ½ ml.
48¼   *Corby Castle* R.
48½   *Wetheral Ferry.* Convenient finishing point for Wetheral stn.
          (Newcastle—Carlisle line.)
48¾   Rly. viaduct. Rapids above viaduct ; keep L of island and take
          centre arch.
49½   *Warwick Br.* Village and inn. Carlisle 4 mls. L.
50   *Salmon Loups, Little Corby.* River divides ; 2nd channel from
          left possible—ledge at end to be shot, R.
50¾   Confl. of Irthing R. Easy water to Carlisle. Rather dull.
58½   *Carlisle Br.* Stn. ¾ ml. through town. 3 mls. further on the Eden
          becomes tidal. Entrance to Solway Firth at Burghmarsh Pt.
          9½ mls. from Carlisle. (See Section 201.)

2. Eamont

The Eamont is, perhaps, chiefly of use as a connecting link between Ullswater and the Eden, but is well worth doing for its own sake, particularly the stretch between Brougham Castle and the Eden. This part is entirely free from weirs, and passes some very fine cliff scenery. In low water the Eamont will entail a great deal of tedious wading, but is excellent if water is good. Between weirs there are many shallows and small rapids. Overhanging trees in places. The final reaches of the river are very rocky, but with deep pools. Generally on this river a canoe cannot be taken down without a considerable amount of rough treatment. The fall of the Eamont to the Eden from Ullswater is approximately 170 feet. The distances given below are approximate. Permission should be sought for the upper part.

O.S. 83 ; Barth. 34, 38

O.S. Lake District Tourist

Miles

0	*Pooley Bridge*, at N end of Ullswater. Low weir at $1\frac{3}{4}$ mls. composed of heaps of boulders. Opening wide enough to shoot, or in low water to pull canoe through.
$1\frac{3}{4}$	*Dalmain Footbridge.*
2	Weir demolished, but watch for masonry just below surface.
$3\frac{1}{2}$	"Weir" and "Ford" marked on O.S. 1-in. map. Weir no longer in existence, but there is a pronounced fall round an island.
$3\frac{3}{4}$	Footbridge.
$4\frac{1}{2}$	Railway Bridge. Rapid in front of bridge, round bend.
$5\frac{1}{4}$	Weir No. 2. A high weir. Lift down left, or portage right. May be shootable L but beware of tree branch.
$5\frac{3}{4}$	Weir demolished.
6	*Eamont Bridge, Penrith.* Town L. Stn. 1 mile. King Arthur's Round Table and Mayburgh Rings R. $\frac{1}{2}$ ml. Just below is : Weir No. 3. Vertical drop of 6 feet. *Land right* and portage, or lift down.
$6\frac{1}{4}$	Footbridge. 200 yards below the footbridge is an artificial ledge about 1 ft. high. In low water lift over.
$6\frac{3}{4}$	Weir No. 4. Line or carry down, or portage right. Can be shot in high water.
$7\frac{1}{2}$	*Brougham Castle Weir.* Immediately past bathing station. Weir is 10 feet high. Lift or carry down, or portage R. On right 50 yards below weir, are ruins of Brougham Castle, followed in another 50 yards by the Penrith-Appleby road bridge.
$7\frac{1}{2}$	Bridge for pipe-line.
9	Pools and rapids under high cliffs.
10	At bend to right under cliff with farm on top keep to channel on right. Left channel blocked by trees.
$10\frac{1}{2}$	Cave and cliffs.
12	*Junction with Eden.*

3. THE LAKE DISTRICT

The charms of the Lake District for the walker need no recommendation. Sufficient to say that the addition of a canoe to a walking and camping holiday in the Lake District is a distinct advantage, and enables the lakes and their surroundings to be seen from a new angle. From the canoeing point of view it is unfortunate that the lakes are not connected (except Derwentwater and Bassenthwaite), and a canoe tour of the Lake District necessarily implies the conveyance by road of the canoe from one lake to another. To those who do not possess or cannot hire a motor car this is a matter of some inconvenience (unless the baggage can be accommodated on a bus), as it means walking, with baggage on trailer, considerable distances, including, between Ullswater and Windermere, the crossing of the Kirkstone Pass.

O.S. Lake District Tourist. Barth. 34

Windermere. Length 10½ miles ; greatest breadth 1¼ miles ; 130 feet above sea level. No permission required. Lake Side station is closed. Windermere Town station is over a mile from the water at Bowness. No landing on Belle Isle.

Running into Windermere at its northern end are the Rivers *Brathay* and *Rothay*, which meet ½ mile from the lake.

River Rothay. There is a fall of 76 feet between Grasmere and Windermere (3 miles of river excluding the lakes). In low water the river is rather shallow and some wading will be required. In full water it affords considerable sport. The river rises rapidly after heavy rain. Permission should be obtained from Major R. E. Porter, Estates Office, Ambleside, for Rydal Water and much of the River.

Miles
0 *Grasmere.*
1 End of Lake. Enter River Rothay. First ¼ mile of rapids full of large boulders. Inspect. Care required, especially if river is full.
1½ Wooden foot bridge.
1¾ *Rydal Water.*
2¼ End of *Rydal Water.* Enter River Rothay. Clear run to footbridge. 50 yards beyond this (just before reaching a stone bridge) is a short rapid full of large boulders. Inspect. Care required, especially if river is full.
2¾ *Loughrigg Cott.* Stepping stones. Canoe will have to be carried round. Then easy but interesting river for 2 miles with miniature rapids and a few tree stumps.
4¾ *Coniston—Ambleside Road Bridge.*
5 Confl. with Brathay.
5½ Head of Lake Windermere.

River Brathay. This carries more water than the Rothay. Start from Elterwater Village if the river is not too low. A better starting point is from the boathouse at the west end of Elterwater Lake but permission should be obtained first from E. W. Hodge, Esq., Elterwater Hall, near Ambleside. The lake consists of three "dubs." There is a fall of 59 feet to Lake Windermere (3 miles). The river rises rapidly after heavy rain.

Miles
- 0   *Elterwater.*
- ½   End of lake. First ½ mile of river is uninteresting. Where trees come down to the left bank at the entrance to a gorge, *land* and portage round Skelwith Force. *Take great care not to overshoot this point.*
- 1   *Skelwith Force.* If sufficient water, embark immediately below the falls, after inspecting the rapid below. In low water the portage can be continued by road to stone bridge over the river at Skelwith Bridge.
- 1¼   *Skelwith Bridge.*
- 2½   *Brathay Church (Skelwith Church).* Near Brathay Church (marked on O.S. as Skelwith Church) care required approaching stone footbridge and again 50 yards further on where there is a rapid that should be inspected from the bank before attempting. Keep to the left of the island below this rapid. Wading may be necessary in low water.
- 3½   Confl. with Rothay.
- 4   *Windermere.* The west side of Windermere is the most interesting to follow. Of the islands Thompson's Holme is a good place to stop for a picnic meal or a bathe.

River Leven. From its exit 1 mile above Newby Bridge the waters of Windermere reach the sea by the River Leven in 14 miles, including 5 miles of tidal water. The fall of 130 feet means fast water.

As objection to canoeing on this river will probably be raised by the fishing interests, permission should be obtained beforehand. The fishing on the Leven is owned by the Leven Anglers Association (Secretary, Ulverston) but permission to canoe down the river would also have to be obtained from the riparian owners mentioned above. It is rarely given except on dates of Leven Wild Water Tests of the Lakeland Canoe Club to whom anyone wishing to canoe the Leven should write beforehand (c/o B.C.U. Headquarters). Lord Richard Cavendish owns the left bank down to Backbarrow, and the Duke of Devonshire part of the right bank. Reckitts own the ultra-marine works at Backbarrow and claim the river in their grounds, Imperial Chemical Industries have a gunpowder works lower down, and enforce strict regulations regarding smoking and access to the river near their property. The tidal portion of the river extends to Greenodd. Boating and fishing on this part are free. Quicksands in parts.

Miles
  0   Exit from Windermere.
  1   *Newby Bridge.* Weir below. Fall at old mill 200 yards beyond,
          followed by rapids (Grading RW III).
  2½   *Backbarrow.* Dam. Portage 200 yards.
  3   Between here and Haverthwaite a high weir, two low weirs, and
          a rocky fall (Grading RW IV in high water).
  4   *Haverthwaite.*
  7¾   *Greenodd.* Tidal below here. Tide runs and turns quickly.
  9   *Mearness Point.*
  12½ Railway Viaduct. Much rough water when tide is flowing.
  14½ *Chapel Islands.* Conishead Priory R.

Buttermere. 1¼ miles long ; ½ mile wide ; 329 feet above sea level. Apply for permission to National Trust Warden : Mr. K. Vickers, Nether Close, Loweswater, near Cockermouth.

Crummock Water. 2½ miles long ; ¾ mile wide ; 321 feet above sea level. Apply for permission to National Trust Warden as above.
  These lakes are connected by a small river ¾ mile in length.

Derwentwater, Bassenthwaite, and River Derwent. The Derwent flows through Derwentwater and Bassenthwaite Lake to the sea at Workington. The course of the river runs through private lakes and land on which the public have no rights. Fortunately it has not been found necessary to obtain permission for all parts, but in case difficulty should arise the names of the people interested are given.

The river from Grange to Derwentwater may be considered as part of the lake, the eastern half of which belongs to Keswick Urban District Council, and the western half to the National Trust. Permission unnecessary for a short stay.

The fishing rights in the river between Derwentwater and Bassenthwaite belong to the Keswick Anglers. Here again permission is unnecessary.

Bassenthwaite Lake belongs to Lord Leconfield, and if anything longer than a passage through the lake is contemplated, permission from his agent, Cockermouth Castle, should be obtained.

The lower part of the Derwent from Bassenthwaite to the sea is a salmon river controlled by the Castle Fisheries, Court Buildings, Cockermouth, who normally refuse permission.

The absence of difficulty will depend largely on the conduct of the canoeist, and it is desirable that nothing be done to alienate the fishing interests.

The Derwent is canoeable from Rosthwaite stepping stones when the water is at least half way up the stones. Easy Grade II shingle rapids to Grange, except one in the gorge (main road close on R) where there is a concealed rock at the foot of the rapid.

Miles

  0   *Grange in Borrowdale.* Accessible from road.

  1½ *Derwentwater.* 2½ mls. long, 244 feet above O.D. At N end river is shallow in low water. Barbed wire may be met with.

  7¼ *Bassenthwaite Lake.* 3¾ mls. long. 223 feet above O.D. At S end (Ouse Br.) river runs fast over stony bed with occasional boulders and deep stretches. If gauge at Ouse Br. shows 1 ft. 8 in. there will be good water all the way. Below it there may be some wading. Shallow where the river spreads out. Stakes may be encountered below Bassenthwaite (against netting).

 15   *Isel Bridge.* Barbed wire across just after Isel Hall and 250 yds. below.

 19½ *Castle Weir, Cockermouth.* Portage L, or shoot L after inspection.

 20¼ *Fitz Weir.*

 22   *Melgram Fitz Weir.*

 28¼ *Salmon Hall Weir.*

 29¼ *Workington Weir.* Town ½ mile below (Stn.).

Thirlmere. A reservoir belonging to the Manchester Corporation. No canoeing or camping allowed.

Ullswater. 7½ miles long ; ¾ mile wide : 476 feet above sea level. No permission required. Nearest railway station, Penrith ; distant 6 miles. Bus service available.

At its northern end the Eamont flows from Ullswater to join the Eden (see section 2).

No particulars are available as to canoeing possibilities on the other lakes.

4. LUNE

The Lune rises in Westmorland, not far from the Eden valley at Kirkby Stephen, and flows S and then SW to Lancaster and the sea at Sunderland Point between Heysham and Fleetwood.

It has been canoed from Tebay, but the fall of the river in these upper reaches is great, and there are many difficult rocky falls. A start above Sedbergh is not advised. The junction of the Rawthey, 1 mile above Middleton Station is best. From here the Lune is canoeable in normal spring or autumn conditions ; a good deal of wading may be expected in dry weather. From Kirkby Lonsdale the river is always canoeable but in summer water is often very low in many places above Halton. The Greeta and Wenning each bring a fair amount of water and below the junctions there should be good going.

The river provides interesting canoeing ; there are a good number of rapids, but they are not particularly difficult, except for those between the two weirs at Halton.

Advice about the need to obtain prior permission should be sought from the B.C.U.

Bus services : several routes up the valley between Lancaster and Sedbergh (Ribble Motor Services, Preston).

Grading : Rawthey—Lancaster : Rough Water II (between Halton Weirs III).

O.S. 89 ; Barth. **34, 31**

Miles

0	*Sedbergh Br.* Sedbergh 2 mls. L.
1	*Beck Side Br.*
2	*Junction of Rawthey.* Good starting point.
3	*Middleton.* Very pleasant valley between hills.
11½	*Kirkby Lonsdale.* Just before gas works near K. Lonsdale church is an island—take the narrow channel L as the main channel has a low plank bridge. Serpentine rapid above the bridges.
12	*Devil's Br.*
	New Br.
13¼	*Whittington Ford.* Nether Burrow (inn) ¼ ml. L.
14	*Tunstall.* River split by islands for about 1 ml. Bad water.
16	*Junction of Greeta* L.
16½	Rly. Br.
18½	*Leyn Br.*
19½	*Junction of Wenning.* L.
22¼	*Caton Green.* L.
25½	Rly. and road bridges.
27	*Halton.* Two weirs. Portage upper weir R in low water, but it can usually be shot through salmon cut near the centre. Difficult rapids between—inspect.
	Halton Br. Second weir shootable through salmon cut. Inspect. Rowing boats from Lancaster come up to here.
28	*Lancaster Canal Aqueduct.*
28½	*John o'Gaunt Rowing Club.*
	Weir. Tidal below here.
29	*Lancaster Br.*

5. WYRE

Rising in the Forest of Bowland the Wyre flows along a more or less westerly course to the sea at Fleetwood. Canoeable at most times from Garstang but hardly of more than local interest. The river can be reached along the Lancaster Canal from Garstang and Catterall Stn. (1½ mls.). It is a better starting point than the road bridge a little above. The scenery is not very good and the river, which at first has narrow, shallow rapids later becomes dull and monotonous. The estuary has swift tides. High water, Fleetwood : Dover plus 10 mins.

O.S. 94 ; Barth. **31**

Miles

0	*Garstang—Lancaster Canal Aqueduct.* Easy, shallow rapids : look out for submerged stakes.
1¾	Weir. Portage L.
2	Road Bridge (A.6). The rapids continue to Churchtown. Sandy bed beyond.
5	*St. Michael's on Wyre Br.* Take R arch. The twists and turns are broader and there are high banks.
9	*Cartford Br.* River becomes tidal and the channels and sandbanks are complicated.
13½	*Shard Br.* Estuary nearly ¼ ml. across and broadens out much more near Fleetwood. The tides are very swift. Poulton-le-Fylde Stn. 2 mls. L.
20½	*Fleetwood* L. Landing below ferry jetty, near stn., or at Knott End across the estuary. Buses from Knott End to Garstang; railway disused.

6. RIBBLE

The Ribble rises in Yorkshire E of Whernside, and flows S between Ingleborough and Penyghent to Settle and Hellifield, then SW past Clitheroe to the sea beyond Preston.

It is canoeable from Horton in Ribblesdale in high water; in normal water it is possible to start a short distance below Settle ; in dry weather one must be prepared for a considerable amount of wading above Clitheroe—in such conditions 3 days may well be required from Settle to Clitheroe. Beyond the junction of the Hodder and Calder this is less marked and 2 days should be enough for the remaining 24 miles to Preston. After autumn rains or in spring with favourable water, the whole distance Settle to Preston can be done in 2 days, the river being wild and boisterous. Normally, pools alternate mainly with shingly rapids, with rocks and rocky ledges in places.

The Ribble becomes tidal a short distance above Preston. Below Preston the estuary is noted for its swift tides and shifting sandbanks, and is not recommended for canoeing.

The upper parts are rather bare ; between Gisburn and Ribchester more wooded ; after that the scenery is dull.

Advice about the need to obtain permission should be sought from the B.C.U.

There is good main line rail access at Settle, Giggleswick and Hellifield, and at Preston. Buses (Ribble Motor Services, Preston) serve the valley.

Grading : Rough Water II generally. The stretch between Helwith Bridge and Settle, which is possible only in high water, is very difficult (Grade V) and is best omitted.

O.S. 90, 95, 94 ; Barth. 32, 31

Miles

0   *Settle Bridge.* Town and stn. L. Weir below, followed by Castle Rock, a difficult fall requiring inspection.

½   Road bridge. Large boulders. No apparent channel in low water.

1   Farmhouse. A convenient starting point at cart track marked on map within easy reach of Giggleswick Stn.

1¼   Railway Bridge. Metal spike on post under middle of bridge. Shallow rapids for a mile or two. Then deep, slow water to—

7   *Cow Bridge.* Long Preston Stn. 1 ml. L. From here onwards fair amount of rapids. In two places oblong blocks as stepping stones may be nasty if just covered by water. Ledges at an angle to the stream in one or two places.

9½   *Halton Bridge.* Hellifield 1 ml. L. Stn. 1½ mls. Fast water through and below bridge.

10½   *Nappa.* Ledge across river. Stepping stones, normally require lifting over. Cafe on main road.

13½   *Paythorne Bridge.*

14¾   Confl. of Stock Beck L. Land to inspect weir.

15   *Gisburn Weir.* With low water land on sill and let down slope. Shootable centre on good water. Fast water to—

15¼   *Gisburn Bridge.* Village ¾ ml. L.

16¾   *Hencroft Weir.* With low water land on sill and let down. In high water this weir is sometimes quite covered and resembles an ordinary rapid.

20½   *Sawley Abbey* and *Weirs.* Inn. Two weirs just before and after a R bend. Neither presents difficulty.

20¾   *Sawley Br.*

22½   *Chatburn Br.* Village ¾ ml. L.

24   Road bridge.

25¼   *Brungerley Bridge.* Clitheroe L. ½ ml.

    Clitheroe Weir. Perpendicular drop—unshootable. Portage L or R. Alternatively bad water below may be avoided by taking intake to mill L for ½ ml. Land again 100 yds. before stone wall on right and portage 100 yds back to river.

26½   *Roefield or Edisford Br.* Inn R.

29   *Great Mitton Bridge.* 1 ml. L. Series of ledges. Channel to left.

29½   Junction of Hodder R. From here fairly easy. A few shallows still in a dry summer even as far as Preston.

30¼   Junction of Calder L.

31¾   Aqueduct.

32½   Footbridge. At approach to footbridge current swings R with a straight rapid immediately after bridge.

33½   *Sale Wheel.* A rapid approach to a right-hand bend where the river narrows between rocks, making a deeper rapid, followed by a large bay on either side, each with a slow eddy (the "wheel"). In flood the waves are very big and heavy.

34¾   *Ribchester Bridge.* Inn.

35¾   *Ribchester Village* R.

42½   *Thirlmere Aqueduct.*

45¼   *Preston By-Pass Bridge.*

45½   *Lower Brockholes Bridge.* Tide may be met shortly after here.

41

47 *Walton Bridge, Preston.*
49 *Penwortham Bridge, Preston.* Between Walton and Penwortham
     Bridges are several railway bridges. If car transport is
     available, it is best to finish at Walton Bridge. The nearest
     land to Preston Station is in the park under second bridge
     after Walton ; but the mud at low tide is unpleasant.

7. LANCASTER CANAL

Runs from Preston through Garstang, Lancaster and Carnforth and
formerly on to Kendal ; 8 locks at Tewitfield, a few miles N of Carnforth,
above which it is gradually being filled in. From Preston it runs not
far from the Lancashire Fells through quite pleasant
country, crossing the *Wyre* at Garstang, and with a short branch from
Galgate to the *Lune* estuary at Glasson, to Lancaster. Here it crosses
the *Lune* by a fine aqueduct, runs close to the sea at Hest Bank and
Carnforth and then more inland into Westmorland and up the valley
of the Kent. Scenery is good from Lancaster. The Preston—Carlisle
main line is never very far from the canal and there are a number of
stations close to the canal : e.g. Garstang, Hest Bank, Bolton-le-Sands,
Carnforth.

O.S. 94, 89 ; Barth. 31, 34

Preston Wharf to Garstang Stn.   16   miles
                Galgate ...   . $25\frac{1}{4}$ miles
                Lancaster   ...   ... $30\frac{1}{2}$ miles
                Tewitfield Locks   ... $43\frac{1}{2}$ miles

8. LEEDS AND LIVERPOOL CANAL

Runs from Leeds up Airedale to Gargrave, then crosses the Pennines
and drops down the Colne Valley to Burnley and Blackburn. From
here it turns S to Chorley and Wigan and then W and S beyond
Ormskirk to Liverpool. This canal is mentioned more because of its
engineering interest in crossing the Pennines than for its canoeing
interest. But the scenery on the Yorkshire side is quite good, particularly between Bingley and Gargrave where the canal is running high up
the side of Airedale, and across the moors to Barnoldswick.

Forty-five locks rising from Leeds to Barnoldswick ; 52 falling from
there to Liverpool.

            Leeds to Bingley   ...   ...   16 miles
            Bingley to Barnoldswick   ...   25 miles
            Barnoldswick to Blackburn   ...   30 miles
            Blackburn to Wigan   ...   ...   21 miles
            Wigan to Liverpool   ...   ...   35 miles

O.S. 96, 95, 100 ; Barth. 32, 28

9. MERSEY BASIN

The Mersey, its two headstreams the Goyt and the Etherow and its tributary the Irwell, flow mainly through industrial districts though they each have short stretches of quite pleasant scenery. Notes are therefore given only of other tributaries, the Weaver, Dane and Bollin which all cross the Cheshire plain through pleasant country.

10. Weaver

The Weaver rises near Ridley, to the W of Nantwich, and follows a circuitous course by Nantwich, Winsford and Northwich to the Mersey estuary near Frodsham. From Winsford it is a navigation. Canoeable from Ashtree Farm, a short way above Nantwich. The scenery is pleasant all the way except in the immediate environs of the towns. The Trent and Mersey Canal (see section 156) runs fairly close to the Weaver for some miles from Anderton, near Northwich, where there is a barge lift connecting the two.

Grading : Nantwich to Top Flash : Difficulty I.

O.S. 110, 109 ; Barth. 23, 28

Miles

0   *Ashtree Farm* (permission to start here is necessary).
2   *Shrewbridge* (A.530).
2½ Railway Bridge.
3   *Nantwich.* A start may be made immediately below the weir near the town bridge, but to obtain greater privacy for building, walk 100 yds. up the main road on the L bank and turn R to cross some fields to the river. River winds along a narrow but deep channel. (Canal ½ ml. left of bridge.)
3¾ *Beambridge* (B.5073).
6½ Rail bridge.
7   *Brayne Hall* (farm).
8   *Shropshire Union Canal Aqueduct* (Middlewich Branch see section 148).
10½ *Church Minshull Bridge and Weir.* Below the weir is a stretch of shallows.
14½ *Top Flash* (lake).
15½ *Bottom Flash* (lake).
16½ *Winsford Bridge.* Town not very interesting. Stn. 1 ml. R.
18½ *Newbridge Lock.*
20½ *Vale Royal Lock.* Vale Royal Abbey L.
21 *Hartford Bridge.*
21½ *Lock.*
22½ *Northwich Bridge.* Town remarkable for its narrow and irregular streets, caused by subsidence from brine pumping. Stn. ¾ ml. R. Junction of *River Dane.*
23½ *Anderton Bridge.* Trent and Mersey Canal close.

25½ *Saltersford Lock.*

27½ *Acton Bridge.* Trent and Mersey Canal diverges

28¼ *Dutton Lock.*

32½ *Frodsham Bridge.* Village, castle and stn. 1 ml. L.

35½ *Weston Marsh Lock.*

36   *Weston Point.* Junction with Manchester Ship Canal and Mersey.

11. Dane

The Dane rises near Buxton and flows W by Congleton and Middlewich through pleasant country to join the *Weaver* at Northwich. Its rapids are shallow "runs" over shingle, and in places there is difficulty owing to overhanging trees. It does not usually carry any large volume of water. From Congleton to Middlewich makes a pleasant day's canoeing. Start below mill a little way below the town.

Grading : Difficulty II.

Ravenscroft Bridge : unshootable weir—portage L. *Croxton Bridge* : weir—shootable centre in high water, portage R. *Croxton Aqueduct* : masonry partly blocks river.

Congleton to Holmes Chapel (weir, portage L)	...	8	miles
Ravenscroft Bridge (Middlewich ½ ml. L)		13	miles
Croxton Aqueduct (Trent and Mersey Canal) ...	... ...	13½	miles
Davenham Bridge	... ...	17¼	miles
Northwich (junction with *Weaver*)	...	20	miles

O.S. 110 ; Barth. 28

12. Bollin

The Bollin rises near Macclesfield and flows NW across the Cheshire plain, mostly in a valley below the general level of nearby country, to the Mersey near Lymm. A small river, with lively little rapids (but involving much wading in low water) with tree stumps and rocks to avoid in places. Has been canoed from Prestbury (Spittle House); from here to Wilmslow is a good run in high water (approx. 5 miles—a weir just before Wilmslow). The stretch from A.34 at Wilmslow to A.538 at Oversley Ford is best regarded as out of the question, as boating is prohibited over most of this stretch, including Styal Park (National Trust) where there is a large weir.

O.S. 101 ; Barth. 28

0   *Oversley Ford* (A.538).

3¼ *Castle Mill Bridge.*

3¾ *Pigley Stair*, footbridge. New road bridge under construction just below.

6   Railway viaduct.

6¼ *Ashley Mill*, footbridge.

8¾ *Newbridge* (A.556).

10¼ *Bollington Weir.* The Bridgewater Canal crosses the Bollin a short distance below.

12¾ *Warburton Weir.* The Bollin continues to the Mersey (Manchester Ship Canal).

RIVERS FLOWING EAST

13. TYNE

The **North Tyne** rises in the Cheviot Hills, and after being joined by the *Rede* near Bellingham flows S to the confluence of the two headstreams above Hexham. It is best done in semi-flood conditions from Bellingham, when it runs fast. On the other hand in low water it can be so shallow as to be practicable only with much wading. It is very beautiful, wild and wooded all the way down.

Grading : Rough Water II-III.

O.S. 77, 78 ; Barth. 39

Miles

0	*Bellingham (Tarset).* Numerous rapids with shingle, some quite long.
5	Two small rocky falls, rather shallow.
5½	Island in midstream ; rapids on both sides impracticable (line down); heavy rapid below. A succession of rapids follows to—
8	*Wark Bridge.* Take rapid on R of island below. More rapids at intervals to—
9½	*Chipchase Castle.* Sharp left and a rocky fall across river (way through under L bank). After several small rapids—
12½	Character of river changes : rocky boulder rapids, several of which are impracticable.
13¼	*Barrasford Ferry.* Rope across river. Dangerous rocky falls ; line down.
13½	*Weir.* Portage.
14¼	*Weir.* Portage. Rapid ¾ mile below.
15½	*Chollerford Bridge and Weir.* Portage L bank. More rapids below, some rocky, between here and Wall.
16	*Chesters* R. (Roman Wall).
17	*Wall* Village L. Near stn. (closed) difficult rapids begin and river enters a gorge.
19	*Warden* R. End of gorge. Several rocky rapids to—
20	Confl. with *South Tyne.*

The **South Tyne** rises on Alston Common, flowing N. then E. to the confluence of the two headstreams above Hexham. It is canoeable in high water from Haltwhistle (stn.), and is fairly difficult, but not so awkward or so beautiful as the *North Tyne.*

From Haltwhistle to the confluence about 15 miles. The river does not fall very fast, but there are many rapids with shingle banks.

Grading : Rough Water II.

The **Tyne** below the confluence is wider, with longer stretches of still water, but still requires to be done after rain if the trip is not to be laborious. It is still pleasant as far as Ryton where it is tidal and industrialised.

Grading : Rough Water II.

Miles

20	Confl. of North and South Tyne.
21	Rapids and shallows past gravel works.
22	Remains of bridge on extreme right and centre of river.
22½	*Hexham Bridge.* Interesting town, R. Abbey. Stn. Take centre then right of island down long stretch of broken water. Look out for dredger wire above river. Slight rapids at long intervals to—
26	*Corbridge Bridge.* Village L.
27½	Cable bridge—heavy rapid under in centre of river. Fairly heavy rapids at approx. ½ mile intervals to—
29	*Riding Mill.* Beyond this there are a number of heavy rapids at intervals of about half a mile.
31½	Look out for row of stakes across river at ordinary levels. In the next half mile two very heavy rapids ; keep L on first ; keep L on second near bank through ruined weir.
32½	*Bywell Bridge.* Two rapids to—
35½	*Prudhoe Bridge.* Keep L. Rapids again at intervals.
37¾	Rly. bridge. Heavy rapid ¼ mile below (keep L).
38	*Wylam Bridge.* Stn.
40	Starts to be tidal and industrialised.
42	*Ryton.*
43	*Newburn Bridge.* Further stretches unpleasant.

13A. WEAR

The Wear rises on Alston Moor, not far from the source of the South Tyne, and flows east to Bishop Auckland, then north-eastwards to Durham and Sunderland. The upper part is in typical high Pennine country, afforested on the hills to the south. Signs of present and past industry are frequent, but little shows from the river. Rowing clubs are active at Durham, where the scenery is fine, and Durham is a pleasant city.

In the upper reaches the bed is rocky or gravelly, with overhanging bushes, and occasionally the river winds in and out of sand and gravel workings. Below Durham passes through a deep valley with rocky slabs, and finally it passes through the Lambton estate and becomes tidal.

Normally the river is bump and scrape from Wolsingham to Witton le Wear, after which there are weirs and it is less shallow. From Durham to Finchale Abbey again bump and scrape normally, but with plenty of white water in flood. Permission from Lord Lambton's agent is required for the stretch from Chester le Street to Fatfield. The river at Sunderland is narrow but busy. Keep to north bank ; best landing is on north beach between the inner and outer piers.

In flood gradings are : Wolsingham-Durham I-II.

Durham-Finchale Abbey II-III.

Finchale Abbey onward I.

The water begins to be dirty at Bishop Auckland, then clears up, but the mouth is fairly foul.

O.S. 84, 85, 78. Barth. 39

Miles

  0   *Wolsingham.* Fast water ; rocky slabs. 200 yds. rubbish from tip. After $\frac{1}{2}$ ml., angled bridge piers.

  3   Remains of broken weir.

  7   *Witton le Wear Bridge.* Two small weirs just before bridge— beware steel rods.

  8   Three small weirs close together, followed by fourth (2 ft. high) on bend, beware steel rods.

  9   Rail and road bridges cross together, followed by concrete ford forming a low weir. Land L. In flood, beware stopper.

 $11\frac{1}{2}$ A 12 ft. weir just round a sharp bend. Portage L. Access to town by road R.

 $12\frac{1}{2}$ *Bishop Auckland road and railway bridges.* Town R.

 15   Island as river enters gorge. Keep L. Sewage effluent pipes R.

 16   Old weir on L with gap on R.

 17   Bridge. Willington L.

 19   *Page Bank Bridge.*

 22   *Croxdale.* Railway viaduct, then arched bridge with weir under. Portage L or shoot R. Inspect. Road bridge (A.1). After 1 ml. Butterby Scar. Approach R, half-way down go centre.

 26   *Shincliffe Bridge.*

 28   *Durham City* R. River makes a big loop round the city. Two old road bridges followed by weir. Usually shootable L. After another road bridge comes a second weir. Inspect for best portage, probably L, or scramble over weir in low water. Shootable L in high water. (*Grade III*).

 30   Fast water for next 5 mls. (*Grade II to III*.) Site of Roman bridge and ancient hospital at Kepier, R. 1 ml. after weirs.

 32   Railway bridge and piers.

47

34   *Finchale Abbey.* Wooden footbridge. Ruined monastery, and cafe and camp site L. Land above bridge.

35½   Bridge.

40   *Chester le Street* L. Two bridges close together and weir.

41½   Double bridge. Go R. Not easy. River enters Lambton estate (permission required).

43¼   Bridge. Lambton Castle L.

44½   *Fatfield Bridge.* High water about 1 hour after Wearmouth.

48½   *North and South Hylton.* Floating shipyard, balks and rubbish.

50½   *Alexandra Bridge.* Shipyards. Keep to L of river.

52   *Sunderland.* Railway and road bridges.

53   *Monkwearmouth.* North beach between inner and outer piers, known as Roker Block Sands. Access to road. Many sea anglers on inner pier.

14. TEES

The Tees rises on Alston Common and flows SE and E to the sea near Middlesbrough. It has been canoed in flood from Winch Bridge, 2 miles below High Force, but is only for experts (Grade IV-V).

In dry weather the river is often too shallow to be practicable. In high water it is very fast with few quiet deep stretches, but slow progress is to be expected owing to the need to prospect numerous rapids. The river is extremely rocky, often with reefs ; much of the upper stretches are in gorges (Middleton to Greta Bridge). Two sections of rapids steepen and narrow to a final tricky fall, the first above Woden Croft, the other the first series of Abbey Rapids. Below Whorlton Falls the river is wider and, except for shallow reefs, easy.

Grading : Middleton to Whorlton Falls—Rough Water II-III (Abbey Rapids Grade III).

Below Whorlton Falls to Yarm—Rough Water I-II.

Advice about the need to obtain permission should be sought from the BCU.

O.S. 84, 85 ; Barth 35

0   *Middleton Bridge.* Wide river with rocky rapids under grassy hillside L.

1¼   Rapids on two consecutive bends : first is a steep drop into a side-current beating up against a rock-buttress ; second is a small fall between a reef L and bank R. At second in high water the wave breaks from the reef and twists into a kind of cone. Mixed pebbly and rocky rapids follow.

4½   *Eggleston Bridge.* (Not to be confused with Egglestone Abbey 2¾ miles below Barnard Castle.)

5   Gorge starts—*Inspect.* Fast water and succession of rocky rapids. A steep rapid on a bend leads into a fall with a large boulder in centre and a narrow passage on either side. Stream may break on to rock. Further rapids, then the gorge widens at—

7½   *Cotherstone.* Iron bridge. Village R. The gorge wall often present on one side only. Fall under Towler Hill—shoot R.

9½   Rly. viaduct. Take on R for shallow rocky approach to a steep rapid ; then L for long rapid down L bank.

10½   Footbridge followed by new weir. The centre break should *not* be shot—dangerous. Shallow approach to steep rocky descent to a stone bridge.

11   *Barnard Castle.* Shallows below, then iron bridge round bend. Broken weir : shoot centre.

11½   Mill L. Partially broken weir, not normally shootable. Boulder-strewn stretch.

12¾   *Abbey Rapids* start. Gorge. Shallow approach to rapids on R ; these steepen, worsen and culminate in three falls. *Inspection imperative, as conditions can easily make this part impossible.* The middle fall is constricted into a "strid," with a tongue of rock in the L of the flow. Approach so as to keep on R side of the fast flow and swing boat to R on the fall.

13   *Abbey Bridge.* A quiet stretch is followed by the second series of rapids. These are easier than the first with a few easy falls ; one is an appreciable drop—inspect first.

    The Abbey Rapids can be avoided by a portage from near Egglestone Abbey where the road is low near the stone bridge over a tributary, but launching below is difficult because of the gorge.

    Further rapids follow with rock reefs just under the surface.

14¾   *Mouth of River Greta* (R). River wider, but reefs continue.

16½   *Whorlton Bridge.* Rapid under. Keep R, then L on rapids to—

16¾   *Whorlton Falls.* Portage over reefs R in low water. In high water portage either bank.

    After this the river presents few difficulties. There are still rapids, shallow and rock-strewn stretches but the chief hazard is grounding on reefs. Shallowness particularly noticeable at Winston and Gainford. The river gradually becomes more and more placid.

19¼   *Winston Bridge.*

20½   Two rly bridges in ½ mile.

Miles

21½   *Gainford* L (stn.).
25   *Piercebridge* ; village L.
31   Weir. Right hand chute passable if water not too low. Portage
       either bank.
32½   *Blackwall Bridge* (A.1) (outskirts of Darlington).
35½   *Croft Bridge.*
39   *Hurworth* L.
50   *Dinsdale Bridge.*
51½   *Middleton One Row* L.
60½   *Yarm.* Road bridge (A.19). The river then starts to become
       industrialised and tidal.

YORKSHIRE OUSE BASIN

15. URE (or YORE) and OUSE

The **Ure** rises on Abbotside Common, NW of Hawes, very close to
the headstreams of the Eden. It flows SE down Wensleydale through
Ripon and Boroughbridge to the Plain of York, where it is joined by
the Swale. A few miles further, where the Ouse Gill Beck joins it, its
name changes, and it is known as the *Ouse* all the way past York and
Selby to the estuary, where its name again changes to the *Humber.*

Canoeable from Askrigg in favourable water. From Askrigg to
Aysgarth the fall of the river is comparatively slight, and in low water
pools of still water will be met separated by occasional shallows. The
bed consists of gravel, comparatively kind to the canoe. A short way
above Aysgarth the character of the river changes. The fall of the river
becomes much more pronounced and the bed more rocky and there is a
series of falls. The great Aysgarth Force is quite impossible and must
always be portaged ; the next few miles will require almost continuous
wading between rocks if the water is low ; if the water level is favourable
there will be a good, exciting fast run. (The average fall of the river from
below Aysgarth Force to Wensley is 150 ft. in 6½ mls.—23 ft. per ml.)

At Wensley conditions become easier—long pools separated by
occasional small rapids and weirs—as far as Jervaulx (fall 50 feet in
9 miles—5½ feet per mile) after which they get more difficult again
until a mile or so beyond West Tanfield (fall 150 feet in 15½ miles—
9.7 feet per mile—mostly below Masham). On this stretch there will
be occasional wading in low water and fast, exciting runs in favourable
conditions. Thereafter the river is much easier.

The scenery is good all the way down. So is Wensleydale cheese.

The Ure is emphatically not a river for beginners. In favourable
water conditions it offers fast wild water as good as the Eden, Dee or
Teifi. In low water a start is best made at Wensley Bridge (where,
however, there are "Private" notices), or at Middleham Bridge.

Advice about the need to obtain permission should be sought from
the BCU.

O.S. 90, 91 ; Barth. 35

Grading : Askrigg—Aysgarth footbridge : Rough Water I. Falls above and below Aysgarth impossible. Hestholme Farm—Wensley: Rough Water III. Wensley-Masham : Rough Water II, but Clifton—Rough Water III. Masham to 1 ml. below West Tanfield : Rough Water III (Hack Fall IV). West Tanfield—Ripon : Rough Water I. From Ripon—a navigation.

Miles

0   *Askrigg.* Village ¾ ml. L.

6   Footbridge near road R is the most convenient landing. In any case do not go beyond Aysgarth Mill just below. Long portage (R bank) through Aysgarth and along the main road to well below Aysgarth Force (nearly 2 mls.).

     N.B. Aysgarth Bridge, ½ ml. beyond Aysgarth is *above* Aysgarth Force, and above it are smaller falls and cataracts, which are impassable.

8   *Hestholme Farm* (R bank) (Permission to launch here no longer given). Difficult, rocky water all the way down to Wensley.

9¾   *Redmire Force.* Must usually be portaged L, though it may at some levels be shootable on R. Inspect.

11¼   Rapids.

12¾   *Bolton Hall Bridge.* Hall L. Easier for next 10 mls.

13¾   *Wensley Bridge.* Village L.

16¼   *Middleham Bridge.* Village ¾ ml. R—no shops. Leyburn village 1¼ mls. L—shops.

20¾   *Ulshaw Bridge.* Small weir 50 yds. below, about 1 ft. drop ; shootable with medium water.

22¾   *Jervaulx Abbey* (R). Rocky rapids recommence and should be negotiable at medium levels.

24¾   *Kilgram Bridge.*
29¾   *Clifton Castle.* Large residence on high bank L. A tricky and exhilarating rapid on final bend just below the castle.

31¾   *Masham Bridge.* Village R.

34¼   *Hack Fall.* A rapid worthy to rank with other canoeing "classics." A long heavy rapid round a wooded double bend, straightening out for the fall itself. Land on L to examine before deciding whether to shoot. If in doubt, line down. It may be advisable to wade the top ledge to get a straight run down the remaining falls. From the end of the fall fast water to Mickley.

35¼   *Mickley Weir.* Village R. Portage L. Good, fast water and rapids as far as—

38¼   *West Tanfield Bridge.* Village L. Quieter water from now. Two weirs in the next mile with rocky shallows between, continuing 200 yds. beyond lower weir. Quieter water from now on but easy rapids still as far as—

44¾   *Ripon Bridge.* Town R.
45¾   Confl. of *Laver.* R.
46¼   *Ure Bridge, Bridge Hewick.* Weir under bridge.

48¾   *Ure Navigation* joins on R.   (2½ mls. to Ripon, 3 locks.)   From here the river is a navigation.
50¾   *Newby Hall and Park* L.   Westwick Lock R.   Portage at side of weir (straight on).
54¾   *Boroughbridge.*   Rly. and road bridges.   Town R.   Milby lock.
56¼   *Swale Nab.*   Confl. of *Swale.*
60½   *Aldwark Bridge.*   Inn R.
62   Confl. of *Ouse Gill Beck* R.   From here the river is called *Ouse.*

The **Ouse** is rather a dull river, flowing right across the Plain of York.   There is little fall ; the river is a navigation with only 2 locks before it becomes tidal.   It is not recommended below Selby and below Goole the Humber is best avoided altogether.

O.S. 97 ;   Barth. 32, 33

Miles
62   Confl. of *Ouse Gill Beck.*
64   *Linton Lock.*   Navigation not under Docks and I.W. Executive.
64¾   *Newton upon Ouse.* L   1 ml. R.
65½   *Nun Monkton* R.   Confl. of *Nidd.*
69¼   *Nether Poppleton* R.   Rly. bridge.
77   *York.*   Rly. bridge, followed by three road bridges.   Stn. R of first bridge.   Very interesting walled town ; minster.
80   *Bishopthorpe* R.   Palace of Archbishop of York.
81½   *Naburn* L.
82½   *Naburn Locks* (duplicate).   Tidal below here (approx. 3 hours later than Goole.)
86½   Confl. of *Wharfe* R.
87   *Cawood Bridge.*   Village R.   Ruins of castle.
88½   *Kelfield* L.
93½   *Barlby* L.
95   *Selby.*   Road and rly. bridge.   Fine church.   Stn. R.   Below Selby is Selby Canal, connecting with the Aire.
102   *Barmby on the Marsh* L.   Ferry to Long Drax R.   Confl. of *Derwent.*   Rly. bridge beyond.
105   *Booth Ferry* road bridge.   Confl. of *Aire* R above.   Goole 2½ mls. R.
107   *Howden Dyke* Ferry.
110   *Goole* R.   Stn. ¼ ml.   Docks and mouth of *Don* (*Dutch River*). 9 mls. to Faxfleet L opposite mouth of *Trent.*

16.   SWALE

Rising on Birkdale Common the Swale flows E to Richmond and Catterick, then SE and S with many meanderings across the plain to Swale Nab, near Boroughbridge (confluence with Ure).   It has been canoed in favourable water from Gunnerside between Reeth and Muker.

Between Grinton, near Reeth, and Catterick it flows down a beautiful steep-sided valley with deep stretches alternating with shallows and a number of portages. In low water laborious. There are heavy rapids, falling in three steps, just above Marrick Priory. The river is liable to heavy spates and in high water conditions are not known ; but the fall between Grinton and Catterick Bridge—375 feet in 19 miles (20 feet per mile, approx.)—indicates some excitement. There is no rail access further up the valley than Richmond. Other places with rail access : Catterick, Ainderby and Baldersby.

Below Catterick the river flows between high banks across the plain, the fall being only 4 feet to the mile. The river crosses the 50 foot contour at a point 7 miles before Swale Nab and 60 miles above Goole.

Advice on the need for permission should be sought from the BCU.

O.S. 90, 91 ; Barth. 35

Miles
- 0   *Grinton Bridge.* Rapid below bridge ; keep L. Normally shallow to Marske but continuous heavy rapids after heavy rain. Just above Marrick Priory heavy rapids falling in three steps. Below Marske pools and rocky shallows.
- 12   Road bridge.
- 12½   Rapid ; keep L ; river swings R then L down rocky fall. Shoot centre.
- 13½   *Richmond Bridge.* Town and castle L. Rly. stn. R after second bridge.
- 13¾   Ledge across river ; steep fall. Portage L through gasworks.
- 14¼   Weir—barbed wire on R bank. Shallows below.
- 14½   *Easby Abbey,* L. Double rapid. L at first then land R to inspect rocky rapid beyond. Take L arch at rly. bridge and pass reef on L. Shallows.
- 15   *Red House Farm.* Rocky shallows lead to a heavy fall—approach difficult.
- 16   *"The Batts."* Fast water followed by shallows and pools.
- 19   *Catterick Bridge.* Rly. stn. ½ ml. L.
- 24½   Road bridge. Great Langton L.
- 32   Railway bridge.
- 32¼   *Morton Bridge.* Morton upon Swale L. Plenty of water, minor rapids, sandy banks.
- 40   Railway bridge. Maunby Village L.
- 47   *Skipton Bridge.* Skipton on Swale L.
- 49   *Catton.* Village L.
- 52   *Topcliffe Bridge.* Village L.   Weir ¼ ml. above—portage R ; shallows below bridge.
- 58½   *Thornton Bridge.*
- 59½   *Brafferton Railway Bridge.*
- 60   *Brafferton.* Village L.
- 63   *Myton on Swale.* Village L.
- 64   *Swale Nab.* Junction with Ure.

17. NIDD

The Nidd rises on Great Whernside and flows SE and E through Knaresborough to the Ouse some distance above York. It does not always carry much water in its upper reaches, as the outflow from the two reservoirs on its headwaters is controlled.

Probably canoeable in favourable water from Pateley Bridge, but the very awkward portage at Castlehead Weir makes Glasshouses a more convenient starting point though it is about 2 miles from Pateley Bridge.

Advice on the need to obtain permission should be sought from the BCU.

Grading :   Rough Water II (III in parts above Ripley).

O.S. 91, 96, 97 ; Barth. 32

Miles

0	*Pateley Bridge*. Village.
¾	*Castlestead Weir*. Difficult portage owing to stone wall banks.
1	*Glasshouses Bridge*. Convenient starting point in good water.
1¾	Railway bridge. Confused rocks above and below.
2½	*Ropeworks Weir*. Portage L if not shootable.
3	*Harewell Weir*. Portage R.
3½	*Summer Bridge Weir*. Portage L. Rapid below continuing to bridge.
4	*Low Hall*. Rocky rapid.
5	*Darley*. Old rly. stn. makes good starting point.
6	*Hardcastle Garth*. Rapid and island at sharp bend. Rly. bridge, footbridge and packhorse bridge in next ml.
7½	*Birstwith Weir* and bridge. If landing can be made through trees L, portage will be easier ; otherwise land R and portage to below bridge.
9	*Hampsthwaite Bridge*. Care required ; sharp set by stream above the bridge into a bushy bank. Bridge at an angle and trees below each buttress.
11	*Ripley Bridge* and Weir. Land above bridge and portage through dry arch L.
13	Rly. bridge ; river deep and slow.
14	Mill and weir ; portage L. River flows through steep-sided valley ; small falls and rapids frequent.
16	Small weir under wooden footbridge—shootable in high water, very little headroom. Boating begins.
16½	*Knaresborough*. Stn.
18	*Grimbald Weirs* and Bridge. Boating ends.
19¼	*Goldsborough Mill*. Portage R, difficult.
22½	*Little Ribston* R. Ribston Park.
25	*Walshford Bridge*. Inn. (Great North Road.)
26½	*Hunsingore Mill*.
28½	*Cattal Bridge*. Village L. River starts to wind.
31½	*Kirk Hammerton Mill*. Bridge. Battlefield of Marston Moor (1644) 2 mls. SW.
35	*Skip Bridge*.

Miles
38 *Moor Monkton* R.
39 *Nun Monkton.* Confl. with Ouse.

18.   WHARFE

The Wharfe, after emerging from Oughtershaw Moor, flows east through Buckden, and then south to Kettlewell, Grassington, Bolton, Ilkley, Otley, and Wetherby, to join the Yorkshire Ouse 10 miles or so below York.

In its upper reaches the dale is very beautiful, and even below Ilkley it is quite a pleasant river. The Wharfe has been canoed in high water from Buckden, but even from Kettlewell it often calls for much wading and portaging. From Grassington there is usually enough water, and good water is almost essential since the river runs fast and falls over ledges. The "Strid" a mile or so below Barden Bridge should be treated as impossible and must be portaged, the river at this point rushing through a very narrow rocky and undercut reef. There are strong undertows and downward drags.

After Bolton Bridge there are mills with many portages but with plenty of water, and some of the weirs may be shot.

Advice about the need to obtain permission beforehand should be sought from the B.C.U.

Buses to Grassington and Kettlewell. (West Yorks. Road Car Co., East Parade, Harrogate.)

O.S. 90, 96, 97

Grading :   Kettlewell—Bolton Bridge : Rough Water II ; but— Ghaistrills IV, Loup Scar III, Appletreewick III, Strid impossible. Below Bolton Bridge : I.

Miles
  0 *Kettlewell Bridge.* Village and inn L.
  3 Confl. of River Skirfare R. Rapid.
  5 *Coniston Bridge.* Village L. Kilnsey R.
  6 Rocky falls. *Portage.*
  7 *The Ghaistrills*, etc.   Following high, wooded bank on left. Portage or line down if in doubt. A minor version of the Strid. This is followed by a fall and strong rapid.
  8½ *Grassington Bridge.* Village L. Inn.
  9 *Linton Falls.* Portage L. River now fast and shallow.
  11 *Hebden.* Village ½ ml. L.

12   *Loup Scar*. Heavy rapid. Channel fairly obvious.
12¼   *Burnsall Bridge*. Village R. Inn.
14½   *Appletreewick* (L up hill). Island. Rapid with ledges. Survey and portage if in doubt.
15½   Confl. of Gill Beck. Visit waterfall up the beck.
16   *Barden Bridge*. Barden Tower R. Approaching the Strid.
17   *The Strid*. Should be treated as impossible. *Land well above* and portage well below.
18¾   Wooden bridge. Park House L.
19¼   *Bolton Abbey*. Ruins R.
20   *Bolton Bridge*. Hotel R.
23   *Addingham High Weir*. Low Weir a mile further on.
26   *Ilkley Bridges*. Town, stn., etc. R.
27½   *Ben Rhydding Bridge*. Stepping stones. Shallows deepening. Stn. R.
28½   *Greenholme Mill Weir*.
30½   *Burley-in-Wharfedale*. Weir. Village R.
33   *Otley Bridge*. Town and stn. R. Weir at mill beyond.
37   *Poole Bridge*.
38¼   *Arthington Railway Bridge*. Weir below.
44   *Harewood Bridge*. Weirs above—portage weir under bridge with two steps—portage extreme L arch, which is usually dry.
48   *Woodhall Bridge* (footbridge). Rapid with jagged rocks and no clear channel.
50   *Linton*. Road and rly. bridges.
52½   *Wetherby Bridge*. Weir. Town L.
54   *Flint Mill Weir*. Jackdaw Crag ½ ml. below.
56   *Thorpe Arch Weir and Bridge*. Thorpe Arch L. Boston Spa R.
60   *Newton Kyme Hall* R.
61½   *Tadcaster Bridge*. Weir. Town R. River now tidal.
65½   *Ulleskelf*. Ferry. Village R.
68½   *Ryther Ferry*.
71   Confl. of Ouse L. One mile above Cawood.

19. YORKSHIRE DERWENT

The Derwent rises not far from the coast in the N. Riding and flows SW to join the Ouse a few miles above Goole.

It is one of the loveliest of the northern rivers, with very easy navigation despite a good current. Below Sutton Lock it is tidal and less interesting, and the tides run fast for the last six miles. Mileages are given from Ganton at the junction of the River Hertford, though both rivers have been canoed some way above this, and canoes are said to have made their way once upon a time from Forge Valley through the Sea Cut to the coast just N of Scarborough. The stretch from Forge Valley to Ganton is, however, obstructed with barbed wire and over-hanging trees and is not really worthwhile. Buses, Scarborough-Leeds, pass frequently through Ganton. The river is small until the River Rye enters. From Malton there is good water all the way. The best stretch of the river is between Malton and Stamford Bridge. The York and Scarborough line follows the river closely between Malton and Kirkham. High water at Barmby-on-the-Marsh : Dover —3¼ hrs.

O.S. 93, 92, 97 or 98 ; Barth. ½ in. to 1 ml. Sheet 36, 33

Miles
0	*Ganton.* Village L. Fast but shallow water and artificial straightened course to—
5	*Foulbridge.*
7	*Yedingham Bridge.* Village R. Small rapid 200 yds. below.
14	Confl. of River Rye. River widens.
17	*Old Malton* R.
18	*New Malton.* Market town R. Rly. stn. L. Inns. If starting here launch above the last bridge.
20	*Cherry Islands.* A lovely corner.
21	*Low Hutton* R. Railway and footbridges.
24	*Castle Howard.*
25	*Kirkham.* Abbey ruins L. Derelict lock. New floodgates L. Weir shootable on extreme R only in high water. Portage over island on L of weir.
28	*Howsham* L. Derelict lock. Weir shootable on R in good water. Portage down centre of weir except at high water. Bridge.
30¼	*Scrayingham* L.
31¼	*Buttercrambe R.* Derelict lock. Take R channel, pass under road bridge and portage on R of mill.
34¼	*Stamford Bridge.* Very deep weir on L channel (portage L), or enter lock cut R, and portage R at derelict lock. Village and site of battle (1066) L.
35¾	*Low Catton* L.
37	*Kexby Bridge.* Main road (York 7 mls. R.)
40	*Elvington Bridge.* Village R. Sutton L and lock. Portage R. River now tidal (3 hours up, 9 hours down).
42¾	Wooden bridge.
44	Wooden bridge. Pocklington Canal enters L, this can be explored, weedy in summer.
49	*Bubwith* L. Bridge.
50	Railway bridge.
51	*Menthorpe* L then *Breighton* R.
53	Railway bridge.
53¾	*Loftsome.* Two road bridges.
55¾	Junction with Ouse. Barmby on the Marsh L.

20. Rye

A tributary of the Derwent, and carrying three times as much water at the confluence, the Rye rises among the bare Cleveland Hills and flows down Ryedale past the ruins of Rievaulx Abbey out into the Vale of Pickering, joining the Derwent a few miles above Malton.

Canoeable from a small concrete weir a mile above Helmsley. Lord Feversham permits canoes to pass through Duncombe Park only in winter and spring. Prior permission to pass through the 4 miles from the rly. bridge above Nunnington to Ness should be sought from the Estate Office, Nunnington. It will not be given between mid-March and end of September.

Shingle banks, shallow scours, broken twisting rapids as far as Nunnington. Inspect the fall at railway bridge 5 miles below Helmsley. After the high lateral weir at Nunnington (unshootable) the Rye twists deep, unobstructed and fast between high tussocky mud banks. Breaks only where numerous tributaries enter. Falls under the bridges at East Ness and Ryton.

From Helmsley Bridge : Rly. bridge 5 miles ; Nunnington Weir 6½ miles ; East Ness Br. 7¾ miles ; Ryton Br. 16¾ miles ; Malton-Pickering road br. 17¾ ; Junction with Derwent 19 miles.

O.S. 98 ; Barth. 33

21. AIRE and DON

In its upper reaches the characteristics of the **Aire** resemble those of the other Pennine rivers, but it flows through a number of small manufacturing towns, and then Leeds, and is not likely to appeal to canoeists. The valley between Skipton and Kirkstall is pleasant enough, and can be seen to advantage from the Leeds and Liverpool Canal (section 8).

The Aire probably has the distinction of being the only river in the country canoeable from its source. An inspection from the bank reveals that in a rainy season it may be canoed from the point where it bubbles from the rock at the foot of Malham Cove.

Below Leeds the Aire is a navigation, and beyond Ferrybridge the countryside becomes pleasant again. From here the river pursues a winding course to the Ouse at Booth Ferry.

Leeds-Ferrybridge 15 miles, 10 locks, then 3 locks to Haddlesey (23½ miles), then an open navigation to Booth Ferry (40¼ miles).

The *Don* and *Trent* can be reached from the Aire *via* the Knottingley and Goole, New Junction and Stainforth and Keadby canals. At Haddlesey the Selby Canal diverges to the left.

The **Don** has some pleasant stretches between Conisbrough and Doncaster and beyond, but then becomes a fenland river with high banked artificial cuts. It also is not likely to appeal to canoeists generally.

22. HULL

The Hull is canoeable from Driffield. It is mostly high banked and not very interesting. From Driffield to Hempholme Lock it is best to take the parallel Driffield Canal as the river is weedy ; below it is tidal. No landing except at high water between Beverley and Hull. Hornsea Mere is private.

Driffield - Hempholme Lock 7 miles.
Hempholme Lock - Hull 18 miles.

O.S. 99 ; Barth. 33

TRENT BASIN AND EAST MIDLANDS

23. TRENT

The Trent is our third longest river and rises in North Staffordshire. After flowing in a south-easterly direction to Alrewas, it turns north-east to Newark, and then north to the Humber.

Immediately after leaving the Potteries the Trent flows through very pleasant country, and although the scenery can never be described as exciting the river has a pleasant charm of its own all the way to Newark. The valley is at its best where the river flows close under the low hills that fringe it.

The river is known, from inspection at the bridges, to be practicable for canoes except after dry weather from Trentham Park, close to Stoke-on-Trent, but is here narrow and twisting. Rail access is, however, rather more than 1½ miles from the river, and it would be better to start at Stone.

Alternatively, a start can be made from Penkridge on the Penk or from Stafford on the Sow, which unites with the Penk and flows into the Trent at Great Haywood (see details below).

From this point the river is pleasant, easy canoeing, but a number of weirs and shallows will be encountered above Newton Solney, where the River Dove enters on the left. As the river is frequently near the Trent and Mersey Canal, it is possible from time to time to carry over into the canal for a few miles if desired.

The windings make the river appear longer than it is. The Trent has a good current and right down to Swarkestone easy rapids may be expected frequently, especially when the water level is low, making an interesting trip, the water conditions resembling those of the Wye. In high water a number of the weirs above Derwentmouth may be found to be shootable. Below Derwentmouth the river is much wider, the weirs are higher and unshootable, but the scenery remains good through Nottingham all the way to Newark.

Below Derwentmouth the river is a navigation and was once a navigation from Burton. No permits required, but a charge of 1s. is made for the passage of a canoe through a lock. This covers return on the same day. No charge when rollers are used or if canoes are carried round the weirs.

The *Trent and Mersey Canal* follows the Trent valley and joins the navigation at Derwentmouth.

An *Aegre* or bore comes up the Trent from the Humber to Gainsborough at the time of spring tides. This fast moving wall of water can be very dangerous, and canoeists should enquire about tides before leaving Newark.

Camping : Camping sites are easy to find all the way down this river, and villages frequently lie well back on account of flooding.

Places of interest: Nottingham and Newark are well worth a stay of several hours, the former for its castle, inns, rock caves, etc., and the latter for its castle, church and many old inns. Burton, Nottingham and Newark are all famous for home-brewed ale and there is an interesting inn built on to, and dug out of, the Castle Rock, called "The Trip to Jerusalem" from connections with the Crusaders.

From Fiskerton, a few miles above Newark it is a short distance to Southwell, where the cathedral is well worth a visit. The stone carving in the chapter house is particularly noteworthy.

Rail access is easy all down the Trent valley and provides good connections to all parts.

British Waterways' Inland Cruising Booklet No. 2 covers the Trent Navigation from Shardlow to Gainsborough.

O.S. 119, 120, 121, 112, 113, 104 ; Barth. 23, 24, 29

Several of the tributaries of the Trent offer interesting alternative starting points, combined with varying lengths of the main river.

Note. No reports have been received of the navigation of the river above Stone. This part of the river is narrow and tortuous but, from inspection at bridges, there should be enough water except after dry weather. There are probably a number of weirs and wire across the river. Scenery through Trentham Park and between Sandon and Great Haywood good. The Trent and Mersey Canal, which runs close all along this stretch, provides a useful alternative (11 miles, 12 locks, falling). The rly. follows the river closely but the stations at Sandon, Weston-on-Trent, Ingestre, Great Haywood and Colwich are closed.

Miles

0 *Trentham.*

1½ *Strongford Bridge.* S end of Trentham Park (A.34).

2¾ Road bridge, Barlaston 1 ml. L.

5¾ *Darlaston Bridge* (A.34).

7 *Stone Bypass Bridge* (A.34), followed by a rly. bridge. Stone Stn. ¼ ml. L.

7¾ *Walton Bridge.* Stone L.

9½ *Aston Bridge* (disused mill).

13¼ *Sandon Bridge.*

13¾ Where river divides above bridge take R channel. Concrete cill on L channel shootable only in spate.

14½ *Casey Bridge.* Salt R.

15¼ Weir.

16 *Weston rly. and road bridges.* Fast and shallow, many sandbanks.

17¼ Road bridge, Ingestre Park R.

18½ Road bridge with weir underneath. If unshootable portage L.

19¼ *Hoomill Bridge.*

20 *Haywood Mill.* Staffs and Worcs Canal aqueduct. Little headroom.

20½ Confl. of *Sow* R. This provides an alternative and quite attractive route starting at Stafford or Penkridge (see section 24 below).

21 *Great Haywood Bridge.*

23 *Colwich.*

25½ Canal aqueduct. Trent and Mersey Canal. Little headroom.

26¼ *Colton Weir.* Easy portage R to lower stream.

26½ *Rugeley Bridge.* Stn. L adjoining . Town ½ ml. R. Power stn. L.

28½ *Mavesyn Ridware Railway Bridge.* Broken weir above bridge. Passage through centre ; islands and scours below.

29¾ *High Bridge.* Road bridge. Island and small rapid below.

30½ *Pipe Ridware* L.

31½ *Nethertown* L. River divides. Take L branch over broken weir, later joined by R. Blythe L. The R branch leads to King's Bromley Mill in ¾ ml. (awkward portage).

32½ *King's Bromley* R. The two branches re-unite.

33 *Yoxall Bridge.* Lichfield—Ashbourne Road A.515.

36¼ *Wychnor Park* L. River divides. Keep R over broken weir.

37 *Alrewas Mill.* Carry L past weir. Village R. Stn. ¾ ml. R. Trent and Mersey Canal enters R and leaves L within a few hundred yds. The Trent flows over a weir (portage L).

38 *Wychnor Bridges.* Lichfield—Burton Road (A.38).

38½ River divides. Keep L.

39 Two railway bridges. Followed by confl. of River Tame R. Trent now much wider.

40 *Catton Hall* R. Island. Rope ferry. ½ ml. below look out in low water for submerged stones and stakes.

43 *Walton-on-Trent Bridge.* Village R. Power stn. R. Rather dull until—

46¾ *Drakelow Park* R. Power stn.

47 *Drakelow Weir.* ¼ ml. below rly. bridge. Rather awkward approach through reeds in summer, but can be shot at all states of the water through the gap in centre. Footbridge ½ ml. below leads to Burton-on-Trent L. Pleasant approach to—

48 *Burton-on-Trent Bridge.* Landing R at bridge. Town L over bridge. Stn. approx. 1 ml. L. Weir on channel L immediately below bridge, but this leads close to gas works. Instead, keep R and portage R of second weir at mill ½ ml. further on.

49½ *"Bladon Castle"* R on hill.

50½ *Newton Solney.* Village R. Confl. of Dove L.

52½ *Willington Bridge.* Village and rly. stn. L. Repton 1 ml. R. Power stn. L. Strong current at intake.

55 *Twyford Ferry.* Village L.

56½ *"Anchor Church."* In cliff on R.

57 *Ingleby* R.

59 *Barrow upon Trent.* Village L.

60 *Swarkestone Bridge.* Small village and inn L. Rapid below bridge. Take R. arch. Submerged masonry each side of channel. Easy portage beneath bridge.

61½   Railway bridge. Trent and Mersey Canal close L.

63½   *King's Mills.* Donnington Park R. The scenery is very pleasant here. The breach in the weir L can be shot at the left-hand side of the opening. Rough water on R. Fast current to Shardlow.

64¼   Power stn. R.

67   *Shardlow* L. Shallow rapid ¼ ml. above requires care. Keep L.

67¼   *Cavendish Bridge.* Leicester-Derby Road (A.6).

68½   *Derwentmouth.* Junc. with Trent and Mersey Canal L. Confl. of River Derwent L.

69   *Sawley Lock Cut* R. Sawley Weir L. Dangerous boil and undertow. Carry past weir L.

69½   *Sawley Bridge.* Village L.

71   *Trentlock.* Canal junctions : Erewash Canal L ; Cranfleet Cut, L (Trent Navigation); R. Soar, R (Loughborough Navigation —Grand Union Canal). Trent Rly. Stn. ¾ ml. L.

71¼   *Trent Railway Bridge and Weir.* Carry past on R.

72½   *Thrumpton* R.

74¼   *Barton Ferry.*

76¼   *Beeston Weir.* Entrance to Beeston Cut L. It is better to carry round the weir R and continue down the river through Nottingham to Trent Bridge.

79½   *Wilford Bridge.* Electricity generating stn. L.

81   *Trent Bridge.* Nottingham City on left. Cricket ground. Boathouse. Good landing and unbuilding on Victoria Embankment Gardens L above bridge. Stns. 1 ml. L.

81½   Canal rejoins river L. Grantham Canal joins R.

83¼   *Colwick Hall* L and Race Course.

83¾   Holme Sluice gates and Locks. High banks make access to river below locks difficult.

87¼   *Radcliffe-on-Trent* R. Village and stn. Wooded cliff R.

87¾   *Stoke Bardolph Weir and Lock cut.* Portage round weir L on concrete embankment. Rollers.

88½   *Stoke Bardolph Ferry.* Village L.

89¾   *Burton Joyce.* Village L.

91¾   *Gunthorpe Bridge and Lock.* Village and inn L. East Bridgford Village R ; portage R at lock.

94½   *Hoveringham Ferry.* Village and inn L.

96½   *Hazelford Ferry.* Village of Bleasby ¾ ml. L. Hotel.

97   *Hazelford Lock.* Rollers R.

98½   *Fiskerton Ferry.* Village L. Rly. stn. ¾ ml. L. Southwell 3 mls. L. It is well worth while visiting the cathedral.

102½   *Farndon Ferry.* Village R.

103½   *Averham Weir.* Generating station L, followed by long weir L. Keep close to R bank for navigation to Newark (R) 2 miles. Canoe can be left at boathouse (near confl. of the River Devon) and the town and castle approached by towing path. Newark Stn. (M.R.) close to bridge and castle. E.R. stn. ¾ ml. through town. If not visiting Newark, portage at weir and continue down main stream.

104   *Averham Church* L.

105   *Kelham Bridge* (A.616). Village L.

106   *Muskham Bridge* (Great North Road).

108   *Crankley Point.* Newark Cut rejoins river. It cuts off 2 mls. Below here the Trent is not particularly attractive ; it is better to stop at Newark.

109½   *North Muskham Ferry.* Village L.

111   *Cromwell Lock.* Unlocked from this point.

112½   *Collingham Wharf.*

114½   *Carlton-on-Trent Ferry.* Village L.

116   *Meering Ferry.* Sutton-on-Trent ¼ ml. L. Girton and Besthorpe R.

120¼   *Marnham Ferry.* Village L. South Clifton R.

123   *Newton-upon-Trent Bridge.* Dunham Village L. Tidal below here.

127   *Torksey-on-Trent.* Here the Foss Dike R (a canal since Roman times) leads to Lincoln (11 mls., 1 lock), and the River Witham.

137½   *Gainsborough Bridge.*

142½   Junc. with *Idle Navigation* L. Also Chesterfield Canal comes in L.

145½   *East Ferry.*

148½   *Susworth.*

150½   *West Butterwick Ferry.*

153½   *Burringham and Althorpe Ferry.*

154½   *Keadby Canal Junc. Stainforth and Keadby Canal* L lead to *R. Don* (Dutch River) (3 locks 13 mls.) from which the *Aire* and *Ouse* can be reached.

164½   *Trent Falls.* Junc. with Humber.

24. Penk and Sow

The **Penk** rises near Codsall, NW of Wolverhampton and flows N to join the **Sow** at a point near Stafford ; the latter flows E to the Trent at Gt. Haywood. Practicable for canoes from Penkridge (stn. on Wolverhampton-Stafford line) and makes a convenient and pretty approach to the Trent. The Staffs and Worcs Canal runs close to the river all the way.

O.S. 119 ; Barth. 23

Miles

0   *Penkridge Bridge.* Build on L bank above bridge if water low. (If river high, start in field adjoining Dunston road below the Roller Mill.)

¼   *Roller Mill.* Sluice shootable in moderate water.

5   *Acton Trussell Bridge.* Village and inn R 1 ml.

7   *Radford Bridge.* Inn R. Stafford L.

8   Confl. with **Sow,** formerly navigable for barges from Stafford
1½ mls. from the mouth of the Penk, but now rather shallow
for the first half mile. It offers a convenient route to the
Trent from Stafford Stn. where many main line trains stop.
The most convenient starting point would be the public
tennis courts immediately across the bridge facing the
station but the groundsman may object and, unless permission has been obtained from the Parks Superintendent in
advance, it is best to turn R on leaving the station and
start from the triangle of waste ground immediately below
the weir 300 yds. away.

8½   *St. Thomas's Priory Bridge.* Take R branch and portage R into
lower stream. Weir on L branch unshootable.

10½   Staffs and Worcs Canal aqueduct.

10¾   *Milford Bridge.*

11½   *Shugborough Park* R. Take L branch.

12½   *Gt. Haywood Bridge.* Take L branch just before bridge. Junc.
with Trent.

25. Tame, its tributaries, and Mease

The Tame rises in the Black Country, flows through Birmingham,
receiving much sewage and trade effluent and then N through Tamworth
to the Trent near Alrewas. The material of the river bed is rather
objectionable but the river has a fast current and flows through pleasant
country. Has been canoed from Castle Bromwich. At second railway
bridge from Castle Bromwich centre arch has concrete pillars under.
Permission to pass between the two rail bridges from Parkhall Farm.
At Water Orton bridge left hand arch (awkward turn and fallen
masonry). The tributary the *Anker* is the usual starting point. From
Tamworth the valley is pleasant (though the water is not) and the
current is good.

O.S. 131, 120 ; Barth. 19, 24

Miles
0   *Water Orton.* Fast water and probably a clear run past Whitacre
and Kingsbury.

12½   *Fazeley.* Coventry Canal aqueduct.

15¼   *Tamworth*, *Lady Bridge.* Castle, stn. ½ ml. R. Confl. of *Anker.*
Take L fork if enough water and portage at weir. Other-
wise the R branch to paper mill.

17¼   *Hopwas Bridge.*

18   Islands. Rly. bridge ¼ ml. below

19   *Comberford.*

20½   Mills L. Road bridge.

20¾   *Elford Village* R. Hall. Church.

22¼   Island—power cables.

24   Island.

24¼   *Chetwynd Bridge* (A.513). Alrewas, 1¼ mls. L, stn. (A.38).

25   Island and rly. bridge. Junc. R with Trent and Canal.

The **Anker** is a tributary of the Tame, is narrow, but has three large, but shallow, meres in its 7 miles from Polesworth, the highest practical starting point.

Miles

0	*Polesworth.* Road bridge.
$\frac{1}{2}$	Railway bridge ; shallows.
$1\frac{1}{4}$	Large mere. Difficult to find exit to L at end of mere.
2	River follows rly. then turns sharp R. Beware of wooden stumps of broken down weir.
$2\frac{1}{2}$	Large mere. Sunken road 100 yds. from entrance on the L. Keep well to R.
$3\frac{1}{4}$	Road bridge ; shallows.
$4\frac{1}{2}$	Large mere. Exit L at end.
$5\frac{1}{4}$	Footbridge ; rapid under.
6	Railway bridge. Take left-hand arch—stumps across right-hand arch.
$6\frac{3}{4}$	*Bole Bridge*—shallows.
7	*Tamworth.* Junc. with River Tame.

The **Blythe**, a tributary of the Tame, is narrow but is canoeable from Stonebridge and has actually been canoed from Barston Bridge. Shallows and barbed wire with stakes where old bridges used to be. At Duke Bridge—sluice gates : portage L.

Mease

The Mease rises near Shackerstone, S of Ashby de la Zouch, and flows into the Trent near Croxall. It has been canoed from Netherseal Mill, 6 miles SW of Ashby de la Zouch. Rather narrow, shallow and laborious in summer ; many meanders with high sandstone banks to Stone's Bridge, near Clifton Campville. Thereafter banks lower, but still shallow through dairying country. Wire fences across the river at times. Other portages at Clifton Mill and Harlaston Mill.

26. Churnet and Dove

(*a*) The **Churnet,** a tributary of the Dove, rises near Leek in N. Staffordshire. It flows through a lovely valley, but is polluted by effluent from several works on its course and is not potable. Through the upper part of the valley run the Leek and Caldon branches of the Trent and Mersey Canal ; the latter runs down the valley as far as Froghall. The 4 mile stretch between Froghall and Oakamoor is thought to be practicable but no reports of attempts have been received; there would be a long portage round the copper works at Oakamoor. The Churnet has been canoed from Oakamoor and gives a fast and beautiful trip past Alton Towers and Denstone to its confluence with the Dove at Rocester. The usual starting point is Alton, 3 miles below

Oakamoor, where the village is close to the bridge. From here it is narrow and twisting and fallen trees may be awkward. A mile or so below Alton is a rocky fall (line down). Between this and Rochester is a weir (portage). At Rocester Bridge another weir, which gives an awkward portage if the river is diverted through the stone works. *Grading* : Rough Water II.

Leek-Cheddleton-Froghall (by canal) approx. 9½ mls.; Froghall-Alton Bridge, 7 mls.; Alton Bridge-Confl. with Dove, 8 mls.

Maps (Oakamoor downwards) O.S. 120 ; Barth 23, 24

(*b*) The **Dove** rises on Axe Edge near Buxton and flows S through the celebrated Dovedale to Ashbourne and thence through a wide, curving valley full of meanders to the Trent at Newton Solney. Practicable from Clifton near Ashbourne. But fast water and obstructions must be expected. The fishing is closely preserved in the higher parts and objections will be encountered above Rocester. The Churnet provides an alternative approach. Below Rocester the Dove is very tortuous.

Grading : Rocester to Tutbury—Rough Water II.

O.S. 120 ; Barth. 24

Miles

0	*Clifton Bridge.* Clifton Village ¼ ml L. Several weirs in next 5 mls. Objections from fishing interests probable.
5	*Norbury Bridge.* Village L ; weir before bridge.
7	Weir. *Rocester Bridge.* Village R.
9	Confl. of *Churnet* R. (See above—provides an alternative approach.)
12	Road bridge. Uttoxeter 1 ml R. Shoot ledge under second arch from R.
12¾	*Doveridge* L.
17½	Weir. Shootable in most states of water, or portage L.
19	*Aston Bridge* (*Sudbury*). Rly. ¼ ml. R.
23	*Scropton.* Village ¼ ml. L.
24	Weir. Must be portaged. A dull loop can be avoided by carrying down the concrete overflow where the weir is first seen. If finishing at Tutbury, best to portage into millstream R.
24¾	*Tutbury Bridge.* Village R.
26	*Dove Bridge.* Rolleston 1 ml. R.
28	*Dove Cliffe.* Weir.
29	Road bridges.
30	*Junction with Trent.*

27. Derbyshire Derwent

From its source in the Peak moorlands on the Yorkshire borders the Derwent flows S through lovely country to Chatsworth Park, through a gorge at Matlock to Ambergate and Derby, and then meanders over flat country to join the Trent at Derwentmouth. It has been canoed from Hathersage and is probably practicable from Bamford in good water. The trouble with the Derwent is the large number of weirs and the difficulty of finding camp sites especially between Ambergate and Derby, but it makes an interesting trip. Also above Rowsley water conditions are problematical as levels are controlled to some extent by the water discharged from three large reservoirs at the head of the valley ; but from Rowsley it should be canoeable at all seasons.

The river is private. Permission needs to be sought to pass through several stretches. Advice from B.C.U.

O.S. 111 and 120 ; Barth. 29, 24

Grading :   Rough Water II.

Miles

0   *Hathersage Bridge.* Take L of centre arch. Shallows for the next few miles which can be negotiated with a lightly laden canoe and a keen eye for rocks and channels.

2   *Nether Padley Bridge.* Grindleford Stn. ¾ ml. L. Soon after this is deep water.

3   *Froggatt Bridge.* Deep water continues.

3½   *Knouchley Bridge and Weir.* Land on L and line down. Difficult water below ; 300 yds. above Calver Bridge is a heavy rapid —shoot centre.

4   *Calver Bridge.* Deep, slow water again.

6   *Baslow Weir and Bridge.* Land in mill lade L. Portage.

6½   *Chatsworth Park* (prior permission required from the Chatsworth Estate Office, Edensor, near Bakewell). Deer-gates hang from footbridge but canoes can be paddled through narrow opening. Shallows in places with soft reed-covered bottom. Shortly below the house there are two weirs each of which should be portaged on L. Below the second weir there are a number of minor rocky rapids continuing to Rowsley.

9   *Road Bridge.* Deer-gates similar to the first.

11   *Rowsley.* Rail and road bridges. Stn. L. Peacock Inn R.

11¼   Confl. of Wye R. River becomes easier after this point but straightforward rapids continue at intervals. Prior permission required from Haddon Estate Office, Bakewell.

14¼   *Darley Dale Bridge.* Inn. Stn. ½ ml. L.

17   *Matlock Bridge.* Building point under dry arch near stn.

18   *Matlock Weir.* Can be shot on extreme right. Portage (also R) difficult owing to high banks.

19   *Matlock Bath.* River used by boats.

20   *Willersley Weir.* Portage L.

20¼   *Cromford Bridge.* Ledge across river ½ ml. below here. Next 2 mls. belong to Matlock and Cromford Angling Assn. who object to canoeing in spring and summer. Cromford Canal on R.

21⅞   *Railway Bridge.*

22   *Canal Aqueduct.*
22¼   *Railway Bridge.*
22¾   *Railway Bridge.* Rapid just below. Submerged poles on R under
          bridge. Shoot.
24   *Whatstandwell Bridge.* Derwent Hotel. Stn. ¼ ml. L.
25½   *Wireworks Weir.* Portage L.
26¼   *Ambergate Bridge.* Long pool used by boats from Belper.
29   *Belper Weir and Bridge.* Land on L and portage over road. After
          this river is easy except for weirs.
31   *Hopping Weir.* Shootable down channel through grass in centre.
31½   *Milford Bridge and Weir.* Portage L.
33½   *Duffield Bridge.*
34   *Paper Mills Weir.* Has been shot middle R but portage R
          recommended.
34½   Rail bridge.
35½   *Allestree Bridge.*
37   *Darley Weir.* Easy portage down sill or shoot through sluice.
38½   *Derby.* Rowing clubs both sides above rail bridge.
38¾   Bridge and Weir. Easy shoot to left of island.
39   Bridge. Land on steps on R for gardens near Trent bus stn.
          River winding, dull and dirty below Derby.
53   *Derwentmouth.* Junction with Trent ; also Trent and Mersey
          Canal.

28. Derbyshire Wye

The Wye rises on Axe Edge near Buxton and flows through a succession of lovely limestone dales, at first rocky and marred in places by
quarrying, then more wooded, to Ashford and Bakewell and then
through the park of Haddon Hall to the Derwent at Rowsley. This
river has been canoed from Millers Dale (rly. stn.) and presents several
interesting rapids but is rather laborious. Below Bakewell the river is
easier through Haddon Park, as far as its junction with the Derwent
near Rowsley. Permission necessary from Haddon Estate Office,
Bakewell, before attempting this section.

O.S. **111**, Peak District Tourist

Miles
0   *Millers Dale.* Stn.
1½   *Litton Mill.*
2½   *Cressbrook* : bottom mill ; may be shot through sluice R if
          conditions permit. Narrow with overhanging trees.
3¼   *Monsal Dale Station* (closed). Low bridge, portage R. No camping
          but good starting point.
4   Weir : portage R ; rapids below for 2 mls., watch for barbed wire
          and fallen trees.
6   Road bridge. Great Shacklow Wood on R.
7   *Ashford* road bridge. Weir : portage L. Village L.

7½   Road bridge (B.6465). Keep R—beware drag of the sluice at
      entrance to L branch.   Small bridge and 2 small weirs
      follow.
9   *Bakewell Bridge*. Town R, stn. ¼ ml. L.
12   Road bridge (A.6). Junction with River Bradford.
13¼   Wye Farm.
13½   Take R. channel.
13¾   Weir may be shot R.
14   *Great Rowsley* (stn.). Junction with River Derwent.

29. Soar

The Soar rises in the high ground between Rugby and Leicester, and
flows northward through Leicester and Loughborough to the Trent
just above Trent Weir. From Aylestone, 3 miles above Leicester, it has
been canalised, and forms part of the Grand Union Canal system.

For these three miles, see the section on the Leicester Canal (Section
154). Below Leicester there are frequent navigation cuts to which the
old river forms an agreeable alternative. The portages at the weirs are
usually shorter than at the locks, and several locks are avoided
altogether by taking the old river. The countryside is pleasant all the
way to the Trent, but naturally there is little current, except in some
places in the old river. Fees may be demanded, if the lock cuts are used.
The itinerary below follows the old river.

Rail access at several points from the M.R. main line.

The Navigation is described in British Waterways Inland Cruising
Booklet No. 10 : Grand Union Canal—Part III.

O.S. 121 ; Barth 24

Miles
0   *Leicester (West Bridge)*. Close to Central Stn. (E.R.).
¼   Weir L. Abbey Park and Meadows L. Keep R. Two locks in
      next mile.
1½   *Abbey Meadows, Lock and Weir*.
2   Road bridge (A.6). Boathouse L.
3¼   *Birstall Mill and Lock*.
4   *Thurmaston Mill and Lock*. The river diverges to the left and the
      navigation cut continues to join the *Wreak*, which it follows
      to the Soar again : one lock just beyond the junction with
      the Wreak.
5¼   *Wanlip*. Village L and bridge.
6½   Junction of *Wreak* (with the navigation). Cossington Mill and
      Lock.
6¾   Junct. of *Rothley Brook* L which can be followed for some way.
7¾   *Sileby Mill and Lock*. Village R.

8½   Weir on R to side channel.

8¾   *Mountsorrel Lock.* Side channel rejoins after a mile.

10¼   Mill and Weir L to old river ; the cut goes straight on to Barrow
       Lock in ½ ml.; the river takes a big loop via Quorndon.

12   *Barrow on Soar Bridge.* Stn. adjoining R.

13   *Pilling's Lock.* This is a stop lock for the cut to Loughborough
       and may be open. The river goes over a weir R and is much
       to be preferred to the navigation which is dirty where it
       passes through the town. The cut passes not far from
       Loughborough Stn. (E.R.) and there are two locks beyond
       the town.

15¼   Mill and weir. Road bridge (A.60). Take R fork ; the second
       arch from the L can be shot after inspection. Loughborough
       Stn. (M.R.) ¼ ml. L.

16¼   *Stanford on Soar Bridge.* Village R. Rly. bridge (E.R.) below.

17¼   Rly. bridge (M.R.). *Caution* : submerged coach bolts stick up
       from old piles to within 3 in. of the surface at summer levels.
       The second arch from L is best.

17½   Cut comes in on R.

18½   *Normanton on Soar.* R.

19¼   *Zouch Mills.* Cut on R with lock at end (¼ ml.). Old river L.

20½   *Devil's Elbow.* (Loop on river.)

22   *Kegworth.* Village L and lock. Another lock and road bridge
       ¼ ml. below ; Kegworth Stn. ½ ml. R.

23½   *Ratcliffe on Soar* (on old river to R). Lock at end of cut L.

24½   *Red Hill Lock.*

25   Junction with *Trent.* If going on down the Trent turn R and
       carry round Trent Weir R ; or turn L upstream and then
       R into Cranfleet Lock cut.

30. Grantham Canal

33 miles long : Grantham to the Trent at Nottingham : 18 locks
descending, mainly in two groups at Woolsthorpe and Cropwell,
separated by a 15 mile level. Closed to barge navigation and the
15 mile level is in bad condition owing to a drop in the water level and
weeds and reeds. Locks unusable. Passes through the fine Belvoir
country with extensive views and canoes might get along parts of it.

O.S. 122 ; Barth. 24, 25

31. Idle

Formed by a number of headstreams flowing through or near the Dukeries. From their junction near Markham Moor (road A.1) it flows N through East Retford (main line stn. E.R. near river) and Bawtry and then across marshes to the Trent at Stockwith.   An ancient navigation from Retford.   It offers a pleasant trip through typical Notts and Lincs scenery, at first well wooded.   Current good, and mostly clear over sandy or gravel bed. From Bawtry the country opens out and the river deepens and straightens, though always with a good current. Gamston-Stockwith, approx. 24 miles.

The *Maun* is believed to be practicable from Mansfield, about 25 miles above Retford.

O.S. 103, 104 ; Barth. 29

32. Chesterfield Canal

Runs from Chesterfield N through mining villages, then E to Retford through pleasant country and then NE to the Trent at Stockwith, this part traversing much the same country as the Idle. The western part is in bad order and there is nothing particular to recommend a cruise on this part of the canal.

Chesterfield-Stockwith 45½ miles, 65 locks ; Retford-Stockwith 15 miles, 5 locks.

O.S. 103, 104 ; Barth 29

33. WITHAM

The Witham rises in Rutland and follows a circuitous course N through Grantham and a few miles E of Newark to Lincoln where it bends SE to the fens and Boston. There is enough water from Londonthorpe road bridge near Grantham, but permission is required to pass through two parks, with artificial obstructions ; it is easier to start at Barkston Bridge where the Witham is still narrow.   It flows partly between low hills and partly across flat marshy country ; it is clear but shallow except above the mills, and should not be tried after dry weather. There is plenty of water from the confluence of the Brant. Portages at the mills at Hougham, Marston, Long Bennington, Claypole, Bassingham and Haddington. Newark Station is about 4 miles from the river at Barnby-in-the-Willows. It is a navigation from Lincoln to the sea ; the Foss Dike connects it with the Trent at Torksey.

From Lincoln it runs through marshland all the way to Boston ; the fall is small—there is only one lock between Lincoln and Boston, and to Boston the scenery is not very interesting.   The lock charge is 2s.

A side excursion can be made from Kirkstead to Woodhall Spa.

British Waterways' Inland Cruising Booklet No. 7 describes the Foss Dike and Witham Navigations.

O.S. 113, 114 ; Barth. 25, 30

34. FOSS DIKE

This ancient waterway, 11 miles long, connecting the Trent at Torksey with the Witham at Lincoln was first made by the Romans ; in the 12th Century it was made navigable and has been widened and deepened since then more than once. There is only 1 lock (lock charge 2s.) at Torksey, which cannot be opened for several hours before and after low water in the Trent. This canal is quite pleasant.

British Waterways' Cruising Booklet No. 7 describes the waterway.

O.S. 113 ; Barth. 29, 30

35. WELLAND

Rising in Northamptonshire near Naseby not far from the Stratford Avon, the Welland flows NE past Rockingham and Stamford to the fens and the Wash. Formerly a navigation from Stamford to the sea. It has little scenic interest below Deeping.

Has been canoed from Harringworth, 16 mls. above Stamford ; but as far as Duddington it is narrow, shallow and apt to be overgrown with rushes, and permission should be sought from Mr. Jackson of Duddington. Below Duddington Mill the river improves and resembles the Nene Valley. Portages at Tinwell and South View Farm, near Stamford. After Stamford much less laborious.

Distances from Stamford : Market Deeping 7 mls.; Crowland 10¾ mls. Spalding 15 mls., Junc. of *R. Glen* 20 mls.

1½ miles below Spalding are lock gates, beyond which the tide flows. At low tide very muddy ; an alternative is to portage a short distance L into *Vernatt's Drain* which rejoins the Welland at Surfleet Seas End—mouth of *R. Glen.*

36. Glen

The Glen rises SE of Grantham and joins the Welland beyond Spalding. It is a fenland river, artificially regulated. There is a sluice at the mouth into the Welland. Of little intrinsic interest, the Glen forms part of a water route using fen drains and the Witham from the Ouse and Nene to the Trent, with a few portages.

Ouse to Nene via Well Creek and Twenty Foot Drain.

Down Nene to South Holland Drain (short portage).

Along Drain to Welland at Peak Hill (portage across Cowbit Wash to Welland).

Down Welland to Glen, and up it to South Forty Foot Drain (portage).

Along Drain to Witham and up it to Lincoln, etc.

Only fenland enthusiasts are likely to attempt it.

O.S. 123 ; Barth. 25

37. NENE

The Nene (or Nen) rises near Badby and flows E to Northampton, thence NE to Peterborough, and then by various artificial channels across the fens to Wisbech and the Wash. Below Northampton it is a navigation, and can also be reached by a branch of the Grand Union Canal from Gayton, near Blisworth (5 miles, 17 locks descending). The navigation has been put in good order by the Nene River Board. Between Wellingborough and Thrapston the scenery is dull. Beyond Irthlingborough the river runs through a pleasant wooded valley as far as Peterborough, with charming villages mostly built of local stone. It is hardly worth continuing beyond Peterborough, though details are given in Section 36 above of a route from the Nene at Peterborough via the Middle Level Navigations to the Ouse at Denver.

Permit for using the locks should be sought from the Nene River Board, 11 North Street, Oundle, Northants. If the locks are not used there is no charge. The paddles or "slackers" on the upper lock gates are used for regulating the flow of the river in wet weather. If the locks are used they should be re-set in the original position. The River Board issue master keys by arrangement but a winch ($1\frac{1}{4}$ inches square) is needed to operate the slackers.

The river often splits into several channels and at the locks there are often two or more weir streams which provide alternatives to some awkward portages. The best part of a week should be allowed for the whole length from Northampton to Peterborough to allow plenty of time to explore the villages. Main lines cross the valley at Northampton, Wellingborough and Peterborough, and the Northampton-Peterborough line (M.R.) follows the river closely, but there are no Sunday trains and some of the stations are closed.

O.S. 133, 134 ; Barth. 19, 20, 25

0   *Northampton Bridge.* Castle Stn. adjoins a tributary where boats can be built close to the station. This, however, flows through the local generating station and it is better to trolley the canoe R out of the station, then L in about 200 yds. along a lane to a mill. Alternatively, Bridge St. Stn. is close to the river.

¾   *Northampton Lock,* followed by 4 more locks before—

5   *Billing Lock and Bridge.*

6¼   *Coggenhoe Lock.* Village R. 1 more lock before—

8½   *White Mills Lock and Bridge.* Inn R. 3 locks before—

12½   *Wellingborough Lock and Bridge.* Wellingborough London Rd. Stn. adjoining. Convenient launching place on promenade adjoining stn. and also on B573—¾ ml. from main line stn.

13½   *Wellingborough Lower Lock.* Easy portage.

15½   *Ditchford Bridge and Lock.* Portage L.

17½   *Higham Ferrers Lock.* May be avoided by portaging into one of the channels L if not overgrown with weeds. Three low footbridges on the channel nearest to Irthlingborough.

17¾   *Irthlingborough Bridge.* Stn. R.

18½   *Irthlingborough Lock.* Alternatively the millstream R can be taken, or portage into channel leaving the millstream immediately after the lock L (barbed-wire at ford).

21   *Ringstead Lock.* Stn. R. Lining down sluice R may be possible. At Ringstead Lower Lock, ½ ml. below, keep to L channel and portage round weir, L.

23¾   *Woodford Lock.* Portage easy.

24¾   *Denford Lock.* Portage R easy.

26   *Thrapston Bridge.* Town and stn. R.

26¼   *Islip Lock.* Keep L ; portage L. Village L.

28¾   *Titchmarsh Lock.* Awkward portage L.

29   *Thorpe Waterville Bridge.* Stn. and village R.

31¼   *Wadenhoe Lock.* Village L. Portage easy R into sidestream opposite church.

32½   *Lilford Lock and Bridge.* Portage close to mill. Lilford Hall R. Scenery very pleasant.

34½   *Barnwell Lock.* Can be avoided by taking stream on L (no weir), fast water but apt to be weedy : Oundle Bridge (town L) on the side stream. Sluice above the bridge—portage R.

35   *Barnwell Lower Lock.* Also avoided by side stream abovementioned. River makes a huge loop to SE.

37   *Ashton Lock.* Portage R easy ; or L over weir.

38   Road bridge. Oundle Stn. R. Town ½ ml. L.

39   *Cotterstock Lock and Bridge.* Village L. Portage on R or mill stream.

39½   *Tansor.* R.

40¾   *Perio Lock.* Long portage R.

42   *Fotheringhay Bridge.* Village L; castle ruins.

43½   *Warmington Lock.* Portage L. Steep bank ; stakes.

45   *Elton Lock.* Village R. Short portage over second weir L.

45¼   Road bridge.

47   *Nassington.* L.

48	*Yarwell Lock.* Portage R easy, close to mill.
49	*Wansford Lock.* Awkward portage L from mill stream into old lock stream. Wansford Bridge and village (Great North Road) $\frac{1}{2}$ ml. below.
51$\frac{1}{4}$	*Stibbington* R. Rly. bridge $\frac{1}{4}$ ml. below.
53	*Water Newton Lock.* Portage L easy. Village R.
54$\frac{3}{4}$	*Alwalton Lock.* Long portage L at lock. Steep bank.
58$\frac{3}{4}$	*Orton Longueville Lock.* Portage R.
60$\frac{1}{2}$	*Peterborough Bridge.* City L. Cathedral. For Peterborough N. Stn. unbuild at rly. bridge furthest upstream and take track along rly. L—$\frac{1}{2}$ ml. For Peterborough E. Stn. unbuild L below Peterborough Bridge, near car park.

The tide runs as far as Dog in a Doublet Lock, 5 miles beyond Peterborough from which it is 26 miles through artificial cuts across the fens to the Wash. The ebb tide runs 4 knots. The 14 miles to Wisbech has long and dreary straight reaches, and no landing except at high water. There can be a tide race under Town Bridge, Wisbech.

BEDFORD OUSE BASIN

The Great Ouse and its tributaries are dredged and kept in order by the Great Ouse River Board. They are canoeable at any time of the year, but during the late summer reeds may prove a serious hindrance in places on the upper reaches. Camp sites are easy to find. River authorities : Great Ouse and tributaries (except for the part of the Cam given below)—Great Ouse River Board, Elmhurst, Brooklands Avenue, Cambridge ; Cam (Grantchester to Bottisham Lock)—River Cam Conservators, Guildhall, Cambridge.

38. GREAT OUSE

The Great Ouse rises in Northamptonshire, about 8 miles E of Banbury, and flows into the Wash beyond King's Lynn. Below Bedford it used to be a navigation, but for many years the locks were out of use. In its upper reaches the river runs through pretty, undulating country fairly well wooded, but after Bedford it passes across the plain to the fens and is very open.

The Ouse is canoeable from Buckingham ; in high water from Westbury, 8 miles above Buckingham (3 portages). Usual starting point, Wolverton, which has better rail access. The growth of weed in high summer is very great above Newport Pagnell or even Olney.

Although the river is private water above Bedford there is usually little objection to the use of the river by well-behaved canoeists, and it is possible that the absence of salmon has something to do with it ; also the river does not traverse many parklands. Though the current is small, the fall being rather less than $2\frac{1}{2}$ feet per mile, including weirs between Wolverton and Huntingdon, and less afterwards, the Ouse makes good canoeing, especially early in the year when there is plenty of water and some of the open weirs can be shot. Below Tempsford the locks are now in good order. After St. Ives it is a typical winding fenland river. Eight miles further on, at Earith, most of the river is carried by artificial cuts, the Old and New Bedford Rivers, along which the tide runs, to Denver Sluice, 20 miles in an almost straight line. It is better to stay on the natural river, called the Old West River, past Ely to Denver Sluice, below which it is tidal for the rest of the way to King's Lynn. Few will wish to follow the Ouse beyond Ely except to reach the Lark or Little Ouse. It is more interesting to turn back up the Cam to Cambridge or beyond.

O.S. 146, 147, 134, 135, 124 ; Barth. 14, 19, 20, 25

Miles
0   *Buckingham, Castle Mill.*   Town.   Bridge.   The Buckingham branch of the Grand Union Canal (now disused) runs along the valley to Wolverton.

½   *Buckingham Mill.*

¾   *Buckingham Weir.*

1¾ *Bourton Mill.*

3   *Maids Moreton Mill.* Portage R at weir. Canal diverges here from river.

4   Confl. of *R. Twin.*

4½ *Thornborough Mill.* Portage L. Road bridge ½ ml. below.

5¾ *Thornton Weir.* Village R. Road bridge.

8   *Beachampton* R.

9   *Passenham Mill.* Village and bridge.

10   *Stony Stratford Mill.* Road bridge (A.5) ¼ ml. below. Village R

12   *Wolverton Mill.* Portage L at weir.

13   *Grand Union Canal Aqueduct.* Junc. of R. Tove L.

14   *Wolverton Rly. Viaduct* and road bridge. Town and stn. (main line) ½ ml. R.

16½ *Haversham Mill.* Village and small inn L.

18   *Little Linford.* Ledge under bridge. Shallow. Can be shot. Motor-way bridge above.

19¼ Site of demolished mill. Low bridge. Portage round both.

21¼ *Newport Pagnell Mill.* (Demolished.) Portage L. Town R. Road bridge and confl. of R. Ouzel below.

22¾ *Sherington Bridge.* Village R.

25¼ *Tyringham Hall* R, *Gayhurst* L.

26¾ *Ravenstone Mill.* Portage at first weir on R. From this point right on to Olney look out for stakes in the water (piers of old foot bridges, etc.). Where river divides, the L channel passes under a low bridge.

30   *Olney Town* L. Weir, road bridge and mill. If the water is fairly high portage at the weir above the bridge ; otherwise keep on the upper river to the mill and then portage down the steep bank (with permission). Shallow below mill.

30½ Footbridge. Fall below bridge ; stony, old bridge pier and stakes —inspect. Clifton Reynes R.

31   Rly. bridge.

32¼ *Lavendon Mill.* Garden on left. Portage on the R.

34   Island. *Newton Blossomville.* Take L channel. Inn and pleasant village.

35¼ *Turvey Mill Weir.* Portage into lower river at sluice gates ; or land R at mill and portage past it. Turvey Bridge below.

36½ *Snelson* L. Islands just above.

38½ *Harrold.* Village L. Portage R at first weir well above the mill. Bridge below. Gravel bar extends below the bridge half way across river from R bank.

40   *Odell* L. Weir broken through.

40¼ *Odell Castle* L.

41½ *Felmersham Bridge.* Village and Inn R.

43   *Sharnbrook Rly. Bridge.* Weir and mill L ¼ ml. below. Village ½ ml. L. Portage on R in weir stream. The rly. crosses and recrosses 5 times before Bedford.

44   *Falcon Inn* L. Roadhouse, bathing pool, etc. Meals.

45½ *Radwell Bridge.* Inn R.

47½   *Milton Ernest.* Village and inns up the lane on the L. Turn sharp R at old broken weir, well above the mill—inspect.

48¾   *Stafford Bridge.* New bridge with remains of old bridge below. Take care.

50¼   *Pavenham.* Village R. Stream narrow and divided by osier beds. Keep L after cottages on R.

51½   *Stevington.* Village and inn lie back R.

52¾   *Oakley.* Road bridge. Several alternatives :
       1. Shoot or portage at first weir R.
       2. Portage over bank below sluice gate.
  On the main weir stream, the R arch carries most water.

54½   *Clapham.* Village L. Ford and inn.

57   *Bromham Bridge.* Mill R. Portage at the weirs L above the mill. Road bridge below—very shallow and stony under bridge.

59   *Kempston Church End* R. If enough water going over, shoot the first weir L just opposite the church. If low water portage between the weirs. The weir stream may be shallow, but it will avoid Kempston Mill.

59½   *Kempston Mill.* It is also possible and quite easy to portage at the mill into the pool, but the owners discourage this.

62¼   *Bedford Bridge,* preceded by a footbridge, three rly bridges and a road bridge. Town L. Boathouses R. For the rly. stns. land L beyond the first road bridge. Main line stn. L ; Bletchley-Cambridge line R ; stn. along A.6 south of Bedford Bridge.

62¾   Weir and lock. Rollers R. Rly. bridge below.

64¼   *Cardington Lock.* Two large sluice gates. Portage round disused lock and follow lock stream. Road and rly. bridge below.

66   *Risinghoe Castle Mill.* Lock disused. Portage R above mill. Awkward.

66¼   *Risinghoe Castle Staunch.* If enough water, shoot weir on L. If low water shoot old staunch gate opening R. Fallen brickwork both sides—keep to centre.

68¼   *Willington Lock* (disused). Portage L just before sluice. Village R.

69   *Old Mills Lock* (disused). Lock on R—shoot through, or portage over weir down L channel—very shallow below.

69½   *Great Barford Bridge.* Village and inns L. Shallow above and under bridges—deep water downstream of bridge.

69¾   *Great Barford Lock* (disused). Shoot through between old sluice gate piers, which have been demolished to just above water level.

72   *Roxton Lock* (disused). Portage R, or if enough water shoot lock. Tempsford village R. Confl. of R. Ivel R.

72½   *Tempsford Staunch* (disused). Shoot R. Tempsford Bridge below. Roxton ½ ml. L.

74½   *Little Barford* R.

76¼   *Eaton Socon Mill and Lock.* Portage R round lock. Village L.

77½   *St. Neots Bridge.* Town R. Inns, etc. Stn. 1½ mls. R.

78¼   Confl. of R. Kym L.

78¾   *St. Neots Paper Mill and Lock.* Portage L around lock—difficult.

Miles

80   *Great Paxton.* Village and inn R.

82   *Offord Darcy.* Village and inn R.

83¼   *Offord Mill and Lock.* Offord Cluny R. Portage on R by sluice gate, or by the weir beyond on L. Bridge. There are a number of side streams between here and St. Ives which can be explored.

85½   *Brampton Mill and Lock.* Portage R round lock.

86¾   *Godmanchester* R. Portage L at lock.

87½   *Huntingdon Bridge.* Town L. Huntingdon North Stn. ¾ ml. L through town.

88¾   *Hartford.* Village and inn L. River very charming to St. Ives.

90¼   *Houghton Mill and Lock.* A youth hostel. Portage R by lock and over boat rollers.

91   *Hemingford Abbots* R—picturesque.

91½   *Hemingford Gray* lock and sluices. Portage L. Village R.

93   *St. Ives Bridge.* Chapel on bridge. Market town and stn. L. Staunch and lock ½ ml. below. Portage R.

95¾   *Holywell* L. Interesting well in churchyard. From here the Ouse is a typical fenland river between raised banks.

97½   *Pike and Ell Inn* L.

98½   *Brownshill Staunch and Lock.* Between Brownshill and Hermitage Lock the river is tidal, the tide flowing up the New Bedford River.

100   *Earith.* Village L. Old and New Bedford Rivers direct to Denver Sluice on L.

100¾   *Hermitage Lock* R. Go through into Old West River (non-tidal).

103½   *Aldreth Bridge.*

108½   *Eldford Closes Bridge.* Cambridge-Ely main road. Inn.

110   Road bridge.

111½   *Pope's Corner.* Confl. of R. Cam R. "Fish and Duck" Inn R.

112¾   *Soham Lode* R leads to Soham 4 mls.—mill—Fordham 8 mls. (rly. stn.).

115   *Ely Bridge.* Stn. L. City ¼ ml. L. Cathedral stands up well on rising ground. It is hardly worth continuing below Ely unless the canoeist wishes to reach the Lark or Little Ouse.

118   *Queen Adelaide Bridges* (rly. and road). Long, straight course between raised banks. Cambridge trial eights course.

119¾   Confl. of *R. Lark* R.

121   *Littleport Bridge.* Village and stn. L. "Black Horse" Inn.

124   *Brandon Creek.* Confl. of Little Ouse R. "Ship" inn.

125½   *Southery* R.

129½   Confl. of *R. Wissey* R.

131   *Denver Sluice.* End of New Bedford River. Tidal sluice.

131½   *Salter's Lode* L. End of Old Bedford River. Salter's Lode leads to Popham's Eau, Well Creek and old course of Nene. See Middle Level Navigations (Section 47).

133   *Downham Bridge.* Downham Market ½ ml. R. Stn.

136   *Stow Bridge.* Village L.

139½   *Wiggenhall St. Mary Magdalene* L. Bridge. Magdalen Rd. Stn. ¾ ml. R.

141   *Wiggenhall St. Peter* R.

142   *Wiggenhall St. Germans Bridge.*   Village R.
146   Road bridge.
147   *King's Lynn.*   Town.   Docks.   Stn.   Confl. of R. Nar.   About
      4 mls. further to the Wash (not recommended).

39.   Tove

Rises W of Towcester and flows into Great Ouse near Wolverton. Has been cleared by the River Board and is canoeable from Towcester Mill. Shallow in summer : 2 weirs before Grand Union Canal Aqueduct (4½ miles from Towcester). The canal runs nearby all the way to the confluence with the Ouse at Wolverton, 10½ miles from Towcester (3 mills and 1 weir in this stretch).

40.   Ouzel (or Lovat)

Rises S of Leighton Buzzard and flows N to Great Ouse at Newport Pagnell. Canoeable from Leighton Buzzard (stn. M.R.); 12 mills and weirs ; scenery pleasant. Leighton Buzzard to Ouse 15 miles. The Grand Union Canal follows the valley for much of the way and can be used as an alternative.

41.   Ivel

Rises near Baldock and flows N through Biggleswade and Sandy to Great Ouse at Tempsford. Much of it formerly a navigation (old canal starting at Clophill a few miles beyond Shefford joins Ivel near Langford —3 portages). The *Hiz*, a tributary, can be canoed from Hitchin (stn.), the *Ivel* itself from Astwick Mill, 3 miles above confluence of Hiz.

From Hitchin down the *Hiz* and *Ivel* to Tempsford 20 miles—11 portages. Stations at Biggleswade, Sandy (E.R. main line), also at Blunham (Cambridge-Bletchley line). A picturesque little river, worth canoeing for its scenery : pine covered hills and small holdings near Sandy.

42.   Cam or Granta

The Cam has three headstreams the names of which are confusing. The western, called *Cam* or *Rhee* on the O.S. Map, rises near Ashwell in Hertfordshire and flows NE past Barrington and Haslingfield. It is practicable for canoes from Guilden Morden. This is difficult of access by rail, being about 6 miles from both Ashwell and Potton stations. Barrington, about 6 miles above Grantchester is as convenient a starting point as any. Foxton Station 1 mile SE, but rail access is also available from Shepreth and Harston stations. All these are on the E.R. Hitchin to Cambridge line. There is one mill between Barrington and Grantchester.

The middle headstream, called *Cam* or *Granta*, rises SW of Newport (Essex) and flows N near Saffron Walden past Gt. Chesterford and Shelford. It is canoeable from Audley End (stn. E.R. main line) about 17 miles above Grantchester. In this stretch there are some 9 or 10 mills. Rail access also at Gt. Chesterford, Whittlesford and at Shelford ($\frac{3}{4}$ mile).

The eastern stream, called *Granta* on the O.S. map, rises in Essex SW of Linton and flows NW to join the middle stream at Stapleford. Canoeable from Babraham.

From the junction of these headstreams Cam, here known as far as Cambridge as the *Granta* flows past Grantchester through charming meadows to Cambridge, and thence NE through the fens to its confluence with the Ouse at Pope's Corner, $3\frac{1}{2}$ miles above Ely.

Although Cambridge station is about 1 mile from the river, it is best to start from Cambridge, spend a while exploring upstream past Grantchester, and then commence the run downstream. The Cam is worth a visit for the beauty of the "Backs" in Cambridge, and the upper reaches are very pleasant. Below Cambridge it is a pleasant fenland river, at times high-banked, and there is little current.

The shortest way from Cambridge Station to the river is to go to the end of Station Road, turn R then L into Bateman Street. At the end turn R along Trumpington Road then L into the Fen Causeway, which leads to the river at Coe Fen about $\frac{1}{2}$ mile above King's Mill.

If going upstream from Cambridge beyond Grantchester Mill, do not go straight up to the mill pool but turn L a hundred yards or so before and carry L round the sluice at Byron's Pool. If coming downstream from Barrington or Shelford, this sluice is on the R a short distance beyond the railway bridge, below the confluence of the headstreams.

O.S. 145, 138 ; Barth. 20

"Cam or Rhee"—western headstream

Miles

0	*Guilden Morden—Hook Mill.* Cambridge-Potton and Sandy road (A.603) 1 ml. NW. Rly. stns. at Ashwell and Potton, approx. 6 mls.
$3\frac{3}{4}$	*Wendy.* Confl. of *Mill R.* R canoeable $3\frac{1}{2}$ mls.
5	Ermine Street road bridge (A.14) and weir. Wimpole Park Avenue beyond.
$9\frac{1}{2}$	*Shepreth Bridge.* (Second road bridge from Wimpole.) Stn. and village $\frac{3}{4}$ ml. R.
$10\frac{1}{2}$	*Barrington.* Bulbeck Mill ; Foxton Stn. 1 ml. R. Good starting point at road bridge $\frac{1}{4}$ ml. below, take L arch. Stones under bridge.
$12\frac{1}{4}$	*Harston Mill.* Village R. Through fine tree-lined stretch to road bridge (Harston Stn. 1 ml. R).
$13\frac{1}{2}$	*Haslingfield* L.
$15\frac{1}{2}$	Confl. of headstreams.

"Cam or Granta"—middle headstream

Semi-private but well worth canoeing in upper reaches where it flows through pleasant country, with low hills. Permission should be asked at the mills. Canoeable from Audley End : easily reached by rail from Bishop's Stortford, head of the Stort Navigation (see Section 79).

Miles

0   *Audley End* rly. bridge. (Saffron Walden line.) Audley End Stn. 1 ml. Mansion 1 ml. below ; a number of low bridges here.

1¼   *Saffron Walden* road bridge. Old town 1 ml. R. Castle. Timbered houses. Weir ¼ ml. beyond.

3   *Littlebury Mill.* River alongside road.

5½   *Gt. Chesterford.* Stn. L and road bridge. Mills at *Ickleton, Hinxton* and *Duxford.*

8½   Road bridge. Whittlesford Stn. L. Mills at *Pampisford, Whittlesford, Sawston, Dernford.*

12½   *Stapleford.* Village R. Confl. of *Granta* R—canoeable from Babraham (5 mls.).

12¾   *Shelford Mill.* Gt. Shelford R. Stn. River shallow.

14¾   *Hauxton Mill* and road bridge. Village L.

16   Confl. of headstreams. Rly. bridge beyond.

16¾   Bourne Brook L. Sluice R. Carry past sluice into *Byron's Pool.* Mill is private.

17   *Grantchester Bridge.* Village L. Trumpington 1 ml. R. Grantchester Village (picturesque) best reached up mill stream ½ ml. below bridge.

18½   River divides, a short way above Coe Fen Bridge. Keep to R branch.

19   *Cambridge, King's Mill.* Boathouses R. Use rollers on left or portage into weir stream L near sluices. Immediately below, the river passes under Silver Street bridge into the "Backs", through lawns and park-like college grounds. Allow plenty of time to wander about the colleges and grounds ; King's College chapel is close by.

20   *Jesus Green Lock.* Toll 6d. Below are University and College boathouses L and Midsummer Common R. Keep clear of college eights and scullers ; these may be encountered anywhere between the lock and Clayhythe. The rule of the river is : keep right, except at Fen Ditton. After a dull stretch by the gasworks the scenery again becomes pleasant.

21½   *Chesterton.* Village L. Inn—"Pike and Eel" L. Footbridge.

21¾   Rly. bridge.

22½   *Fen Ditton* R. Chain Ferry—The Plough R. Changeover to the left of the river at the ferry, just round the first corner. Just below the river makes an S bend through "The Gut." Here change over to the right again.

23½   *Baitsbite Lock.* Toll 6d.

24½   *Horningsea.* Village and inn R.

26   *Clayhythe Bridge.* Waterbeach Village L. Inn by bridge. Stn. ½ ml. L.

26¾ *Bottisham Lock.* Toll 6d. Bottisham Lode R ; canoeable to
     Gt. Wilbraham, 6 mls., 2 mills.

28   Entrance to Swaffham Lode R. Swaffham 4 mls.

30¼ *Upware Ferry*. Inn "Five Miles from Anywhere" R. Lode R.
     leads to Wicken Sedge Fen, preserved in its original un-
     drained state as a reserve for wild life and fen flora.

31¾ *Dimmock's Cote* road bridge. Ely Cathedral forms a landmark on
     its hill over the fens.

33½ *Pope's Corner*. "Fish and Duck" Inn L. Junction with Old
     West River L. 3½ mls. along Ouse to Ely.

43. Lark

The Lark rises S of Bury St. Edmunds and flows NW to the Ouse
between Ely and Littleport. Formerly canalised up to Bury St.
Edmunds. The upper part of the Lark is attractive and passes through
interesting Breckland Country. Below West Row it is a fenland river
embanked on both sides, with few features. The upper reaches are best
done when water levels are high.

Rail access at Bury St. Edmunds. Half a mile below Bury long portage past broken lock at Fornham ; high banks. Portages at the sluices
and locks that follow.

Bury St. Edmunds-Mildenhall—12 miles (13 portages).

Mildenhall-Junction with Ouse—13 miles (one lock at Isleham).
A short distance above Mildenhall a new cut-off channel for flood water
diverges to the right.

Occasional riverside inns and one village (Prickwillow). The *Kennett*,
which joins the Lark 1¼ miles above Isleham lock, is canoeable from
Kennett (7 miles).

O.S. 135, 136 ; Barth. 20, 21

44. Little Ouse or Brandon River

For much of its course the Little Ouse marks the boundary between
Norfolk and Suffolk. It rises near Lopham in the same marsh as the
Waveney and flows W and NW through Thetford and the Brecklands
to the Ouse at Brandon Creek 3 miles below Littleport. It is canoeable
from Knettishall (road access from Thetford and from Diss, on the
Waveney), but a more promising starting point is Thetford which has
good rail access and which can be made the starting point for exploring
the upper stretches of the Little Ouse and its tributary, the Thet.
The river has long been a navigation as far as Thetford, to which a
towpath follows the river. Regulated by staunches. The flood cut-off
channel crosses the river near Hockwold.

O.S. 135, 136 ; Barth. 20, 21

Miles

0   *Knettishall.* No obstacles till water mill 1 ml. above Thetford. The *Sapiston* (canoeable from *Ixworth*, 9 mls., 4 mills, 2 weirs) joins the L. Ouse 4 mls. above Thetford. The *Thet* (canoeable to *East Harling* (Harling Rd. Stn.) 11 mls., 1 mill, 1 weir) joins L. Ouse at Thetford.

11   *Thetford Bridge.* Anchor Hotel close to the bridge. River banks very pretty all the way to Brandon. Land near river : well wooded—afforestation being carried out on a large scale.

11¼   *Thetford Staunch.* Rollers.

12½   *Thetford New Staunch.* Difficult portage.

13½   *Turfpole Staunch.*

14½   *Croxton Staunch (Fison's).* Manure works.

16   *Santon Staunch.* Picturesque spot. River abounds with bird life and fish.

16¾   *Santon Downham Bridge.* Village L. "Grime's Graves" 1½ mls. N.

19¾   *Brandon Bridge.* Town L. Stn. R. Attractive town with many flint steep roofed houses. Centre of flint knapping industry for centuries.

20   *Brandon Staunch.* A small lock in working order. Without a key it will be necessary to carry over. From this point the river has shallows but is very charming and the water is clear.

21¼   *Sheepwash Staunch.*

23   *Wilton Ferry.* Inn. Hockwold-cum-Wilton Village R.

23½   *Hockwold Bridge.* Beginning of fens. Lakenheath Stn. L.

27½   *Lakenheath Lode* L. Leads to Lakenheath.

31¼   *Feltwell.* Anchor Inn.

33   *Brandon Creek.* Junc. with Ouse. "Ship Inn."

45. Wissey

A typical Norfolk river, with good scenery. The Wissey rises near Shipdham, SE of East Dereham, and flows W to the Ouse 1¼ miles S of Denver Sluice. Canoeable from Hilborough, 6 miles S of Swaffham on the Brandon-Fakenham road. No locks ; 2 mills—first 2 miles above Mundford, second near Northwold. At weir ½ mile below take R branch of river. Large motor boats come up to Stokeferry. The flood cut-off channel crosses the river above Stokeferry.

Hilborough to Mundford 7 miles ; to Stokeferry 15½ miles ; to confluence with Ouse 25 miles.

O.S. 124, 125 ; Barth. 20

46. Nar

Rises near Litcham and flows W to Gt. Ouse at King's Lynn. Canoe-able from Narborough (stn.). Tidal lock at junction with Ouse : King's Lynn Stn. ¾ mile. Narborough to King's Lynn 12 miles.

O.S. 124 ; Barth. 25

47. Middle Level Navigations

These are a complex series of navigable rivers and fenland drains connecting the Nene Navigation and the Ouse. The whole area is very lonely, and plenty of food should be carried if exploring it. The water-ways are in general high banked and without perceptible current and would be considered dull except by those who are fenland enthusiasts. The following route connects the Nene at Peterborough with the Ouse at Denver Sluice :

Nene to Stanground (lock); *King's Dike* to Whittlesey (lock), Angle Corner (cross straight over), and Flood's Ferry ; *Old Nene* to March, Upwell (sluice 1 mile before) and Outwell ; turn R into *Well Creek* for Nordelph and Salters Lode sluice (altogether 29 miles). Alternatively, turn R out of *Old Nene* 4 miles beyond March into *Popham's Eau*, direct to Nordelph.

O.S. 134, 135, 124 ; Barth. 20

(Middle Level Commissioners, March, Cambs. Tel. March 3232)

48. The Wash

The Wash is mentioned only by way of discouragement. It is liable to strong winds, the tides run fast between the sandbanks from the river outfalls, and a nasty sea can get up suddenly. It is not as easy as it appears to get from the mouth of the Ouse to Hunstanton because the outfall channels between sandbanks lead well away from the coast and with the full force of the ebb plus the river water and possibly also a SW following wind can carry a canoe seriously out of her course. The whole area is best avoided.

EAST ANGLIA AND ESSEX

49. NORTH NORFOLK COAST

The canoeing possibilities along the north Norfolk coast have not yet been much explored. Those who enjoy sea canoeing and sailing and the exploration of creeks and marshes will find the stretch of coast from Blakeney to Wells and beyond to Scolt Head an ideal area for their activities. The coast is low and marshy, with many promontories of firmer ground running out to sea and there are many navigable creeks flowing in all directions across the marshes. There are no real rivers— only a few streams—and the creeks are mostly entirely tidal and run quite dry at low tide. A glance at the one inch Ordnance map will show better than any written description the wide extent of the canoeing possibilities. Morston, Blakeney and Wells-next-the-Sea all make excellent centres for many good expeditions or starting points for a cruise along the coast towards the Wash.

Blakeney Point, a narrow spit of land running almost due west along the coast and forming the fine natural, though shallow, harbour known as The Pit, is of exceptional interest. It is now a bird sanctuary under the control of the National Trust and is visited by hundreds of people during the terns' nesting season in the spring. Camping is not allowed on the Point. The Point is easily reached by canoe from Blakeney or Morston, or from Cley-next-the-Sea down a winding creek which at low tide could scarcely be navigated even in a canoe. There are many interesting natural and geological features about the formation and shape of the Point, which is continually being enlarged through the action of the tides, the tendency being now for it to curve inland. From the Point it is possible to canoe along the shore and up a wide channel to Wells, an attractive, old-fashioned town, and then to return to the Point through the creeks across the intervening marshes. Care should be taken to see that a point about half way across the marshes on the return journey should be reached at high tide. High water at Blakeney : Dover $-4\frac{3}{4}$ hours. The ebb will then carry the canoeist back into Blakeney Pit, where he started, but if the return journey is left too late all the water will have run out of the creeks before the harbour is reached and a long portage may be necessary. It is doubtful whether any other kind of boat could make this journey through the creeks from Wells, as there are several low-lying bridges ; and at high tide, when there is enough water for navigation these are almost awash and a portage is necessary.

The map suggests the possibility of many other creek explorations, and considerable sport can be had, given decent conditions riding the breakers outside the harbour mouth and watching the seals which now live and breed there in hundreds on the sandbanks.

No reports have been received about the coast beyond Wells, but the possibilities at Scolt Head, another bird sanctuary, Holkham, Overy Staithe, Burnham Deepdale and Brancaster (remains of Roman fort) should be equally good.

O.S. 125 ; Barth. 26
Chart : St. 20

50. NORFOLK BROADS AND RIVERS

The Norfolk Broads, with their rivers and their tributaries, cuts, dykes and broads, must provide well over 300 miles of waterways capable of exploration by a canoeist. Wroxham on the Bure is a convenient starting point.

The Norfolk Broads provide no exciting water—there is no fast water at all—and there are no locks except on the upper reaches of the rivers.

But though there is no fast water the Broads have a charm of their own, and are eminently suitable for exploration by canoe, perhaps more so than by any other type of craft. Wonderful opportunities occur for canoe sailing.

Much interest will be found in the many types of pleasure craft to be met on the Broads—for the most part handled with a fair amount of skill, though canoeists should remember that the Broads is the playground of the novice at boat-sailing and motor-boating. Also, should one be fortunate enough to meet one of the fast disappearing trading wherries (easily recognised by their black sails) paddle clear—they (as also some of the few professionally manned pleasure wherries) give way to no man.

River dues for canoes are 12s. (up to 31st December) and 1s. 6d. registration fee payable to the Gt. Yarmouth Port and Haven Commissioners, 21 South Quay, Gt. Yarmouth, but for visiting craft the registration fee may not be demanded. River Inspectors will challenge and demand payment if not obtained in advance.

Camp sites are not difficult to find in the marshes. Except near villages it may be difficult to find anybody from whom to ask permission. Elsewhere, however, owing to reedy margins to the broads parts of the rivers and arable farming, some difficulty may be experienced.

51. BURE

Rises S of Melton Constable and flows E and SE through attractive broadland country to join the Yare at Yarmouth. Formerly a navigation to Aylsham, but the locks between Coltishall and Aylsham are now disused.

O.S. 126 ; Barth. 26

Stanford's Map of the Broads—Northern Section (St. 21) 2 in.= 1 ml.
Hamilton's Guide to the Broads (with maps)
Esso Map of the Broads (from petrol stations)

Jarrold's "What to do on the Norfolk Broads" (annually)

Miles
0	*Aylsham.* Town, shops, inns.
1	*Aylsham Lock.* This lock and following disused.
3	*Burgh Lock.*
3¾	*Oxnead Lock.*
5¾	*Buxton Lamas Lock.*
9	*Coltishall Bridge and Lock.* Village L. The millstream on R by lock repays exploration.
11	*Belaugh.* A small village on the L bank. It is frequently possible to paddle into the marshy country at this part of the river.
13	*Belaugh Broad.* A small broad on the left.
14¼	*Bridge Broad.* So called because the railway passes across both it and the river.
14½	*Wroxham Bridge.* Stn. L. Wroxham R is a busy village and the centre of Broads yachting. Good shopping facilities on L of bridge (Hoveton). Boat houses. Convenient places to build boats at public staithe, 200 yds. from stn. or on NE bank upstream of bridge behind wooden shops. Beyond the yacht stations are some bungalows and houses and then wooded banks to—
16	*Wroxham Broad.* This is the biggest deep freshwater broad, a mile long, lying alongside the river on the right. Access can be obtained through either of two narrow entrances.
16½	*Hoveton Great Broad.* This is on the left and is private.
17	*Salhouse Broad.* A small broad on the right.
18¾	*Hoveton Little Broad* L. Open for navigation.
19¼	*Horning* L. Inn. Fresh water from pump on green. Shops. Tide flows to here (slight).
20	*Horning Ferry.* Inn. A chain ferry for vehicles.
21¾	*Ranworth Dyke.* On the R, leading in ½ ml. to Ranworth Broad. Do not miss this. Stores at P.O., 100 yds uphill from staithe. Ranworth Church. The same route back to the river is necessary.
23	*Junction of Ant* L.
23¼	*Fleet Dyke* R. Leads in just over a mile to South Walsham Broad. Very beautiful. Its construction in the middle divides it into an inner and outer broad. The former is private but only landing is barred. Return to river by same route.

Miles

24   *St. Benet's Abbey.* A landmark known to all Broadsmen—a ruined windmill built in the ruins of an Abbey. There are still many windmills on the Broads, but they are fast disappearing.

24¾   *Junction of Thurne* L. A somewhat uninteresting flat treeless section to—

27½   *Wey Bridge (Acle Bridge).* Inn. Stores. Sailing wherry "Claudia" R bank ¼ ml. above Acle. Village and stn. 1½ mls. SW. Tides felt below here.

28¾   *Muck Fleet* L. A dyke 3½ mls. long leading to Filby, Rollesby and Ormesby Broads. Well worth exploring. Dam across mouth, but easy portage L. Watch for eel-nets. One portage at low road bridge 1 ml. along. At 2½ mls. take R fork. Stream narrows to 8 ft., then widens on approaching Filby Broad. Filby Broad 2¾, Filby Bridge 3½ (village R), Ormesby Bridge 6, head of Ormesby Broad 7 mls. from the Bure. Camp sites almost unobtainable here, except near Eel's Foot Inn, Ormesby Broad.

29½   *Stokesby Village.* The rest of the Bure to Yarmouth is uninteresting except to yachtsmen and there are few landmarks.

37¼   Rly. bridge. Immediately after is Yarmouth Yacht Station L. Enquire here if proceeding further as there is a double fast tidal race at the junction with the River Yare.
Road Bridge. Yarmouth (Vauxhall) Stn. R.

37½   *Junction with Yare.* Gt. Yarmouth R.

High Water Yarmouth : Dover – 1 hour 50 mins. Tide flows until high water Dover, and ebbs at 4 knots to low water Dover.

52. Thurne

The Thurne or Hundred Stream begins very close to the coast near Horsey. It drains a number of waterways, broads, meres, and dykes within a short distance of the NW coast of Norfolk and is affected by tides nearly to its source. Provides very enjoyable canoeing and sailing.

O.S. 126 ; Barth. 26.

Stanford's Map of Norfolk Broads—Northern Section (St. 21).

Hamilton's Guide to the Broads (with map).

Esso Map of the Broads.

Miles

0   *Hickling Broad.* Inn. (The proprietors may be able to advise about a camp site.) Largest expanse of water in the Broads. though appearing smaller owing to reeds. Ideal for canoes as yachts must keep to the channel. Excellent sailing. Outlet in SE corner leads through White Slea to—

1¾   *Heigham Sound.* Immediately on L the Meadow Dyke leads in 1 ml. to Horsey Mere ¾ ml. in length. 1 ml. up New Cut from Horsey Mere to Bridge Farm, Horsey. Horsey village is about 1 ml. from the coast.

     The New Cut is canoeable for several miles. At road bridge (B.1159) easy portage, and it is possible to paddle along the dykes ("Hempstead Marshes") to within 200 yards of the sea.

2¾   Outlet from Heigham Sound leads in ¼ ml. to the Thurne. (1¼ mls. up the Thurne, to the left, a dyke leads off right to Martham, or Somerton, Broad ; picturesque and overgrown. Somerton Staithe on Martham Broad for Somerton Village.) Down the Thurne (to right)—

4¼   *Potter Heigham.* Rly. and road bridge. Inn. Boathouse. Stores. Village ½ ml. R.

6   *Womack Water* R leads to Ludham Staithe (¾ ml.). Village. Interesting church.

7   *Thurne Village* L. Lion Inn.

7¼   *Junction with R. Bure.*

53. Ant

(and North Walsham and Dilham Canal)

The Ant rises near Thorpe Market about 5 miles SSE of Cromer and flows more or less parallel to the coast SE then S to the Bure near St. Benet's Abbey. Above Dilham it is canalised for a mile or two beyond North Walsham (North Walsham and Dilham Canal) but this is now disused, and there is a portage at each lock and in summer it is overgrown with reeds, though there is talk of clearing the part up to Antingham. Below Dilham the Ant flows through low, marshy country, with Barton and Stalham Broads. Distances given from Spa Common Bridge although the Canal starts 3 miles before this at Antingham. Above Honing there may be little water in dry weather.

O.S. 126 ; Barth. 26.

Stanford's Map of Norfolk Broads—Northern Section (St. 21).

Hamilton's Guide to the Broads (with map).

Esso map of the Broads.

Miles
0   *Spa Common Bridge.* 1½ mls. E or North Walsham (stn.).

1   *Ebridge Mill and Lock.* Road bridge.

2½   *Briggate Lock and Mill.* Road bridge.

3½   *Honing Bridge.* Dilham Broad R. Honing lock.

5½   *Dilham Lock.* End of canalised portion. Wayford Bridge. Stalham 1½ mls. L.

  7¼ *Stalham Dyke* L leads to Stalham (or Sutton) Broad 1 ml. long.
       Stalham (Inns) at far end.
  7¾ *Barton Broad.* A large, shallow Broad 1 ml. long. Barton Turf
       Village at NW corner. Half ml. down a side arm leads W
       towards Neatishead (stores). Outflow is in SE corner of
       Broad.
  9¼ *Irstead Church* R and *Irstead Water* L. Village picturesque.
       Then through marshy country to—
 12¾ *Ludham Bridge.* Stores. Inn. ¼ ml. L. Hundred Dyke L (un-
       canoeable and full of reeds).
 13¼ *St. Benet's Abbey.* Junction with R. Bure.

54. WENSUM and YARE

The Yare rises S of East Dereham in Norfolk but above Norwich is canoeable for some 8 miles only. The Wensum rises near Fakenham and flows S and then E to join the Yare just below Norwich. Below Norwich the Yare (sometimes called the "Norwich River") flows generally E to Breydon Water and Great Yarmouth. The Wensum is canoeable from Fakenham. There are several mills and other obstacles in the upper reaches, but the river flows through pleasant country. These upper stretches are little known. Normally there is enough water from Ringland. Rail access on upper stretches at Fakenham, 22½, Ryburgh, 19½, County School, 15½, and N. Elmham, 14 miles above Ringland. Below Norwich scenery is flatter, and after Coldham Hall rather uninteresting. Tides affect the river below this.

O.S. 125, 126 ; Barth. 26.

Below Norwich : Stanford's Map of the Norfolk Broads (St. 22).
                  Hamilton's Guide to the Broads (with map).
                  Esso Map of the Broads.

High water at Yarmouth : Dover - 1 hour 50 mins. Tide flows until high water Dover, then ebbs until low water Dover at 4 knots.

Wensum

Miles
  0   *Ringland* R. Inn. Ford. Fine scenery below here.
  3   *Taverham Mill.* Portage.
  4½ *Costessey* R. Mill. Portage.
  5   *Drayton* L. Rly. bridge.
  7½ *Hellesdon* L. R Portage at Mill. River Tud R.

10   *Norwich.* The approach to the city is under two road bridges, a footbridge and a railway bridge. Wensum Park and bathing place L. Interesting Cathedral City well worth exploring. In the middle of the city is an awkward portage round New Mills. Below are 4 bridges close together, then Quayside R near Cathedral. The old Cathedral Ferry makes a good launching place. Three more bridges then Norwich (Thorpe) stn. (E.R.) L adjoining river. Tidal variation 1 ft.

12¼   *Carrow Bridge.* Start of the navigation.
12¾   *Trowse Hythe.* Junction with River Yare R.

Yare

13   *New Cut.* Leads straight on. Old river under railway bridge L is pleasanter.
13¼   *Thorpe next Norwich* L.
15½   *Woods End* R. Inn and ferry.
17   *Surlingham Ferry.* Inn R.
18   *Surlingham Broad* R. (Nearly dry.) Brundall Stn. L ¼ ml. below.
18¾   *Coldham Hall Inn* R.
20   Dyke to Rockland Broad (R ½ ml.). Much overgrown.
21¼   *Buckenham Ferry.* Inn R. Stn. L 1 ml.
23¾   *Cantley.* Red House Inn L. Ferry. Stn.
26¼   *Hardley Cross.* Junction of R. Chet R. Navigable 3½ mls. to Loddon.
26½   *Norton Staithe* R. Inn. Reedham Ferry. Reedham Stn. ¾ ml. L.
27½   *Reedham* L. Rly. bridge. New Cut to R. Waveney diverges R. Tide ebbs and flows from this end.
31¾   *Berney Arms* L. Inn and stn. Junction with R. Waveney. Burgh Castle R. Remains of Roman Fort of Saxon Shore (Garianonum) R followed by Breydon Water. Extensive flats at low tide on both sides.
36¼   Railway bridge. Junction of *R. Bure* L. Yarmouth (Vauxhall) Stn. L.
36½   *Yarmouth Bridge.* South Town Stn. R.
39½   *Mouth of Yare.*

55. WAVENEY

The Waveney rises at Little Fen, Lopham, in the same marsh as the Little Ouse and flows E and then N to join the Yare at Breydon Water. It forms the boundary between Norfolk and Suffolk for the whole of its course. It is connected by Oulton Dyke with Oulton Broad and Lowestoft. Tide felt below Beccles but as a rule has little force. Formerly canalised between Bungay and Beccles ; canoeable when water levels high from Diss some 6 miles below Lopham Bridge. Scenery quietly pleasant throughout ; best from Beccles. Breydon Water, a tidal lake, can be very rough with strong winds. High water at Lowestoft : Dover – 1 hour 20 mins. High water at Yarmouth : Dover – 1 hour 50 mins. Tide flows till high water Dover and ebbs at 4 knots to low water Dover.

O.S. 136, 137, 126 ; Barth. 21, 26.
Stanford's Map of the Broads—South Section (St. 22).
Hamilton's Guide to the Broads (with map).
Esso Map of the Broads.

Miles

0	*Diss Bridge.* Town L.
1½	*Stuston Bridges.* Rly. and 3 road bridges. Diss Stn. ½ ml. L.
2¼	*Scole Bridge.* Inn L.
3¾	*Oakley Bridge.* Inn. Confl. of Dove ½ ml. below.
5¼	*Hoxne Mill.* St. Edmund's Monument and Abbey 1 ml. R.
7¾	*Syleham Bridge.* Brockdish Village L. 4 mills to—
11	*Shotford Bridge.* Harleston 1 ml. L.
13¼	*Mendham Bridge.* Inn and village R. 2 mills to—
16	*Homersfield Bridge.*
17½	*Flixton Park* R.
20½	*Earsham* L. Mills. River divides into several channels.
22	*Bungay, West Bridge.* Town R. River makes a huge loop to Falcon Bridge ¼ ml. in direct line through town.
24	*Bungay, Falcon Bridge.* Below here canalised to Beccles but locks not working.
24¾	*Wainford Mills.* Bridge and lock. Portage at mill.
26	*Ellingham Mill.* Bridge and lock. Portage at weir.
28¼	*Geldeston Lock.* Inn L. Portage.
31½	*Beccles Bridge.* Town R. Stn. Interesting old town. Church has a detached tower. Inns and boat houses.
38½	*Burgh St. Peter Church* L. Curious tower. Inn.
39¼	*Oulton Dyke* R. Leads to Oulton Broad 1½ mls. Oulton (stn. L) 2¼ mls. Lake Lothing (tidal) and Lowestoft 4 mls.
42¼	*Somerleyton* rly. bridge. Village and inn R ½ ml. Stn.
44	*Haddiscoe Rly. Bridge.* Stn. L. New Cut L to Reedham (on the Yare) 2½ mls. Tide ebbs and flows from Yare end. Waveney forks R.
44¼	*St. Olave's Bridge.* Inn. Fritton Decoy 1 ml. R.
49¾	*Burgh Castle* R. Remains of Roman Fort of the Saxon Shore (Garianonum). Junction with Yare and beginning of Breydon Water. Extensive mud flats at low tide on either side.
54	*Yarmouth Rly. Bridge.* Confl. of Bure L. Stns. and town.

56. ALDE

The Alde is tidal from Snape, some 21 miles from Shinglestreet, where (as the "Ore") it reaches the sea. At Slaughden, 8 mls. from Snape only a narrow shingle bank separates it from the sea. The winding tidal reaches between Snape (where there is a quay) and Slaughden Quay are attractive. Quay at Orford. Canoeable for a mile or two above Snape Bridge. Rail access at Aldeburgh. The tidal stream runs at about 4 knots on the average.

O.S. 137, 150 ; Barth. 21
Charts : St. 3 ; Y.3

57. DEBEN

Canoeable for 4 or 5 miles above the estuary at Melton. Convenient access at Woodbridge (stn.). Nine miles to mouth at Felixstowe Ferry (Inn R). Bawdsey Manor L. Upper reaches pleasant scenery.

High water : Dover plus ½ hour. Ebb runs up to 6 knots. Local information should be obtained about the mouth, which is sometimes dangerous.

O.S. 150 ; Barth. 21

Charts : St. 3 ; Y.6

58. GIPPING and ORWELL

The Gipping was formerly a navigation below Stowmarket (Ipswich and Stowmarket Navigation), but it was closed over 30 years ago and the river is now claimed to be private. Flows SW through Ipswich. The estuary is known as the Orwell and leads to Harwich Harbour. Yachting centre at Pin Mill. The estuary has long, broad reaches and can be rough with wind against tide. Landing very awkward owing to mud. Scenery pleasant. High water at Harwich : Dover plus 40 mins.

O.S. 136, 149, 150 ; Barth. 21, 16

Charts : St. 3 ; Y. 6 or 16

Miles
0	*Stowmarket.* Stn. There were 3 locks to—
4	*Needham Market* R. Stn. There were 5 locks to—
9	*Claydon Bridge.* There were 2 locks to—
12	*Bramford.* There were 2 locks to—
16	*Ipswich.* Stn. R. Convenient access from stn. to quay if starting here. Below, the estuary has mainly mud at low water but is otherwise quite pleasant.
21	*Pinmill* R. Inn ("Butt and Oyster") and hard. Only good landing at low water until Felixstowe Pier. Bus to Ipswich at Chelmondiston ½ ml.
26	*Bloody Point* R. Junction with Stour Estuary. Ebb tide runs very fast off Harwich.
28	*Felixstowe Pier* L.
28	*Harwich* R. Landing close to pier convenient to stn.

59. SUFFOLK STOUR

Rising in Cambridgeshire a few miles S of Newmarket, the Stour flows generally ESE to Manningtree and Harwich. For most of its course it forms the boundary between Suffolk and Essex and passes through many picturesque villages and towns. The lower part of the valley is Constable's Country. Little water above Long Melford during summer months. The Stour was once a navigation below Sudbury but the locks are now derelict ; weeds may be encountered, especially after July. High water Harwich : Dover plus 40 mins.

O.S. 149, 150 ; Barth. 21, 16
Charts : St. 3 ; Y.6 and 13

Miles

0	*Stoke-by-Clare* (stn.).
2½	*Clare*. Stn. L. Portage R at mill sluice.
5½	*Cavendish Bridge*. At mill above bridge portage L. Village and stn. L.
6¾	River divides ; L branch usually best.
7	*Glensford Bridge*. Rly. crosses twice.
8¼	Mill. Shoot or portage L.
9	*Long Melford Bridge*.
9½	Mill. Shoot sluice or portage R. Village (fine church) and stn. L. Launching place at concrete ramp 50 yds. below mill sluice.
10¾	Mill. Portage L. Concrete ford below sluice.
11	Mill. Portage L into pool.
12¼	*Sudbury Mill and Bridge*. At mill portage R at sluice. Stn. and shops L. Boathouse.
13¾	Mill. Portage R at slipway opposite church or at sluice.
15	Site of mill. Line over or portage L.
16	Derelict lock. Portage at weir. Rly. bridge.
18¾	*Bures Bridge*. Stn. R.
19¼	Mill. Portage L (ask for permission).
21	*Smallbridge*. Derelict lock shootable in high water—or portage L.
23	Mill. Portage L or lift over.
24	*Nayland*. Take R branch. Portage R at weir below road bridge.
27	*Boxted Mill*. Mill house private. Ask permission in advance to portage and where (Mr. C. C. J. Bullough, Boxted, Colchester). Remains of Langham Lock followed by waterworks pumping station just above Langham Bridge. Submerged timber culvert below.
29½	*Stratford St. Mary* L. Lock, portage R. All this stretch very pleasant.
31	*Dedham* R. Lock and mill, portage R. ½ ml. down take L branch.
32¼	*Flatford Mill and Lock*. (National Trust.) Cafe. Reedy banks to—
34	*Brantham Lock* (tidal). Arrange to arrive here at or *before* high water as the gates automatically close on the ebb, though for 2-3 hours after high tide portage can be made into creek R. This dries out.
34½	*Cattewade Bridge* and rly. bridge. Manningtree stn. 1 ml. Landing possible at road bridge at high water but liable to be muddy.
35	*Manningtree* R.
35½	*Mistley* R. Stn. Slipway at end of quay. Landing until 4 hrs. after H.W., then mud. Shops, cafes, etc. in Manningtree. The estuary below here is very muddy and the channel narrow at low tide for some distance.
44½	*Harwich*. Landing upstream of first pier convenient for station. Mouth of Orwell L. Felixstowe Pier opposite across Harwich Harbour. Tide runs out past Harwich very fast. Care needed ir windy weather.

60. ESSEX COLNE

The Colne is not really practicable above Colchester. Tidal sluice at Colchester. Rail access at Colchester, Wivenhoe and Brightlingsea. Distances along estuary from Colchester (Hythe) : Wivenhoe 3, Pyefleet Channel 7, Brightlingsea (on Brightlingsea Creek) 8½ miles. Hard at East Mersea opposite Brightlingsea Creek. High water at Brightlingsea : Dover plus 40 mins.

O.S. 149 or 162 ; Barth. 16
Charts : St. 4 ; Y.6 or 15

61. ESSEX BLACKWATER

It may at times be possible to canoe the Blackwater from Coggeshall, some 15 miles above tidal waters at Maldon, but Kelvedon (stn.) is a more promising starting place. The river may be weedy and there are a number of mills that must be portaged. The river becomes tidal at Beeleigh Weir where the Chelmer and Blackwater Canal crosses it, and it dries out below. The Chelmer from Chelmsford is, however, to be preferred to this upper part. The estuary is canoeable between Maldon and West Mersea. Pleasant scenery particularly on south shore. Tidal streams are swift and wide mud banks are left at low tides, as indicated on map or chart. Keep to the marked channels except near high water. In bad weather the S bank may give shelter from the prevailing wind.

From Maldon, or the causeway at the SW corner of Northey Island, to Bradwell and back is a comfortable day's run working with the tide. To reach the causeway take road B.1018 and turn left in the middle of the Corporation housing estate, 1½ mls. from Maldon Bridge past South House Farm. No attempt should be made to go east of Bradwell unless the weather is very settled and the tide suitable.

Lawling (or Mayland) Creek, which opens into the Blackwater 4½ mls. from Maldon on the South bank provides more shelter than the larger estuary and there is always water in the SW branch.

Heybridge basin extends from ½ mile north of Maldon station to the tidal lock into the Blackwater (see Chelmer, Section 13).

Eastern National and Osborne's buses from Maldon.

High water Maldon : Dover plus 1 hour 10 mins.

High water Bradwell : Dover plus 37 mins.

O.S. 162 ; Barth 16
Charts : St. 4 ; Y.6 or 12

G

Miles	Landings

0   *Maldon.*   Start at bridge at or about high water (stn. about 200 yds. N), or at any boat yard on S bank by permission.

⅝   Public park known as Marine Parade. Good landing but may be crowded.

(*N. Bank*)

2   *Heybridge Basin.*   Hotel.
2½   *Mill Beach.*   Hotel.
3   *Decoy Point.*   Causeway to Osea I.

(*S. Bank*)

2   *Causeway* to Northey I.   (South House Farm.)
4½   Mouth of *Lawling Creek.*   (2 mls. long, good landings at Old Yacht Club jetty and at boatbuilder's hard (Cardnell Bros.). Supplies in Mayland Village).
5½   *Stansgate Abbey Farm.*
7   *The Stone.*
9½   *Bradwell Waterside.*   Hotel.

(*N. Bank*)

10   *West Mersea.*

62.   Chelmer

The Chelmer rises north of Dunmow, flows S to Chelmsford, then E to join the Blackwater at Heybridge (Maldon). From Chelmsford it is canalised (Chelmer and Blackwater Canal). A licence from the Proprietors of the Chelmsford and Blackwater Navigation Ltd., 71 Duke Street, Chelmsford (normally £2. 2s. 0d. per annum), is required, but members of recognised canoe clubs can apply through their club secretary to the proprietors for a licence at reduced rates (annual £1 ; week-end 5s.). It is understood that a new scale is under consideration (1960).

The Chelmer is canoeable from Little Waltham but this part may be weedy or low in summer. Its tributary the *Can* is canoeable from Writtle, near Chelmsford.

Chelmsford is the most convenient starting point. From station trolley through Chelmsford Central Park to the *R. Can.* After half a mile portage at mill (Chelmsford Boating Club at rear) into Chelmer. The canal joins the river about 200 yards below. All locks must be portaged (best by the locks). Bathers and fishermen may be found most of the way along the canal.

O.S. 162 ; Barth. 16

63. CROUCH

The estuary only is canoeable (from Battlesbridge at high water). Burnham-on-Crouch is a famous yachting centre ; be careful to keep out of the way of racing yachts. Tides are very swift, banks in many places faced with stone. Do not go E of mouth of Roach unless prepared for full sea conditions.

Rail access at : Battlesbridge Station, $\frac{1}{4}$ mile, convenient access ; Althorne Station, 400 yards to hard on Bridgemarsh Creek ; Burnham Station, $\frac{1}{2}$ mile.

O.S. 162 ; Barth. 16

Charts : St. 4 ; Y.6, 7 or 11

High water Burnham : Dover plus 48 mins.

Miles	Landings
0	*Battlesbridge.* Stn. $\frac{1}{4}$ ml.

(S. Bank)

2$\frac{1}{2}$	*Hullbridge Ferry.* Supplies.

(N. Bank)

5	*Fambridge.* Stn. 1 ml.
9	*Bridgemarsh Creek.* Althorne Stn. $\frac{1}{4}$ ml.

(S. Bank)

10	Burnt out inn. Just short of this Paglesham Pool connects with R. Roach at H.W. Spring tides only. Considerable portage necessary at other tides.
10$\frac{1}{2}$	*Creeksea.* Boatyard and ferry landing stage.

(*N. Bank*)

11½   *Burnham-on-Crouch.* Hard leading to camp site behind sea wall.

(*S. Bank*)

14   Mouth of *R. Roach* (which see).

17   *Foulness Point.*

64. Roach

Tidal branch of Crouch, canoeable at high water from Stambridge Mills, 1½ miles from Rochford station. Current swift, banks muddy.

O.S. 162 ; Barth. 16

Charts : St. 4 ; Y.7 or 11

Miles

0   *Stambridge Mills.*

(*S. Bank*)

3½   *Potton Creek.* Like *Middleway* (see below) this connects with Havengore Creek.

(*N. Bank*)

4½   *Paglesham East End.* Pleasant village with ancient inn and supplies. Good hard at boat building shed. Tide : Dover plus 48 mins.

5   *Paglesham Pool.* (See R. Crouch.)

(*S. Bank*)

5½   *Middleway.* Connects with Havengore Creek giving short cut across Maplin Sands to Swin. *Havengore Creek* can only be used at H.W. and the 3 ml. width of Maplin Sands is only covered by a few feet of water at ordinary springs. Havengore Creek passes through Foulness Island, which is military property.   The crossing of Maplin Sands may involve danger from firing practice from Shoeburyness.   But Havengore Creek is a right of way for small craft. There is a swing bridge where the road crosses the creek.

THAMES BASIN

65. THAMES

Although sometimes looked upon as a river too quiet and gentle for interesting canoeing, the Thames has much to recommend it from the point of view of river scenery and picturesque old villages. Some think the prettiest—and certainly the least known—part lies above Oxford. The river, known here as the Isis, is always navigable from or to Lechlade, and in the winter and early spring from Cricklade, some 11 miles higher up and 155 miles from London Bridge. The river from Cricklade to Lechlade has no locks or weirs, but many little rapids and pools, and is well worth visiting, especially early in the year before weeds make progress difficult. Lock-keepers can often advise about camp sites.

Starting from Cricklade the river twists and turns through pretty country, passing Castle Eaton and Kempsford to Inglesham (at which point the derelict Thames and Severn Canal joins the river) and Lechlade, an old Cotswold market town.

From Lechlade to Oxford the scenery continues similarly, but with no riverside villages except Eynsham, and even that is over a mile from the river. There are, however, some very fine old inns such as the "Swan" at Radcot, the "Trout" at Tadpole Bridge, the "Rose Revived" at Newbridge and the "Trout" at Godstow. There are also some of the oldest Thames bridges at Radcot and Newbridge.

The passage through Oxford down to Folly Bridge is very ugly for a couple of miles and then the river changes its character completely. It is larger, more boats are seen, the hills close in, larger and more frequent villages are found. The river from Oxford downstream is too well known to need a long account here, but the following towns and villages, some of them off the main channel, are well worth visiting : Nuneham Courtney, Abingdon, Sutton Courtney, Clifton Hampden, Dorchester, Streatley and Goring, Sonning, Henley, Hurley, Marlow, Cookham, Bray, Eton and Windsor. Locks are not so frequent as to be troublesome, and some of the lock-keepers are good gardeners and take pride in their lock-side gardens.

From Staines onward the river banks begin to display river-side bungalows, mostly used for summer or week-end residences, and large waterworks appear on the banks at intervals right down to Kingston. However, there are still very pleasing reaches, as between Laleham and Shepperton, and at Chertsey the Canoe Camping Club maintains a canoe house on the Permanent Site of the Camping Club of Great Britain and Ireland, lying up a little creek on the right above the bridge.

Below Teddington the river is tidal, although a half-tide lock at Richmond prevents too strong a current down to that point, and keeps up the river level. Below Richmond lock the tide runs very strongly and one of the chief joys of canoeing on these otherwise rather uninteresting tidal waters is in using the fast current to carry one down through the heart of London and the Docks, among all the shipping.

Fees and Charges : A registration fee of £1 per annum is charged by the Thames Conservancy, 15 Buckingham Street, Strand, London, W.C.2, for keeping a canoe on the Thames between Lechlade and Teddington, and this is charged for however short a period the river is used. Below Teddington the Port of London Authority is in control and makes no charge for canoes, neither does it require any licence to be taken out.

There are 45 locks between Lechlade and Richmond, and a charge of 9d. is made for each canoe passing through, by or over, so there is nothing gained by portaging at the lock. The charge covers a return journey on the same day. There is also a period return for 1s. per lock for a minimum of three locks, available for return within one month.

Maps and Guides : O.S. 157, 158, 159, 170 ; Barth. 14, 8, 9 ; excellent strip maps in Salters' "Guide to the Thames"; and in Stanford's "Map of the Thames" (St. 77). Many excellent books on the river, such as Gibbings' "Sweet Thames Run Softly," and S. R. Jones' "Thames Triumphant."

By making use of the locks, portages can be avoided, but those who do not mind the extra trouble of lifting round a weir or over an obstacle will find added interest in exploring a number of side-arms of the river, some of them by-passing one or more locks. In some cases care has to be taken in their navigation, for one may come up against fallen trees, wires stretched across to prevent cattle from straying, etc. Some are only navigable in the early part of the year when the water is high and the vegetation not fully grown, but mention may be made of two or three shown on the map that are worth exploring :

Great Brook : leaves the river on the left before Rushy Lock and appears to lead back, but soon turns and is pleasant and intimate. As a result of recent drainage alterations the first ¾ mile or so may not have much water, but after it is joined by the artificially straightened Sharney Brook N of Tadpole Bridge it is much better. Various obstacles such as bridges, a sluice, fences and small rapids ; some care is required, but avoids two locks, Rushy and Shifford.

Seacourt Stream : leaves on the right 2½ miles below Swinford Bridge ; this can be followed into Oxford, or taken together with the *Hinksey Stream*, comes back into the Thames below Iffley Lock, thus by-passing Oxford and its approaches. Several obstacles, such as the mill at Wytham, several low bridges, shallows, fallen trees, but passes four locks—King's, Godstow, Osney, and Iffley.

Backwater : on the left ½ mile above Abingdon Lock—only in high water. Carry round sluice. The arches of the road bridge at Culham may be obstructed by poles.

Old River : through Sutton Courtney, keeping right where Culham Cut begins, passes through the Sutton Pools ; avoids Culham Lock.

Old River : through Long Wittenham, keeping right where Clifton Cut begins ; avoids Clifton Lock.

St. Patrick's Stream : leaves river on the right 1 mile below Sonning Bridge ; joins later with the River Loddon and re-enters the Thames below Shiplake Lock ; beware low hanging willow trees in strong current.

Miles

0   *Cricklade Bridge.* Old market town. Launch at Rose Cottage. Stn. on Andover-Swindon-Cheltenham line.

4½   *Castle Eaton Bridge.* Shallows. Village, inn R.

6   *Kempsford* L.

7¼   *Hannington Bridge.*

11   *Inglesham.* Footbridge. Round House, entrance of derelict Thames and Severn Canal L.

11½   *Lechlade Bridge.* Inn. shops. Boathouse. Old market town.

12¼   *St. John's Lock.* Bridge, Trout Inn. First lock on the Thames.

13   *Buscot Lock.* Village R. No lock-keeper.

17   *Grafton Lock.*

18   *Radcot Bridge.* Swan Inn.

19   *Radcot Lock.*

20½   *Rushy Lock.* Entrance to Great Brook above lock on left.

22   *Tadpole Bridge.* Trout Inn.

23¾   *Tenfoot Bridge.*

25   *Shifford Lock Cut* L. Old River goes off on the R to Duxford Village.

28¼   *Newbridge.* Old bridge. Confl. of Windrush above on L. May Bush Inn on R above, Rose Revived on L below.

29½   Footbridge. On site of old weir (Ridge's Weir).

30¼   *Northmoor Lock.*

32   *Bablock Hythe.* Ferry and inn, the Chequers.

35   *Pinkhill Lock.*

36   *Swinford Bridge and Eynsham Lock.* Village of Eynsham 1¼ mls. L. Wytham Woods R.

37   *Confluence of Evenlode* L.

38   *Seacourt Stream.* Branches off on the R rather inconspicuously and passes through Wytham and Hinksey.

38¾   *King's Lock.* Cut to Oxford Canal (½ ml.) above L (Duke's Cut).

39½   Road bridge.

40   *Godstow Bridge and Lock.* Trout Inn L. Ruins of Godstow Nunnery R. Backwater L to the mill and old bridge, also another way to the Oxford Canal, awkward.

43   *Binsey.* The Perch Inn L. Boat sheds L and junction with Oxford Canal.

44¼   *Osney Bridge, Oxford.* Nearest point to Oxford stn.; land below bridge.

44½   *Osney Lock.* Branch of Seacourt Stream comes in ¼ ml. below R.

45   *Folly Bridge.* Good point to leave canoe for tour of Oxford. Salter's Boathouse. Cherwell enters ¼ ml. below L.

46   *Donnington Bridge.*

46½   *Iffley Village and Lock.* Hinksey Stream comes in ½ ml. below R.

48   *Sandford Lock.*

52   Sluice L. Leads to backwater (often dry) by-passing Abingdon.

52½   *Abingdon Lock.* Bridge and town R ½ ml. below ; inns, shops.

54½   *Culham Lock Cut* L. Leads to Culham Lock. Sutton Courtney, picturesque village on old river R below weir.

Miles

56½   Railway bridge. Village of Appleford R.

57½   *Clifton Cut.* Long Wittenham down old river R.

58½   *Clifton Hampden Bridge.* Pretty village. Barley Mow Inn R.

61   *Day's Lock—Little Wittenham Bridge.* Dorchester 1 ml. L.

62   *Confluence of River Thame* L. ½ ml. up the Thame to Dorchester (Abbey).

64   *Shillingford Bridge.* Inn.

65   *Benson Lock.* Inns and village L.

66¼   *Wallingford Bridge.* Town L, shops, inns, boathouses   Old market town.

69½   Railway bridge.

70½   *Moulsford* R. Beetle and Wedge Inn.

71¼   *Leather Bottel Inn* L.

71½   *Cleeve Lock* then *Goring Lock* and Bridge ½ ml. beyond. Goring L (stn.); Streatley R. Inns, boathouse.

73½   Railway bridge.

76   *Pangbourne—Whitchurch Lock and Bridge.* Inns, boathouses. Stn. in Pangbourne R.

78½   *Mapledurham Lock.* Picturesque mill on L.

82¼   *Caversham Bridge.* Hotels, boathouses.

83   *Reading Bridge—Caversham Lock* below. Reading town and stns. R ; land on L bank.

83¾   *Confluence of River Kennet* R.

85¾   *Sonning Lock.* Picturesque village and inns R.

87   *St. Patrick's Stream.* Doubles back on R under footbridge ; navigable and fast to River Loddon.

88½   *Shiplake Lock—*Railway Bridge—Wargrave R. Confl. of River Loddon ; inn, stn.; Hennerton Backwater leaves on R and re-enters above Marsh Lock ; many kingfishers.

91   *Marsh Lock.*

92   *Henley Bridge.* Town and station L, shops, inns, boathouses.

93   *Remenham* R. Farm and church.

94½   *Hambleden Lock.*

96½   *Medmenham Abbey—*on L bank below the ferry. Frogmill Farm R behind islands, ½ ml. below.

98   *Hurley Lock.* Village R, inns, shop.

99   *Temple Lock—*mill and pretty backwater. Bisham Abbey R. ½ ml. below ; dates from 12th century ; eventful history.

100   *Marlow Bridge and Lock.* Town L, shops, inns, boathouses ; stn. ½ ml.

103   *Bourne End.* Sailing reach ; village L, stn.; Upper Thames Sailing Club.

104   *Cookham Bridge.* Village R ; river divides ; lock about ½ ml. down cut.

106½   *Boulter's Lock.*

107   *Maidenhead Bridge.* Town R ; shops, inns, boathouses ; Taplow Stn. (1 ml. L).

108½   *Bray* R and Lock. Inn.

108¾   Motorway bridge. Monkey Island ¼ ml. below.

112   *Boveney Lock.*

Miles

114 *Windsor Bridge* followed by *Romney Lock*. Inns, Windsor Castle, Eton College ; shops ; stns. (R). Windsor Home Park on R.

115½ *Datchet* L. Stn.

116 *Albert Bridge*—Old Windsor Lock. Cut leaves R.

118 *"Bells of Ouseley"* Inn R. Beginning of Runnymede. Bridge (Staines Bypass).

118½ *Magna Carta Island.* Passage either side, better view on the R.

120 *Bell Weir Lock.* Colne Brook enters L ; Egham ¾ ml. R.

121 *Staines Bridge.* Boathouses, inns, shops ; nearest point to SR stn. below railway bridge on L ; River Colne enters on L below the bridge.

123 *Penton Hook Lock.* Laleham ½ ml. downstream L.

125 *Chertsey Lock*—Chertsey Bridge below. Inns, shops, stn. 1 ml. R ; Permanent Site of Camping Club of G.B. & I. up creek just above bridge.

127 *Shepperton Lock*—River Wey and Wey Navigation enter R below lock. Desborough Channel (flood relief) R ; keep L for Shepperton and Halliford.

129 *Walton Bridge.* Walton on R below the bridge ; boathouses.

130½ *Sunbury Lock.* Sunbury Village L bank ; Hurst Park Racecourse R below.

133½ *Molesey Lock.* Molesey on R bank.

134 *Hampton Court Bridge.* Hampton Court Palace on L bank below the bridge ; inns, hotels ; stn R, confl. of Mole R.

135 *Thames Ditton* R. Inns, pleasant village ; Hampton Court Park L.

136 *Surbiton* R. Town on R ; rly. to Waterloo ½ ml.

137 *Kingston Bridge.* Kingston on R ; Turk's boathouse ; stn. R.

138 *Royal Canoe Club.* On L at the upper end of Trowlock Island.

138½ *Teddington Lock.* Limit of normal tides ; Teddington L. For tidal constants see end of Section 66.

139 *Ham Dock* entrance R (Surrey C.C. Youth Centre).

139½ *Twickenham* L. Opposite Eel Pie Island ; inns, shops, rly., etc.

141 *Richmond Bridges*—Richmond Lock just below. The tidegates are opened about 2 hours before highwater and closed about 2 hours after it. Rollers on L bank. Richmond Hill R ; boathouses R. Inn, Richmond Old Deer Park and Kew Gardens R.

142¼ *Isleworth* L. Inn.

144 *Kew Bridge.* Stn. L ; Strand-on-the-Green L ; boathouse.

145½ *Chiswick Bridge.* Mortlake R below bridge ; stn. at Barnes Bridge.

146½ *Chiswick Church* L. Good landing at ferry slip or Chiswick Dock L, 200 yds below.

147 *Hammersmith Bridge.* Shops, inn L ; Met. Rly. to Paddington (½ ml. L).

149 *Putney Bridge.* Rly. stns ; District Line L ; S.R. ¼ ml. R ; rowing and sailing clubs R ; good landing.

66. THAMES TIDEWAY AND ESTUARY

The Thames Tideway and Estuary provide excellent cruising ground for the London canoeist. Southend, Leigh or Chalkwell are easily reached by train or bus, the last two are on the seafront, and from there access to the creeks and rivers N of the estuary is not difficult. The journey down the Thames from Hammersmith to Southend is full of interest and may be conveniently carried out in three stages, making use of the ebb tides. The tide varies in different places, running up to 6 knots, but to all intents and purposes it is useless to paddle against it above Shellhaven. The estuary is always full of shipping and care should be taken to keep well out of the way of all vessels. There are large flats of soft mud below Gravesend, and the landing thereabouts should be chosen with care. It is worth remembering that by using something flat, like a plywood seat, you do not sink in quite so far into soft mud. Spring tides occur when high water at London Bridge is about 3 o'clock.

Hammersmith to Greenwich : About 3 hours canoeing. Canoes can be built near the "Old Ship" at Hammersmith and there is a boathouse just below the Royal Naval Hospital at Greenwich. "The Turk's Head" and "The Prospect of Whitby" public houses on the N bank below Tower Bridge are convenient stopping places en route. The journey through the Pool of London is of great interest, especially if there is much shipping about.

Greenwich to Purfleet : About 3 hours' canoeing. The river widens considerably and care should be taken to avoid the large washes of the bigger steamers.

Purfleet to Leigh or Southend : About 4 hours to "The Lobster Smack" at the entrance to Holehaven. Here there is a choice of routes.

- (a) Round Canvey Island to Benfleet and on to Leigh. At Benfleet there is only about 3 hours water in each tide and at low tide the creek is not navigable even by a canoe. See below.
- (b) Direct to Leigh and Southend down the Thames. There are several boathouses at Leigh.

O.S. 160, 161, 162, 170, 171, 172 ; Barth. 9, 10, 16

Charts : St. 6 ; Y.4

Miles

0	*Hammersmith Bridge.*
2	*Putney Bridge.* Good landing at boathouses R.
4	*Battersea.* Landing at "dock" near Battersea Parish Church R.
7¼	*Westminster Bridge.* Landing at steps R, near County Hall ; also at Cleopatra's Needle L ¼ ml. below ; several other steps and stairs before—
9¼	*London Bridge.*
9¾	*Tower Bridge.* Landing on L bank.
11¾	*"The Prospect of Whitby."* N bank side ; the landlord welcomes canoeists ; bad landing at low tide.
13¾	*Deptford Dockyard.* Near "The Duck and Gun," S bank, a stairway with concrete runway makes a good landing.
14	*Greenwich Pier.* On the S side ; good landing just above pier.
15¾	*Blackwall Pier.* Good landing at most tides.
20¼	*Barking Creek.* On the N bank.

25¾   *Erith Pier.* Good landing and shopping centre on S bank ; from here the banks begin to show country and camping is possible with care.

27¾   *Purfleet.* N bank ; good landing opposite the inn ; a good train service from London.

30¾   *Greenhithe Pier.* S bank.

35¾   *Gravesend Town Pier.* S bank ; opposite the Tilbury Landing Stage a ferry runs across and throws a moderate wash ; from here the banks are rather bleak ; camping behind the sea wall is possible in most places.

45   *Holehaven.* (N bank.) Landing at steps by coastguard stn., about 50 yds seaward of P.L.A. floating pier. Hidden behind the sea-wall is "The Lobster Smack" Inn. Taxi to Benfleet or ¾ ml. level walk to bus route. For 1½ mls. seaward of Holehaven the sea can be extremely rough on the ebb at spring tides (the overfalls are shown on the Admiralty chart).

45¾   Line of obstructions extends 1¼ mls. from S bank to the edge of the steamer track. It is like a high, lightly constructed wooden jetty. Just to seaward—

45¾   *St. Mary's Bay.* (S. bank.) Landings can be made 2 hours either side of H.W. and camping sites found.

47½   *Chapman Light* (N bank). Last lighthouse on tideway.

49   *Allhallows* (S bank). Small pleasure resort. Stn.

50   *Yantlet Creek* (S bank). Entrance marked by a small obelisk (The London Stone) near the shore. Whilst there is no longer a sea route through to Colemouth Creek and the Medway, Yantlet Creek provides an entrance 2 hours either side of H.W., and camping.

50½   *Benfleet and Leigh Creeks* enter (N bank) forming the Ray (or Ray Gut).

51¾   *Southend Pier* (N bank). 1¼ mls. long.

55½   *Sheerness and mouth of Medway* (S bank).

The Nore Lightship has been replaced by a fort on stilts. Note : The 1-in. O.S. map does not show the Nore Sand between Southend Pier and Sheerness, which is sometimes uncovered. It can cause a nasty sea at times when covered.

Holehaven, East Haven and Benfleet Creeks

Towards high water these form a pleasant and safe route round the north of Canvey Island from Holehaven. The two tides meet at the sharp bend where East Haven Creek and Benfleet Creek meet ¾ of a mile from Benfleet Station.

At low water there is water for 1½ miles only in Holehaven, and no water in East Haven Creek or Benfleet Creek until Leigh Marsh is reached.

Chart : St. 6 ; Y.4

0   *Holehaven.* Numerous yachts lie in the first ¾ ml. The main
channel is about 50 yds. from the E bank for about a mile
and then crosses to the L bank, between the first island,
known as the Lower Horse and the second island the Upper
Horse. From 3 hrs. after H.W. it is desirable to keep to
the main channel.

1½   Jetty on W bank.

2   Jetty on E (Canvey Island) bank. Keep close to E bank until—

2¼   *East Haven Creek* branches squarely off NE. Entrance about
30 yds. wide.

4   Sharp bend where tides meet.

4¾   *Benfleet.* Stn. L. Benfleet Yacht Club L. Benfleet Slipway L.
Dauntless Boatbuilding Co., S. R. Hearn & Sons, R. Best
place to unbuild is Benfleet Yacht Club (if permission is
obtained) or immediately below the road bridge over creek
(mud is sticky in places).

       Main channel is on S side for ½ ml. below Benfleet bridge
and then crosses to N side to—

6¼   Salvation Army Jetty N side in ruins. This was used for a
cement industry many years ago. Surrounding fields now
owned by Salvation Army. Hadleigh Castle ruins (13th
century) stand on hill up to Hadleigh Village. Immediately
below the jetty **Leigh Creek** branches off (see below).

7¾   *Small Gains Creek* S bank leads up to a part of Canvey Island
known as Leigh Beck. Hard at Canvey Island Yacht Club.
Here are shops and buses to Benfleet Stn. Boatbuilders
(G. Prout & Sons).

9¾   Junction with Leigh Creek in *Ray Gut.*

11¾   *Southend Pier.*

Leigh Creek. Leigh Creek forms a useful short cut from *Benfleet
Creek* to Leigh and Southend, but there is sufficient water for a canoe
only for 2 hours each side of high water.

Charts : St. 6 ; Y.4

0   *Junction with Benfleet Creek.* Near the Salvation Army Jetty on
the N bank. The entrance is very narrow. The hull of a
barge about ¼ ml. beyond the jetty means a portage at low
water.

1½   *Leigh-on-Sea Stn.* Johnson & Jago Ltd., boatbuilders. Numerous
cockle-boats and yachts lie in the next ½ ml. This part of
the creek may be foul ground owing to the frames of broken
up houseboats.

2   *Bell Wharf,* which is just by the old Leigh Stn. There is sand
here, convenient access to the few shops of Old Leigh and
of new Leigh up the hill. Also boatbuilders. The creek then
opens into the sea at H.W., but at L.W. it winds across
Southend mud flat to join Benfleet Creek at—

Miles
3½   *The Ray* (or *Ray Gut*). The creek is marked across the mud by withies on the W bank. There are usually cockle-boats moored just at the junction. For 1 ml. E and W of the junction the Ray provides water at all states of the tide.
4½   Entry into the Thames Estuary.
5½   Southend Pier end.

TIMES OF HIGH WATER ON THE THAMES

	Dover		London Bridge		Average Duration of			
					EBB		FLOOD	
	hr min		*hr min*		*hr min*		*hr min*	
Teddington Lock	*plus* 4	4	*plus* 1	25				
Richmond Lock	,, 3	50	,, 1	11	9	10	3	7
Kew Bridge	,, 3	34	,,	55	8	18	4	6
Hammersmith	,, 3	18	,,	39	7	50	4	40
London Bridge	,, 2	39			7	6	5	18
Greenwich Pier	,, 2	25	*minus*	14	6	45	5	25
Gravesend	,, 1	35	,, 1	4				
Holehaven	,, 1	23	,, 1	16				
Benfleet	,, 1	29	,, 1	10				
Southend Pier	,, 1	9	,, 1	30				
Mouth of Medway	,, 1	20	,, 1	19				

67. Windrush

Rises in the Cotswolds and flows SE through charming Cotswold villages and countryside, past Burford and Witney to the Thames at Newbridge. The river is canoeable from Bourton-on-the-Water, where it is still narrow. There are numerous obstacles—wire, low bridges, mills ; there are also stretches of private trout fishing, and difficulties may be encountered with water bailiffs. The banks are low, and landings easy. Bourton-on-the-Water to the Thames approx. 21 miles.

O.S. 144, 145 and 158 ; Barth 14

68. Evenlode

Rises in the Cotswolds near Moreton-in-Marsh and flows SE through Charlbury to the Thames near Eynsham. For much of its course it is followed by the Oxford-Worcester railway line, which crosses and re-crosses it. It is canoeable from Charlbury (station). Four mills and numerous small obstructions (low bridges, wire). The banks are low, and landings easy. Attractive woodland, parks and low hills ; no villages close to the river. Shallows after dry weather will necessitate some wading. Charlbury to the Thames approx. 15 miles. Care needed under most bridges.

O.S. 145 ; Barth. 14

69. Cherwell

Rises in the Northamptonshire uplands NW of Banbury and flows S to join the Thames at Magdalen Bridge, Oxford. The upper parts are canoeable, but are rather narrow, dull and weedy from Banbury ; it is better to start lower at Aynho (station) or Somerton. A pleasant meandering course, with fairly frequent portages. The Oxford Canal follows the valley and provides an alternative as far as Hampton Gay ; the Oxford to Banbury railway line runs with the Canal. Aynho to Oxford approx. 20 miles.

O.S. 145, 158 ; Barth. 14

70. Thame

The Thame rises to the NE of Aylesbury. It flows through fairly wooded and thinly populated country to the Thames near Dorchester ; the banks are fairly low. In early summer the river becomes very reedy and from then until the first winter floods a trip is inadvisable.

From January to June the river is possible from Aylesbury. High water (the river floods easily) makes many of the low bridges very low, but gives a good flow. Fallen trees and wire may be encountered.

Below Wheatley road bridge the river is wider in parts. Many interesting houses can be half seen from the river, and bird life is plentiful. Camp sites are easy.

A branch of the Grand Union Canal terminates at Aylesbury and may make a circular tour possible.

O.S. 158, 159 ; Barth. 14

Miles
0	*Aylesbury*. Road bridge A.413, 1 ml. N of Aylesbury centre.
1	Footbridge. Remains of deserted village of Quarrendon R.
1½	Road bridge (A.41). Rly. bridge ¼ ml. below.
3¼	*Eythrope Park* R. Small wooden sluice L opposite house. It is best to lift over this to left-hand stream. The lake in the park is very pleasant. Either return to the sluice (better) or carry over road.
3¾	Road bridge. After ¼ ml. field bridge. Lift round.
5¼	Fall under low bridge. Make sure there is enough headroom.
6¼	*Lower Winchendon Mill*. Either go up to the mill and portage L, or in H.W. take the first possible of the several falls L.
6¾	Concrete weir R. Haul over if possible so as to avoid the next mill.
7	Road bridge. Little clearance in H.W. ¼ ml. beyond is a mill, avoided if concrete slip has been taken ; otherwise portage R 50 yds. before mill.
7¾	Low footbridge. Chearsley Village R.
8½	Railway bridge. Easy rapid beyond wire across.
9	*Notley Abbey* R. Easy rapid under bridge beyond.

Miles

9¼ Site of old mill. Right-hand branch has been shot in high water.
11¼ *Thame Bridge.* Town L. Land L and walk through churchyard to
High Street.
13 Field bridge. Take middle arch.
13½ River divided—go L over fall or lift round.
14 *Shabbington Bridge.* Village R. Inn.
16 Road bridge. Ickford R. Small fall—take L arch.
18¼ *Waterstock Mill.* Go up to mill and portage L or shoot on R of
mill.
19¾ *Holton Mill.* Paddle beyond weir, which is unshootable. Portage
over concrete 5 yds. beyond L.
20 *Wheatley Bridge* (A.40). Wheatley 1 ml. R. Hotel. Railway
bridge.
21¼ Double sluice L. Shoot either, preferably R, or portage L.
22 Road bridge by mill.
23¾ Field bridge.
25¼ *Chislehampton Bridge* (B.480). Inn R. Shoot second arch from L.
26½ *Stadhampton Bridge.* L arch.
29 *Queensford Mill.* Take L channel, avoiding weir.
30 *Dorchester Mill.* Portage R at first weir on R a short distance
before the mill is possible but the owner has objected and
disclaims any responsibility for damage in portaging. A
portage at the mill would be through private grounds.
Access on L branch to lane above mill ; ¼ mile to main road.
30¼ Low footbridge, broken. Unshootable fall just beyond. Portage R.
30½ *Dorchester Bridge* (A.423). Village and Abbey R.
31 Confl. with Thames, by Little Wittenham Wood.

O.S. 158 ; Barth. 14

71. Kennet

Rises in the Marlborough Downs and flows E through Newbury to
the Thames at Reading. The main railway line from Paddington
through Reading, Newbury and Hungerford follows the river most of
the way, continually crossing and recrossing. The valley is also the
route of the Kennet and Avon Canal, which below Newbury often makes
use of the river itself. The upper reaches are private and preserved for
trout, and should be regarded as impracticable. There is usually enough
water for canoes from Hungerford where it is a clear, fast chalk stream,
but there are numerous obstructions (mills, low bridges, etc.); the Canal
is always available as an alternative. Below Newbury, the windings of
the old river can, in many places, be followed instead of the Canal cuts ;
though they involve some portages they also avoid portages at locks
on the Cuts. *N.B.* The last lock (Blake's Lock) belongs to the Thames
Conservancy, whose fees and dues are chargeable if this point is passed.
Hungerford to Reading 30 miles.

O.S. 158, 169 ; Barth. 8

111

72. KENNET and AVON CANAL

Runs from Reading to the Avon at Bath, 76 miles ; was opened in 1810 ; has 101 locks, with 6 more on the Avon between Bath and Bristol.

The canal passes through some pleasant country with delightful villages off the beaten track ; from it there are magnificent views of the Avon Valley at Devizes and between Bradford and Bath. At present (1960) the canal is low between Bradford-on-Avon and Avoncliff, and drained between there and Limpley Stoke. For the rest, parts of the canal are weedy at certain times of the year, but it provides much interest for the naturalist.

The locks between Reading and Garston are workable, and between Weston and Hanham on the Avon Navigation. In between only occasional locks are workable.

The canal is possible for canoes at any time of year, though conditions vary with water level, weed, etc. The main drawback is the number of locks : 53 rising from Reading, of which 20 occur in 7 miles between Hungerford and Crofton, and 48 falling (to Bath), of which 29 occur in a ladder in 1¼ miles at Devizes. The portage round the Devizes ladder is best done on A.361 and B.3101. There is one tunnel, at Savernake, 500 yards straight. Special permission necessary to pass through. The Crofton pumping station has the original two James Watt beam pumping engines. There are lock-keepers only at every 6 or 7 locks.

The first lock from the Thames (Blake's Lock) is under the control of the Thames Conservancy, whose fees apply.

Controlling authority : British Waterways. Further detailed information is obtainable from the Kennet and Avon Canal Association, c/o the Inland Waterways Association, 114 Regents Park Road, London, N.W.1.

O.S. 156, 166, 167, 158, 168, 169 ; Barth. 7, 8

73. Loddon

Rises near Basingstoke and flows in a generally NW direction to the Thames at Wargrave through rich meadows and well timbered parkland. Above Swallowfield the river is shallow and fairly narrow, and there are obstacles (*e.g.* a fish screen, a decayed sluice, three mills and overhanging trees, etc.). Permission to pass through Stratfield Saye Park (two weirs —easy portages) should be sought from the Agent to the Duke of Wellington. Silchester (a Roman township) is 4 miles W of the road bridge at the north end of Stratfield Saye Park. Private water all the way, at least as far as Twyford. Sherfield to Swallowfield approx. 6 miles.

O.S. 169, 159 ; Barth. 8

Miles

 0   *Swallowfield Bridge.* Old Mill House (restaurant).
 3   *Arborfield Bridge.* Portage on L 100 yds. beyond into small side
      stream, in order to avoid Arborfield Weir, by the Hall.
 5½ *Sindlesham Bridge and Mill.* Portage in front of mill through
      gate on R past mill house.
 6¼ *Loddon Bridge.* Inn, cafe. Rly. bridge beyond.
 8   *Sandford Mill and Bridge.* Portage on R before weir.
 8¼ River divides. Right branch—easy deep water under a road
      bridge and rly. viaduct past Twyford Mill. Left branch—
      shallows and a ford.
10¼ *Twyford Mill and Bridge.* Portage on L of weir. Shallows to
      junction with left branch on L. Inns, shops, etc. in Twyford.
      For Twyford stn. land at rly. viaduct (¼ ml. R).
11   Road bridge (A.4).
12   Entrance of *St. Patrick's Stream* L.
13   Confl. with *Thames.* Wargrave R.

74. Middlesex Colne

Rises near St. Albans and flows S, splitting into two or three streams
which join the Thames near Staines. Of these the River Colne itself
(the most easterly) and the Colne Brook (the most westerly) carry
enough water and can be canoed from West Drayton, above which the
Grand Union Canal follows the Colne Valley for some way. There are
numerous portages, some awkward, on either stream, both of which are
private water. It would be best to explore them beforehand and obtain
permission. The country through which they flow is flat market garden
land. West Drayton to Thames approx. 7 miles.

O.S. 170 ; Barth. 9

75. WEY

A tributary of the Thames, coming in on the R at Weybridge,
immediately below Shepperton Lock. It has two sources, one near
Alton in Hampshire, and the other near Haslemere in Surrey. Both
streams may be descended by canoe, the former from above the town
of Farnham and the latter from Frensham ; the two branches join at
Tilford. The mileage in the itinerary is given from Farnham as this is
more accessible.

The Wey is a pleasant river ; its upper reaches run through the
sandstone belt of heathland and its lower reaches through lowland
pasture. Above Godalming the river runs fast and clear over a sandy
bottom ; below here it is a navigation. From Guildford the river and
the navigation keep coming together and then parting again, and it is
worthwhile taking the natural stream where possible. The branches
above Tilford may call for occasional wading and portages, but there
are no really difficult places. Waverley Park on the Frensham branch
is well worth a visit, for it contains the ruins of Waverley Abbey.

The river below Godalming has been canalised. The National Trust is the navigation authority. Annual licence 15s.; if a period lock-permit is not held a fee of 9d. per lock is charged, available for return the same day. For unlicensed visiting craft a permit for a return journey and locks between Guildford and Thames costs 15s., Godalming and Thames £1. Applications for licences or permits should be made to the River Wey Navigation, Guildford Wharf, Guildford. Lock charges are payable to lock-keepers. A lock key is obtainable against a small deposit on application to Guildford Wharf. There is a lock-keeper every two or three locks. Camp sites are difficult to find below Godalming.

O.S. 169, 170 ; Barth. 8, 9

Medium Water : starting point—Farnham Bridge, or a short distance downstream along by-pass.

Low Water : starting point—Moor Park, some 2 miles below Farnham and reached by a short cut over the hill from the station.

Miles

0   *Farnham*. S.R. stn., town, castle, shops, etc.; portages at 2 mills.

2   *Moor Park Bridge*. Portage.

3   *Waverley Bridge and Weir*. Awkward portage ; Waverley Abbey R $\frac{1}{2}$ ml. below.

5   *Tilford Mill Bridge*. Portage R ; fast water.

6$\frac{1}{2}$ *Tilford Bridge*. Confl. of the two branches ; inn, village. (The southern branch is canoeable from Frensham Bridge, 3 mls. above Tilford.) From the confl. of the two branches there should be plenty of water, but occasional snags such as tree trunks may be encountered ; between Tilford and Elstead there are many rapids, twists and turns ; watch out for trees.

9$\frac{3}{4}$ *Elstead Mill*. Portage 100 yds. above mill on L ; carry to road and down to the bridge ; river continues fast with many bends.

13   *Somerset Farm Weir*. Drop of 1 to 2 feet then rapids below bridge ; Peper Harow Park $\frac{1}{2}$ ml. below ; current not so fast.

14$\frac{1}{2}$ *Eashing Mill*. Just below Guildford by-pass viaduct short portage on L into weir stream ; Charterhouse School on left below, on hill.

16$\frac{1}{4}$ *Godalming Mill*. Portage on R beyond low bridge around mill (a tannery) into mill pool ; landing is awkward ; it is easier but longer to land L 300 yds. above the mill where a path leads to the road. Follow road under rly. bridge to river bridge below mill pool. Godalming stn. R close ; shops R.

16$\frac{1}{2}$ *Godalming Wharf* R. Beginning of Wey Navigation.

17   *Cotteshall Lock*. Leroy's Boathouse.

18$\frac{1}{4}$ *Unstead Bridge and Lock*. Junction of Wey and Arun Canal (now derelict and impassable) is up a small river on the R below the first rly. bridge ; this river is possible as far as Bramley (1$\frac{1}{2}$ mls.) where there is a weir, but permission to pass may be refused.

114

19½   *St. Catherine's Lock.* Ruins of St. Catherine's Chapel on hill on L; fine approach to Guildford.

20½   *Mill Mead Lock, Guildford.* Most convenient landing for Guildford.

20¾   *Guildford Bridges.* Interesting old town with ancient buildings ; fine walks ; river very ugly through town ; stn. ¼ ml.; there is a landing very close to the stn., between Guildford bridges up an alley on the L.

22½   *Stoke Mill.* Road bridge (A.320). Navigation cut diverges to L. Old river over weir to R, rejoins just below Stoke Lock.

23   *Stoke Lock* (keeper). Scenery improves again.

24   Navigation cut R. Old river L.

24¼   *Bower's Lock.* Old river leaves on R ½ ml. below and rejoins below Trigg's Lock.

25¾   *Trigg's Lock* (keeper). Send Grove and Church on old river R.

26½   Flood lock, usually open.

26¾   *Cartbridge.* Old Woking L. Send on R ; old river goes off on L via Old Woking ; possible to portage out of this into new flood channel between this and the canal cut, which it rejoins below next lock.

28½   *Paper Court Lock* (keeper).

29¼   *Newark Lock.* Newark Priory on L ; numerous channels leave navigation R and L ; some shallow.

29¾   *Walsham Flood Gates* (usually open—keeper)

    The natural river over weir R goes through Wisley and Brooklands. The initial portage into the old river should be made about ½ ml. below Walsham Gates, where the river and Navigation are very near together ; numerous shallows. Just after iron footbridge about ½ ml. above Byfleet Mill, turn sharp L into side stream, narrower than mill stream, and portage L on footpath near the mill. Do not try to portage at the mill itself. Byfleet Mill is a private residence whose owners do not permit portages through their property. At fork above A.245 road bridge take L branch (pipe across R branch). If you do not wish to go on through Brooklands, stop here.

    The owners of Brooklands (Vickers-Armstrong Ltd.) allow canoes to pass through but landing is forbidden. Just before Brooklands a low girder bridge ; in high water portage R. *N.B.* Half-way through Brooklands there is a bridge which in very high water is too low to pass under and no portage is possible.

31   *Pyrford Bridge and Lock.* Inn.

32   Road bridge (near Byfleet) (A.245). West Byfleet Stn. 1 ml. W.

32¾   Railway bridge. Junction of Basingstoke Canal L.

33¾   *Newhaw Bridge and Lock.* Lock-keeper ; inn ; Byfleet and New Haw Stn. ½ ml. R.

34½   *Cox's Lock.*

35¼   *Weybridge Lock.* River joins below the lock. Butler's boatyard ; facilities for assembling canoes, leaving cars, etc.

35¾ *Thames Lock*—junction with Thames just below. 10 feet rise and
         fall ; care required in use ; Shepperton Lock (see Thames
         itinerary) just above on Thames.

Link with the River Arun: As the Wey and Arun Canal is now derelict,
access from one river to the other can only be had by road ; the road
portage between the bridge on A.281 near Shalford and New Bridge,
Billingshurst (see Section 93) on A.272 is about 18 miles.

76. BASINGSTOKE CANAL

The Basingstoke Canal (privately owned) runs from the Wey Navigation at Byfleet to Basingstoke, but beyond Greywell is now impossible.
It is a very pretty canal all the way, passing through heath and woodland, but the summit level between Aldershot and Greywell Tunnel may
be weedy. Proprietors : The New Basingstoke Canal Co. Ltd., Green-
ways Farm, Winchfield, Basingstoke, Hants. Charges £1 per annum,
or 1s. per person per day, 2s. 6d. weekend, 5s. week.

Byfleet to Greywell—31 miles. There are 29 locks, 28 of which come
in four flights in the first 10 miles : Nos. 1 to 6 at Woodham ; Goldsworth
Locks (Nos. 7 to 11) ; Brookwood Locks (12 to 14) ; and Frimley Locks
(Nos. 15 to 28). There is another lock at Ash Vale, 6 miles above
Frimley locks. Only pleasure craft now use the canal. Many stretches
weedy in summer.

O.S. 169, 170 ; Barth. 8, 9

77. MOLE

The Mole rises near Horsham and flows generally northwards to the
Thames at Molesey, except for a few miles where it flows W under the
escarpment of the North Downs, breaking through them between
Dorking and Leatherhead in very fine country. Beyond Leatherhead
the country remains pleasant all the way until just before Molesey. It is
all private water, and tact and discretion may be called for, especially
at the portages, if canoeing is to be tolerated on it at all. Objections
to any canoeing have been made by fishing interests between Oldmill
Bridge and Street Cobham.

At many times of the year there is insufficient water below Burford
Bridge. Between Dorking and Leatherhead the river dries up after dry
weather, such flow as there is in the upper reaches flowing here underground. Between Leatherhead and Cobham many shallows and some
fast water will be encountered except in times of spate ; a watch should
be kept for overhanging trees, etc.

O.S. 170 ; Barth. 9

Miles

0   *Horley.* Bridge on main Brighton Road (A.23); stn. 1 ml.; for a starting place this is rather public, and a water bailiff lives nearby ; Lee Street Bridge is better (see below).

¾   *Court Lodge Farm Mill.* Weir and portage on L ; Lee Street Bridge below.

4   *Kinnersley Manor and Bridge.*

5¼   *Sidlow Bridge.* Reigate-Gatwick Road (A.217).

8   *Flanchford Bridge.*

9   Low footbridge near Ricebridge Farm. Valley pleasant, good views of the North Downs.

11¾   *Betchworth Bridge.* Stn. 1¼ mls. on R.

12¾   *Betchworth House.* Weirs. River divides ; weir on L channel can be shot in high water with care ; the best portage is R of the weir on the R channel.

13½   *Brockham.* Low footbridge. Rapid ; remains of old bridge under.

13¾   *Brockham Bridge and Weir.* Brockham, shops, inns, L.

14½   *Betchworth Castle.* Ruins on hill, L ; snags in river. Two road bridges, then—

15¾   *Dorking—Castle Mill.* Portage R a little way above mill into pool below sluices ; town, shops, stns., L ; current quickens and river turns N under foot of Box Hill.

17   Stepping stones. Covered at high water ; spaces between stones are too narrow for canoes. Footbridge below.

17¾   *Burford Bridge.* Inn ; Boxhill Stn. ¼ ml. L ; between here and Leatherhead the river dries out after dry weather ; rly. crosses twice, then—

20¼   *Mickleham Bridge.* Village, inns, etc. R ; remains of weir just below.

20¾   *The Priory Weir and Bridge.* Plenty of water in time of spate but strong undertow in boil below—caution ; portage R ; in low water line down L.

22   Road bridge. Leatherhead by-pass.

23   *Site of Leatherhead Mill.* River divides just beyond Thorncroft Bridge ; best portage on L of L channel if there is enough water in it ; otherwise go to end of R channel and portage R.

      Leatherhead Bridge. Immediately below Mill ; many arches ; shallows and cross currents make approach tricky ; town, shops, stn. R ; road bridge and two rly. viaducts below ; between here and Cobham shallow rapids and pools alternate ; the river no longer flows underground in dry weather but some wading may be necessary.

24¾   *Oldmill Bridge.* Sluices removed. Bridge R usually shootable, but a steel girder limits headroom when water is high. In spate a portage is necessary unless the weir channel on L (usually dry) is carrying enough water.

25½   River divides. Either channel practicable.

27¼   Small weir. Slyfield Bridge just below ; Stoke d'Abernon House ¼ ml. below on R.

29   *Downside Saw Mill.* Just after rly. bridge ; portage into weir stream R, or at mill ; nearest point to Cobham Stn. ¼ ml. below mill.

31   *Church Cobham Mill.* Now demolished. Portage on L, rather awkward, easier but longer on road R. Village, shops, etc., R.

       Church Cobham Bridge. Awkward cross current.

33¾   River divides. Line down weir on R or portage past water wheel on L channel.

35½   *Street Cobham Weir and Bridge.* Portsmouth Road (A.3); village, shops, etc., on R ; shallows under the bridge, then 6 mls. of good water.

40½   *Esher Bridge.* Wainfleet's Tower and Esher Place on R below.

41½   *Esher Railway Bridge.* Royal Mills ; awkward steep portage on L ; Esher stn. 1 ml. on R ; shallows and pools recommence.

42¾   River divides, enclosing Island Barn Reservoir. There is usually not enough water in the R branch (the *Ember*), which at Ember Court is led down two steep and narrow slippery concrete culverts. Take the L branch (the *Mole* proper).

44   Sluice ; portage R. (The L branch leads into private grounds.) A short distance beyond where it rejoins the Mole and Ember flow close together. Portage R near a footbridge across meadow about 10 to 20 yds. into *Ember.* The Mole continues under Esher Lane Bridge (portage R about 80 yds along Summer Road to Ember at a ford) and on to a new sluice where sheet steel piling makes a portage down into the Ember impossible.

44½   (*Ember*) Ford (Summer Road). Shallow step under footbridge and large pipe just awash below necessitates lining over at normal levels.

45   Road and rly. bridges. Hampton Court Stn. adjoins.

45¼   *Confluence with Thames* opposite Hampton Court Palace.

78. LEA (or LEE)

The Lea rises near Luton and flows S and E to Ware, then S again to the Thames at Limehouse. Its upper reaches are pretty but very private. Below Hertford it is a navigation. Whilst it affords access to the Thames from the north it is not recommended nearer London than Enfield Lock, owing to the many factories along its banks.

Lock fees 9d. per lock, paid to lock-keeper. This charge covers return on the same day. British Waterways' Inland Cruising Booklet No. 3 describes the Lea and Stort Navigations.

O.S. 160 ; Barth. 15

  0   *Hertford Town Mill.* Stns., shops. etc.

  ½   *Dicker Mill Bridge.*

  ¾   *Hertford Lock.* Junction of *Rib* ¼ ml. beyond.

2¼   *Ware Lock.*

  3   *Ware Bridge.* Town and stn. L. 200 yds. beyond weir at SE end of Ware one can carry over to the old river channel with the help of a small overflow from the navigation. This channel passes through Stanstead Abbots (portage at mill in village) and rejoins the navigation in 2¾ mls. On the navigation there are locks at Amwell Hard Mead and Stanstead, where St. Margaret's Rly. Stn. is close to the river.

6½   *Rye House Bridge.* Rye Park Stn. R.

  7   *Feildes Weir and Lock.* Junction of *Stort Navigation* L which gives access to Bishops Stortford and thence by short rail link to the headwaters of the Cam (see Section III—5).

  8   *Dobbs Weir and Lock.* One can carry over above the weir to the old river R which can be followed for 1¾ mls. to Broxbourne Mill, where a portage through the mill grounds to the navigation is necessary (Broxbourne Stn. adjoins the old river). On the navigation there is one lock between Dobbs Weir Lock and Broxbourne.

9¾   *Broxbourne Mill.*

10¼   *King's Weir.* The old channel diverges L and runs through Waltham Abbey before rejoining the navigation at Waltham Bridge. There are 3 locks on the navigation before—

13¾   *Waltham Bridge and Lock.* Waltham Cross (stn.) ¾ ml. R.

14   *Romney Marsh Lock.*

14¾   *Enfield Lock.* Stn. ¼ ml. R ; 8 more locks to the Thames at Limehouse.

28   Junction with Thames, 2½ mls. below London Bridge.

79. Stort

The Stort flows SW through Bishop's Stortford and Harlow to the Lea near Hoddesdon. A navigation below Bishop's Stortford passing through a pleasant valley and giving, with a short rail connection from Bishop's Stortford to Audley End, access to the Cam and Bedford Ouse. The navigation is apt to be weedy. It is followed all the way by the Cambridge-Liverpool Street main line (E.R.) and there are several stations with convenient access to the river ; 15 locks—13¾ miles.

Charges : as for the Lea (see above).

British Waterways' Inland Cruising Booklet No. 3 describes the Stort.

O.S. 160, 161 ; Barth. 15

KENT AND SUSSEX

80. MEDWAY

Rises in Sussex not far from East Grinstead and flows NE through Kent to Thames Estuary. *The* river of Kent, dividing Men of Kent from Kentishmen. At high water possible from Balls Green ; at medium levels from Penshurst ; always from Tonbridge. Above Tonbridge hilly countryside, deeply scoured channel, liable to severe flooding in wet season. At low water shallows and a number of dams, some shootable with care. Below Tonbridge canalised, countryside flat, current sluggish. Below Yalding hills again to Rochester. Near Maidstone notable for fruit blossom in spring and for hopfields. Much frequented by fishermen at weekends and holidays. Permission to use locks (some unattended) from Divisional Engineer, Kent River Authority, London Road, Maidstone ; but portages are straightforward. Below Allington tidal ; banks very muddy at low tide ; not recommended except on the ebb just after high tide. Below Rochester widens into very broad estuary with extensive shoals and saltings. Apt to be rough when wind is fresh, especially when against the tide. Beware of being stranded on a falling tide on a mud or sandbank. Rail access at Withyham, Ashurst, Leigh (Lyghe Halt), Tonbridge ; railway follows river closely, Yalding-Strood; Sheerness.

O.S. **171**, **172** ; Barth. 10

Charts : St. **6** or **8** ; Y.5

Miles

0   *Balls Green Bridge* (Withyham Stn.). Launch into pool by bridge. River about 10 ft. wide. Narrow, sharp bends, fairly fast stream. Various obstructions and scours, not requiring portages.

1½   Junction of Groombridge stream R. River widens ; good flow.

3   *Ashurst Bridge*. Stn. (Croydon-T. Wells Line). Inn. Mill no longer exists. Portage L at sluice. Shallows at first, but soon deepens.

5   *Chafford Bridge*. Automatic sluice, fall about 10 ft.; portage L. A heavy object pressed by the force of water against the base of the sluice may at times cause it to open without warning, causing a sudden rise in the water level below. River swift and shallow below with several dams.

Miles

6   Road bridge (B.2188).
10½ *Penshurst. R. Eden* L. Village picturesque ; shops, inn ; Pens-
     hurst Place, mangificent mansion, 1½ mls. below : dam.
14½ Railway bridge. ½ ml. below : weir ; portage L.
16   Railway bridge. River divides. Left-hand branch more direct ;
     right-hand passes boathouses near Tonbridge Stn.
16½ *Tonbridge.* Town, castle, shops, hotels. Stn. Launch upstream
     of road bridge near boathouses. From stn. take first L, then
     footpath R leads through playing fields to river.
16¾ *Tonbridge Town Lock.* If using locks, get permit here. Little
     current. Often better to portage into weir stream, not at
     lock.
17   Road bridge.
18½ *Eldridge's Lock.*
19¼ *Porter's Lock.*
19½ Road bridge ; footbridge below. Two more locks then a footbridge.
20½ *East Lock.*
21¼ *Oak Lock.*
22   River divides ; either branch practicable.
22½ *Sluice Weir Lock*—automatic floodgates on R.
23½ *East Peckham Bridge.* Beltring Halt ¾ ml. R.
24   Rly. bridge and remains of old lock (no gates).
25¼ *Twyford.* Yacht basin R. Inn. Weir and road bridge. Mouth of
     River Teise. Yalding Village ½ ml. R. Lock cut leaves on L
     above the weir, alongside the road. The weir stream is
     joined after ¼ ml. by the *River Beult.*
25¾ *Hampstead Lane Lock.* Yalding Stn. close by L. Country more
     hilly and populated.
27¼ *Wateringbury Bridge.* Stn. adjoining. Village L. Inn.
28¾ *Teston Lock and Bridge.* Inn.
29¾ *East Barming.* Church L and bridge.
30¾ *East Farley Bridge and Lock.* Stn. L. Village R. Inn.
32¼ *Tovil Bridge.*
33   *Maidstone Bridge.* West Stn. ¼ ml. L. County town ; shops,
     hotels, etc. Fine church ; remains of Archbishop's palace.
33½ Railway bridge. Maidstone East Stn. R.
35   *Allington Castle* L.
35¼ *Allington Lock* (tidal). Best to wait for high water here. H.W.
     approx. 2 hrs. after Dover. (The lock is usable only between
     3 hrs. before and 2 hrs. after high water.) Motorway bridge
     just below the lock.
36½ *Aylesford Bridge.* Picturesque village. R "Kitts Coty House,"
     1½ mls.
37   *Mill Hall.* Aylesford Stn. L.
38   *New Hythe* L. Stn. River now passes through North Downs.
     Cement works are frequent.
40   *Snodland L.* Stn.
41½ *Halling* L. Stn.
42   *Wouldham* R. Landing possible at all states of tide.
44   *Borstal* R.

Miles

46¼ *Rochester Bridge.* Stns.—Strood L ; Rochester R. Shops, hotels, castle, cathedral. Landings above bridge R ; or below bridge L near Strood Stn., at all states of tide.

47¼ *Chatham* R. Naval Dockyard for two miles.

48¾ *Upnor* L. Good landing at hard 150 yds. above Upnor Castle. Supplies at village.

49¼ *Lower Upnor* L. Training Ship "Arethusa." Inn. Good landing except at extreme low water at wide concrete slipway just below "Arethusa." For the next ½ ml. there is a pleasant bathing beach L at the foot of Cockham Wood, which is on a steep hillside. N of Upnor as far as the mouth of the Medway is the "Hundred of Hoo," scene of Dickens novel "Great Expectations."

50¾ *Gillingham* R. Landing at hard marked with large signboard, "Gillingham Borough Causeway." Last low water landing for miles. The estuary becomes very wide, with extensive shoals, saltings and creeks. Its navigation requires some care.

57½ *Port Victoria* L. Big oil refinery L.

58½ Junction of the Swale R. Queenborough (stn.) 1 ml. along Swale.

60½ *Sheerness* R. Stn. Large naval town. If passing round Garrison Point to land on sea front, beware of groyne running out to dolphin.

Mouth of Medway. Opposite to Sheerness there is a Martello Tower—"The Grain Tower." This is joined to the shore by a long line of obstructions.

High water at Mouth of Medway : Dover plus 1 hour 20 mins.

81.   Eden

Rises near Lingfield, Surrey, flows E through Edenbridge to Medway at Penshurst. Shallow with gravel bed in low water, with numerous weirs and obstructions. Possible from Edenbridge (stn.) at high water. Edenbridge-Penshurst approx. 8 miles. Private water near Hever Castle.

O.S. **171** ; Barth. 10

82.   Teise

Rises E of Tunbridge Wells, flows E then N ; 1 mile below Horsmonden bridge it divides and flows down two separate valleys, the left-hand stream joining the Medway near Yalding, the right-hand stream joining the Beult near Hunton. Possible only in high water from Goudhurst Stn. The left-hand stream is reported to be the better. Very narrow and tortuous, and requires skill where current swift. Frequent portages at low bridges.

O.S. **172** ; Barth. 10

83. Beult

Rises SW of Ashford, flows WNW past Headcorn (stn.) to Medway at Yalding. Possible only in high or moderate water from the Staplehurst Road at Headcorn. Inns at Stile Bridge (6 miles) and Hunton Bridge (8½ miles). Two miles lower portage at sluice R or 50 yards further on L ; below is a weir. Yalding Bridge (village, inn) (12 miles). Confluence with Medway ¼ mile below.

O.S. 172 ; Barth. 10

84. SWALE

The Swale is the tidal channel extending from the Medway Estuary at Queenborough to the Thames Estuary at Shell Ness along the S shore of the Isle of Sheppey. Interesting and pleasant in good weather. Tides run strongly and should be carefully studied. Flood flows in from each end ; the Swale empties on the ebb both ways from Elmley Ferry. Best low water landings : Garrison Point, Sheerness ; Queenborough Hard ; Queen's Bridge ; Elmley Ferry ; and Harty Ferry. At low water extensive mud banks ; care required when exploring creeks on falling tide. Elmley Ferry makes a good centre. For day cruises from here a high tide between 6 and 8 o'clock is most suitable. Access by rough road from Sittingbourne via Tonge Corner, or (at high water only) by Milton Creek from Sittingbourne (stn.).   Approx. distances from Elmley Ferry : Queen's Bridge 3½ ; Queenborough Hard 7 ; Sheerness 9½; Conyer 3 ; Harty Ferry and Faversham Creek 5 ; Shell Ness 8 (landing only within 2 hours of high water).

High Water at Harty Ferry : Dover plus ¾ hour approx.; at Queenborough : Dover plus 1 hour 18 mins.

O.S. 172 ; Barth. 10

Charts : St. 8 ; Y.5

85. KENTISH STOUR

The **Great Stour** rises near Charing, joined by the East Stour near Ashford, flows NE through the North Downs and Canterbury, turns SE across Ash Level and after a huge loop past Sandwich flows into Pegwell Bay, near Ramsgate ; the *Wantsum* leaves the Great Stour NW past Sarre to the sea on the North Kent coast near Reculver. This stretch of country was formerly covered by the sea before reclamation and divides the Isle of Thanet from the rest of Kent.

A navigation below Sandwich. Easy throughout. Above Canterbury private water, scenery good ; fair current, frequent shallows ; some difficulties in portaging over private grounds. The lower reaches should be done only with the tide. Tidal limit Fordwich. Starting point at high or moderate levels—Wye ; at low levels—Sturry or Grove Ferry ; Plucks Gutter is a good centre (Dog and Duck Inn ; camp site) for tidal parts of Stour, Little Stour and Wantsum ; or a run back can be made on the tide to Grove Ferry.

High Water at Grove Ferry (2½ miles below Fordwich) same as for London Bridge (Dover plus 2 hours 40 mins.). The tide floods for 3 hours only.

O.S. 173 ; Barth. 10

Miles

0	*Wye.* Stn. (50 yds.). Build below bridge L.
1¼	*Olantigh Park.* Avoid mansion by easy portage L into small stream which re-enters below main weir.
3	*Godmersham Church* L. Road bridge.
5¼	*Chilham* L. Road and rly. bridges. Stn.
5½	*Bagham Mill.* Portage L at sluice.
7½	*Chartham Mill* and Tea Gardens. Portage R close to sluice.
8½	*Chartham Paper Mills.* Portage R through private grounds into small branch.
9	*Horton.* Portage back into main stream.
9¾	*Milton Bridge.*
11¼	Railway bridges. River divides. R branch to Canterbury Weavers. L branch to Westgate Towers. Both interesting.
12	*Canterbury.* Interesting city ; cathedral. Stns. Difficult portage at Old Mills and sluices.
12¾	Flour Mills. Carry L into side stream. Pipe across river ½ ml. below.
13¾	*Sturry.* Take R branch. Mill and road bridge. Portage L across road.
14½	*Fordwich Bridge.* River becomes tidal and deep. Inn R.
17	Flooded fields caused by subsidence.
17½	*Chislet Colliery.*
19½	*Grove Ferry.* Stn. and chain ferry. Inn. Camp site L. Shops at Upstreet.
22¼	*R. Wantsum* L. Sluice and barrier.
23¼	*Little Stour.* Enters R. Plucks Gutter Bridge. Inn. Camp site R. Double boom to catch weed.
27	Railway bridge.
28¼	*Stonar Cut* L. By-passes the Sandwich loop when river is in flood. If wishing to portage across obtain permission from sluice-keeper to carry through garden and across road. Tide must be fairly high on seaward side. Red flag hoisted means sluice open—danger.
29	*Richborough Castle* R. Remains of Roman Fort of the Saxon Shore.
31	*Sandwich Bridge.* Stn.

35   *Stonar Cut.*
36   *Shell Ness* (Pegwell Bay).   Exposed camp site—no drinking
      water.

86.   Little Stour

Rises near Lyminge, and called Nailbourne in upper stretches. Clear chalky stream ; in summer may be obstructed by weed dams—easy portage. Numerous portages between Bridge and Wickhambreux ; then no difficulties. Accessible below Seaton (Wickhambreux). From Plucks Gutter up to here 6 miles—useful shopping trip.

87.   Wantsum

Of little scenic interest but may be followed to the sea 2 miles E of Reculver. Enter by portage from Stour. Short portage at Sarre ; 6 miles to sea. Carry over at sea wall. Coast exposed.
At Reculver : Remains of Church and Roman Fort of Saxon Shore.

88.   STRAITS OF DOVER

The Straits of Dover have been crossed by canoe on a number of occasions. Although the direct distance to Calais is not more than 22 miles, the crossing should not be lightly attempted as the tidal streams are tricky and run at several knots through the straits. They are particularly difficult at the mouth of Dover harbour, and must be studied carefully so that full advantage can be taken of the tides. If they are misjudged, the canoeist may find himself in difficulties, and will be able to make land only with laborious paddling. Directions for the crossing have been deliberately omitted ; the canoeist must seek them for himself from yachting manuals and charts of tidal streams.

Charts : St. 1 ; C.8

89.   ROTHER (EAST SUSSEX)
(and the Royal Military Canal)

The Rother rises not far from Rotherfield, Sussex, and flows E to the levels near Rye, then S past Rye to the sea at Rye Harbour. Mileages are given from Etchingham, but above Bodiam much depends on how recently the undergrowth and bushes along the river banks have been cleared.

The *Royal Military Canal* (see below) follows the Rother for the last 3 miles before Rye. The tributary R. Brede can be explored up to about 1½ miles west of Winchelsea. Some other tributaries and subsidiary channels may be possible.

O.S. 184 ; Barth. 10

Miles
0   *Etchingham*.   Stn. very close.   Portage R for weir.   Scenery
       pleasant.
3   *Robertsbridge*.   Stn. Portage at mill.
6   *Udiam Bridge*.
7   *Bodiam Bridge*.   Inn ; castle interesting ; Rother now flows
       through flat country ; little current.
11   *Newenden Bridge*.   Village ; inn.
15½   Road bridge. Wittersham L. 1 ml.
17½   Main road bridge.
19   Road bridge. Royal Military Canal through lock on L.
20   *Scots Float Sluice* (tidal). Lock may be portaged without charge.
       Inn R.
22   *Rye*. Stn. Very interesting old town. R. Brede joins R.
24   *Rye Harbour*.   No landing at low tide between Rye and Rye
       Harbour. This should be done within an hour either side
       of high water. High tide approx. = Dover.

The **Royal Military Canal** was constructed as a defence work in Napoleonic times. It runs from Hythe in a wide sweep behind the Romney Marshes to Appledore, then SSW to join the *Rother* near Iden. Beyond Rye it continues to Winchelsea and Pett. A short stretch at Hythe is controlled by the Hythe Corporation, who grant seasonal licences (Borough Treasurer, Municipal Offices, Stade Street, Hythe). From West Hythe Dam it is under the jurisdiction of the Kent River Authority, London Road, Maidstone, who grant annual licences expiring on 31st March. The stretch between West Hythe and Appledore may at times be weedy. From Appledore Bridge to a new dam at Priory Lands, about ½ mile SW of the bridge, the canal is silted up. It is necessary to portage Iden Lock to get into the Rother. The stretch between Winchelsea and Pett is unnavigable. There are no charges on those parts of the Rother and the canal south of Iden Lock.

O.S. 193, 184 ; Barth. 10

90. CUCKMERE

The Cuckmere rises near Heathfield, Sussex, and flows S through South Downs to sea at Cuckmere Haven. Only the lowest 7 or 8 miles where it flows through South Downs are worth while, but they make a very pleasant double run, down on the ebb from Chilver Bridge and back on the flood (Berwick Stn. 1 mile). The river is tidal below Alfriston Bridge. Cuckmere Haven is pleasant for "surfing." The flood does not top the bar at the mouth until about 1½ hours after low water. But let the flood run for at least another ½ hour before starting up, or you will get ahead of it into slack and shallow water.

High Water approx. = Dover.

O.S. 183 ; Barth. 6

91. OUSE (SUSSEX)

From its source near Handcross the Ouse flows E and then S through Lewes to the sea at Newhaven. In former times it was a navigation from above Lindfield and the old locks are to be seen in several places. Now, however, the Ouse has in these upper reaches been allowed to find its natural level, and has a deep, narrow channel with very little depth of water except after rain. The lower Ouse is tidal from Hamsey, and is still functioning as a navigation. The upper parts are very overgrown at present, and are impracticable. The usual starting point now is Barcombe Mills (stn.) from where there should be no difficulty except with weeds in summer. Below Lewes the river runs between embankments, but the valley is rather pleasant as it cuts through the S Downs.

Miles

0   *Barcombe Mills.* Stn. Tunbridge Wells-Brighton line.

2½   *Hamsey Church* R. Tidal from just above. High water : Dover
        plus 1 hour.

4½   *Lewes.* Stn. County town.

6   *Glynde Reach* L. Practicable at high water for some distance
        beyond Glynde.

7   *Itford Bridge.*

10   *Newhaven Bridge.* Stn. High water approx. = Dover.

11   *Newhaven Harbour.* Land at bridge or continue through harbour
        to beach on R within the mole.

O.S. 183 ; Barth. 6

92. ADUR

Two streams, both called Adur, rising near Billingshurst and Haywards Heath, unite near Henfield, Sussex, and the river is then tidal all the way through the South Downs to Shoreham Harbour. From Henfield it flows through flat marshlands, rather lonely, between tidal banks to Steyning. The South Downs are in view practically all the way. The western Adur was once a navigation called the Baybridge Canal from West Grinstead from where it has been canoed. Three minor weirs before Bines Bridge (B.2135) 1 ml. S of Partridge Green and another before the confluence. On the eastern Adur a start could be made at high tide at the A.281 road bridge 1½ mls. N of Henfield. The river should always be done with the tide—it is, of course, possible to start at Shoreham and paddle inland, or Bramber makes a good centre. Below Bramber very shallow at low water.

Miles

0   *Bines Bridge* (B.2135). Tidal shortly below here.

½   Unites with eastern Adur (1½ mls. to road bridge A.281).

1   Bridge. Ashurst ¾ ml. R. Henfield 2 ml. L.

3   Railway bridge.

O.S. 182 ; Barth. 6

93. ARUN

The Arun is tidal for 18½ miles from its mouth at Littlehampton to Pulborough. It was once connected by the Wey and Arun Canal with the Wey above Guildford, but this canal has long been abandoned. Above the old lock at the entrance to the disused canal, near Pickhurst, the stream is very narrow and may be choked with reeds, but a passage can be made or forced to Pallingham Farm. In spring a canoe might start at New Bridge, Billingshurst, when the weeds would not be as thick; Gibbons Mill, ref 071308 is highest point from which it is known to have been canoed.

There are no obstacles from Pallingham Lock to the sea, and the river runs through pleasant country throughout its course—between fields and woods above Stopham, through open, marshy country between Pulborough and Amberley (Amberley Wild Brooks) with good views of the Downs, and then through the Arundel Gap to the sea. The current on the ebb is strong (4 to 6 knots). On the flood there is little if any flow upstream above Amberley.

Littlehampton Harbour dues—payable on the river below Arundel. For harbour purposes canoes are subject to the same regulations as shipping. Harbour dues—2s. 6d. week ; 1s. day.

Fees to be paid to Harbour Master at Harbour Offices, Littlehampton, Sussex.

O.S. 181, 182 ; Barth. 6

9½   Railway bridge.

9¾   *Pulborough Bridge*. S.R. stn. Swan Inn on L. Canoes may be left here. Best starting point for Arun cruise. On leaving stn. go R of Railway Hotel to river bank.

12¼ *Greatham*.

13   *Greatham Bridge*.

15½ Railway bridge.

16¼ *Bury and Amberley Ferry*. Bury church R. Amberley L ½ ml ; interesting church and ruined castle. High water : Dover plus 2 hrs. 40 mins. The tide flows 4 hrs. and ebbs 8 hrs.

17½ *Houghton Bridge*. Amberley Stn. and Bridge Inn 100 yds. L. Private landing stage. Camping is discouraged on the Arundel Estate below here.

19½ *South Stoke*. River makes great bend E. South Stoke bridge is on the cut R. There is a similar bend past Burpham L, also with a cut (Offham Bridge).

21   *Offham*.

21¼ *Black Rabbit Inn*, beyond end of cut.

23   *Arundel Bridge*. Stn. L. Landing places above bridge R. Tide runs strongly. Arundel Castle, seat of Duke of Norfolk, and park. Shops, inns, etc. High water : Dover plus 1 hr. 20 mins Tides rise 8 to 12 ft.

25   Railway bridge. Ford junc. Stn. ¼ ml.

28   *Littlehampton*. Stn. High Water : Dover plus 20 mins.

28¾ Mouth of Littlehampton Harbour.

94. Rother (West Sussex)

The Rother rises in Hampshire, near Empshott, flowing SE for 30 miles to join the Arun near Stopham.

It has been canoed in the early part of the year from Rogate but is hardly worth while above Midhurst. From Rogate is runs fairly fast over sand and gravel bed in a twisting course between steep, overgrown banks. Depth varies considerably ; there is about 10 feet drop at each mill. Fallen and overhanging trees and wire may be encountered above Selham.

The average current on the Rother between Midhurst and Stopham is about 2 knots, the fall of the river being about 45 feet.

In 1791 the Rother was rendered navigable for barges, which used to ascend to Midhurst, but it is over 80 years since the locks were used and all are now completely broken down. The Rother Navigation Act of 1791 did not give any right of way to pleasure craft, and the position of canoeing on the Rother is as on other private waters. In 1935 those responsible for the Navigation made application to the proper authority for its abandonment—the position of canoeing is not thereby affected, but riparian owners are likely to be less tolerant towards canoeists.

The locks on the Rother have no gates left, but most have a step, and some of these may be shot when there is sufficient water.

The Rother passes through attractive well-wooded country, and as the river has recently been cleared in parts, it forms a delightful canoe trip with plenty of variety.

The railway between Petersfield and Pulborough is closed.

O.S. **181** ; Barth. 6

Miles

0   *Rogate Bridge.* Barbed wire underneath.

2½   *Terwick Mill.* Portage between sluices and mill. Two barbed-wire fences across river below.

2¾   *Trotton Bridge.* Stream swings awkwardly through bridge over shallows against L bank. Church L. Barbed-wire fence and broken hurdle weir beyond. Further on a barbed-wire barrier on T-iron stakes, difficult to lift over because of depth of water.

3¾   *Chithurst Bridge.*

5   *Iping Mill and Bridge.* Land R bank above main sluices at mill and portage along mill lane to bridge. River now deeper.

6½   *Stedham Bridge.* Little head room. Hall on R.

7   *Stedham Mill.* Portage L above sluices. Stony shallows below.

9   *Woolbeding Weir.* Just after church L a stepped weir. Portage R.

11¾ *Midhurst Mill and Bridge.* Portage over bank below first (small) sluice on R bank. Millstream leads to fenced-off gardens. Obstructions under bridge. Midhurst R ; pleasant town.

     If starting here a launching place may be found just below the mill (N of town). Or near pumping station along second road on R from the station. Cowdray (ruins) and Cowdray Park L.

14   *Todham Lock.* Lock cut dry—take channel through old weir.

14½ *Ambersham Bridge.*

Miles

15½   *Moorland Lock.* Impossible to shoot—stakes in channel. *Caution*: fast current and a drop of 10 ft. just under a small wooden bridge. Portage on R bank.

16   *Selham Lock.* Lock-cut dried up. Take the channel to the R. In low water there may be shallows and stakes in the channel. Road bridge, Selham Village R.

17   *Handwright Lock.*

19   Footbridge.

19¾   *Coultershaw Bridge and Mill.* Portage L bank just before road bridge, cross it and go down path on R bank along out-buildings.

20½   *Shopham Lock.* Clear run through on R. The stream about 200 yds. above the lock could be taken, but is rather shallow. Bridge ¼ ml. below.

23¼   *Fittleworth Lock.* A private house and garden make portage on L bank impossible, and there is difficulty on the R bank. The old lock-cut is completely overgrown, but a portage may be made through a field on the R, about 100 yds. altogether. Land just before first sluice on R at a small building. Walk through field to bridge and launch above.

24   Pipeline across river. Stopham lock cut (L) is dry.

24½   *Site of Hardham Mill.* Sluice. A high fence by the sluice makes a difficult portage.

24¾   *Junction of Arun.* Slightly over a mile above Pulborough.

HAMPSHIRE, DORSET, DEVON
AND CORNWALL

95. CHICHESTER, LANGSTONE and PORTSMOUTH HARBOURS

A series of three inland waters popular with yachtsmen.

Chichester Harbour in particular is attractive, and the exploration of the various branches of it, working the tides which run strongly, makes a very pleasant cruise. A camp site convenient for all channels or for starting to explore Spithead can be found on the inside of East Point at the mouth of the harbour where the landing is sandy, but there is no fresh water nearby. Further inland it is muddy.

Access :
> *Bosham.* Picturesque village, shops, inns, boatyard adjoining church. Good landing at most stages of the tide. Stn. 1 ml.

> On *Chichester Channel* :
> *West Itchenor.* Yachting centre, inn.
> *Birdham.* Entrance to Chichester Canal. Yacht basin.
> *Dell Quay.* Inn. Chichester Stn. 2 mls.

> The *Chichester Canal.* Basin close to Chichester Stn. Good for building boats. Can also be used to reach Chichester Channel (3 mls., 2 locks—unusable). Weedy in summer. A barrier at road bridge (A.286) will have to be portaged. The canal is not used except for a short distance between Birdham and Casher Lock.

> On *Emsworth Channel—Emsworth.* Town and Shops R. Stn. ¾ ml.

> *Sweare Deep* leads to Langstone Harbour. There is an old hard at West Thorney.

The entrance to Chichester Harbour lies well over to the W, close to the Treloar Hospital between Eastoke and Sandy Points. The E side is shallow and can provide a very nasty sea. Best time to go out is at high water.

Flood runs for 7 hours until High Water Dover plus 15 mins.

Distances from harbour entrance : Bosham 5 miles ; West Itchenor 3½ miles ; Birdham 4½ miles ; Dell Quay 6 miles ; Head of Thorney Channel 5 miles ; Emsworth 4½ miles.

Langstone Harbour is extensive and similar but not so attractive as Chichester Harbour. Landings at all states of the tide at the ferry slips at the harbour entrance. The tides run strongly.

High Water : Dover plus ½ hour

133

Portsmouth Harbour is interesting more because of its ships than its scenery. Access at all states of the tide at gravel hard at end of Old Portsmouth High Street, and at Gosport ferry slips ; also at Porchester (remains of Roman castle, stn. 1¼ miles) and Fareham (shops, etc., stn. 1 mile). Tides strong, up to 4 knots.

High Water : Dover plus ¼ hour

Chichester and Langstone Harbours : O.S. 181 ; Barth. 5

Charts : St. 10 ; Y. 29 or 33

Portsmouth Harbour : O.S. 180 ; Barth. 5

Charts : St. 11 ; Y. 29 or 31

96. SOUTHAMPTON WATER, SOLENT, HAMBLE RIVER and BEAULIEU RIVER : ISLE OF WIGHT

A cruise on these waters always provides plenty of interest : much traffic, numerous yachts, and very pleasant scenery. There are a number of interesting places to visit, and the crossing to the Isle of Wight can be made.

O.S. 180 ; Barth. 5. Charts (general) : St. 11 ; Y.31. More detailed charts mentioned below.

Tides. The tides are peculiar, and repay study as they can be of great assistance. There is a double high water.

In the **Western portion of the Solent** the tide starts to run NE from H.W. Dover plus 5 hours until H.W. Dover minus 1 hour. In the **Eastern portion of the Solent** the tide runs NW from Spithead past Lee-on-Solent from H.W. Dover minus 2 hours.

In **Southampton Water** the flood tide rises for 2 hours, then is slack for 1 hour, then rises for 3½ hours to first H.W. Then there is a slight ebb and flood, till second H.W. The ebb occupies only 3½ hours and consequently the tide runs very strongly. First H.W.: Dover minus 20 mins. Second H.W.: H.W. Dover plus 1¾ hours.

Landings at Cracknore Hard (Inn) opposite Southampton West Quay.

Hythe (shops).
Ashlett Creek (Fawley).
Millbrook Sailing Club.

Hamble River. Tides as for Southampton Water. Practicable, with the tide, from the road bridge at Botley (stn.). Pipe and footbridge with little headroom below. On the ebb beware submerged snags and stakes above Curbridge. Access also at Bursledon (stn. close). *Landings* at ferry and at Warsop. Charts : St. 11 ; Y.35.

Beaulieu River. A most charming waterway, winding and well wooded. Very popular for yachts. Canoeable from road bridge at Leygreen Farm.

Landings at Gilbury Hard (E shore) 2½ miles ; Exbury Village ½ mile (shop, P.O.); Buckler's Hard 3 miles (inn) ; Bailey's Hard 5 miles ; and Beaulieu 6 miles from the entrance. Charts : St. 11 ; Y. 39.

    1st H.W.: H.W. Dover minus 35 mins.
    2nd H.W.: H.W. Dover plus 1¼ hours.

Newtown River. On the Isle of Wight—makes an interesting cruise from the Beaulieu River. Landing at Newtown and Shalfleet (attractive village). Tides as for Beaulieu River. Charts : St. 11 ; Y. 22.

Lymington River can be followed to Lymington (shops). Tides as for Beaulieu River. Charts : St. 11 ; Y.34.

Keyhaven. Pleasant, rural harbour, at the back of Hurst Castle. Landing at hard at Key Point. At Keyhaven, shop and inn etc., or at Milford. Charts : St. 11 ; Y.20.

    1st H.W.: H.W. Dover minus 20 mins.
    2nd H.W.: H.W. Dover plus 1 hour.

Yarmouth (Isle of Wight). Peaceful and picturesque, good shopping. Landing either at quay or at steps beside the bridge further up (stn.). The *River Yar* can be explored up to Freshwater which is only a short distance from the S coast of the Island. Charts : St. 11 ; Y.34.

    1st H.W.: H.W. Dover minus 1 hour.
    2nd H.W.: H.W. Dover plus 1 hour.

Cowes (Isle of Wight). Famous yachting centre. Shops R. The *Medina* can be explored towards Newport. Chart : St. 11.

    1st H.W.: H.W. Dover minus 40 mins.
    2nd H.W.: H.W. Dover plus 20 mins.

Wootton Creek provides a place of call halfway between Cowes and Ryde (steamer to Portsmouth). Slipway at Fishbourne car ferry. Shops at Wootton Bridge where landing is possible above half tide. Charts : St. 11 ; Y.22.

    H.W.: H.W. Dover plus 15 mins.

Circumnavigation of the Isle of Wight. This makes a fine trip in settled weather. Consult yachting manuals and local information about tidal streams. The Needles can be avoided by a portage at Freshwater into the Yar. Chart : Y.30.

97. ITCHEN

The Itchen rises near Cheriton, Hants. At Itchen Stoke, it is joined by the Alre, and flows W and then S through Winchester to Southampton Water. It has been canoed in winter from New Alresford on the Alre to Winchester, but there are many obstacles—low bridges, wire ; mills, trout hatcheries, etc. Below Winchester it used once to be a navigation, but several of the artificial cuts are derelict. It is tidal below South Stoneham. See Section 96. *Landings* at Woodmill, Cobden Bridge, Northam Bridge and Woolston ferry hards.

Distances : New Alresford-Winchester, 10 miles.
Winchester-South Stoneham, 12 miles.
South Stoneham-Southampton Water, 4 miles.

O.S. 168, 180 ; Barth. 8, 5

98.   TEST

The Test rises near Whitchurch and flows S through Stockbridge and Romsey to Southampton Water. It flows through a charming valley, and is undoubtedly practicable for canoes for a considerable distance. It is a closely preserved trout stream, however, and should be regarded, in practice, as out of the question.

99.   SALISBURY AVON

The Avon has two headstreams, both in the Vale of Pewsey, through which runs the Kennet and Avon Canal and the W.R. main line, and flows S with many twists and turns, and lower down many channels and islands, through Salisbury Plain, along the western edge of the New Forest through Ringwood to Christchurch Harbour. In the 17th century the river was canalised up to Salisbury but the works were washed away soon after and the river is now all private water. The coarse fishing on the lower parts of the Avon is famous ; there is also salmon fishing below Fordingbridge, and trout fishing over the whole length. All is strictly preserved. Permission needs to be sought to pass through some of the principal estates, and may not be given. B.C.U. may be able to advise. Difficulties from water-bailiffs may be encountered if permission is not granted, and it is not likely to be given in spring and early summer. The river is everywhere pretty, sometimes really beautiful. It runs through many private parklands. Above Salisbury there are many obstacles and little detailed information is available, except that a rowing boat was reported by the Press to have been taken the whole way from Pewsey to the sea for a wager in 1920 and again in June, 1947. Detailed notes would be welcomed.

O.S. 167, 179 ; Barth. 8, 5
Chart of Christchurch Harbour : St. 12

Miles

0   *Pewsey.* Stn. ¼ ml. Pewsey Wharf (Kennet and Avon Canal) 1 ml.

5   *Scales Bridge.* Confl. of western headstream. There is said to be always sufficient depth of water from here.

5¾   *Upavon.* The river cuts a winding valley through Salisbury Plain. Numerous bridges and weirs and other obstacles. Many villages.

17   *Bulford.*

18½   *Amesbury.* Stonehenge 2 mls. W.

27   *Avon Bridge,* Stratford-sub-Castle. Old Sarum ½ ml. E.

27½   *Stratford Mill.* Portage into weir stream. A number of low bridges.

29   Railway bridge.

29½   *Salisbury.* Land at mill R. Cross river and trolley through streets to Fisherton Bridge. Launch (with permission) at County Hotel steps. Crane Bridge immediately below.

29¾   Confl. of R. Nadder R. Cathedral close L. If starting at Salisbury build and launch at one of the bridges below Fisherton Bridge (no building facilities at this); a possible alternative is at Fisherton Mill or Long Bridge just below it on the Nadder ; this is close to Salisbury stn.; access from stn. by Church Street.

30½   *Harnham Bridge* and *New Bridge.* Inn. Just beyond, ignore the weir L ; continue and take L channel immediately before sluice house, then at hatchways portage R back into R channel. A second portage at other hatchways a short distance further on.

33¾   *Longford Bridge.* Castle R. Weir ; may be shootable through scoop.

35   *Charlton* R.

35½   *Standlynch Weir and Mill.* Trafalgar House L. Portage or line down weir (awkward). Barford Park L.

37   *Downton Weir.* Portage into weir stream R before mill.

37¼   *Downton Bridge and Mill.* Village L. Shops.

38   Railway bridge. ½ ml. below ; Charford Weir ; portage L. Then Hale Park L.

40¾   *Breamore.* Portage at mill sluices L. Bridge ; village R.

42¾   *Burgate Weir.* Line down or portage L.

44½   *East Mill Weir.* Portage R. Camp site, Sandy Balls Wood above weir.

45½   *Fordingbridge Bridge.* Town, shops, etc., R.

46½   *Bickton Mill.* Portage R at either weir.

48¾   *Ibsley Bridge.* Weir ; line down R. Village L.

50¼   *Somerley Park* R.

53   River divides immediately after a very sharp double bend. Left-hand channel : to Ringwood Weir and mill (54 mls.); portage R.
Right-hand channel : weir (53¼ mls.); portage R into "King Stream"; rejoins main stream at Ringwood.

54   *Ringwood Bridge* and rly. bridge. Town, shops, etc.

56   *Avon Castle* R. (Hotel).

59¾   *Avon Tyrrell Bridge*. Inn ¾ ml. below L.

61¼   *Avon Causeway Bridge*.

62¾   *Sopley Mill*. Portage R into weir-stream. Village L, inn.

63¼   *Winkton Weir*. May be shootable.

65½   *Knapp Mill Weir*. Tidal below here.

66   Railway bridge. Nearest point to Christchurch Stn. R.

66½   *Christchurch Bridge*. Town R interesting. Priory, Saxon keep,
       etc.

66¾   *Christchurch Quay*. Confl. with Dorset Stour R.

70   *Christchurch Bar*. Mudeford L. "Haven" Inn.

Tides : 1st flood tide runs 4½ hours, then ebb 2½ hours ; 2nd
flood 1 hour, ebb 4 hours. 1st H.W. approx. 2¼ hours before
H.W. Dover ; 2nd H.W. approx. 1¼ hours after H.W. Dover.

It must be emphasised that any canoeing on the Avon is by the
tolerance and goodwill of the riparian owners and fishing interests.
Courtesy is essential, if canoeing on this lovely river is to be possible.

100. DORSET STOUR

The Stour rises not far from Mere and flows S then E through the
Hardy country to Christchurch Harbour. A quiet river, passing through
little known country with ancient bridges of great beauty. The current
is good for such flat country. Weeds and rushes are plentiful and may
be a nuisance in late summer. Apt to be shallow just below each mill
weir, but long, beautiful, wide, placid stretches above the weirs.
Private water all the way. Access from Southern Region main line at
Gillingham, and from the Exeter road (A.30) at High Bridge, 5 miles W
of Shaftesbury (4 miles below Gillingham). Except under dry conditions
the Youth Hostel at Marnhull also makes a feasible starting place.
These upper reaches are narrow and twisting, and the most convenient
starting point is Sturminster Newton, 18 miles from Gillingham. There
are about 9 mills, sluices or weirs between Gillingham and Sturminster
Newton.

O.S. 178, 179 ; Barth. 4, 5

Chart (Christchurch Harbour): St. 12

Miles

0	*Sturminster Newton.* Shops. Inns.
1¼	*Fiddleford Mill.* Line down. Rly. bridge beyond.
3¾	*Hammoon Bridge.*
5½	*Site of Marsh Mill.* Weir gone. Submerged masonry at 90 deg. turn to L.
6	*Hayward Bridge.* Inn.
7¾	Ford ; ground weir of sharp stones. Shoot in good water, otherwise line down.
10½	*Durweston Mill.* Portage into weir stream on R of weir on L, ¼ ml. before the mill.
10¾	*Durweston Bridge.* River broadens and enters Bryanston Park.
13	*Bryanston Weir.* Portage R. School and boathouse L.
13¾	*Blandford Bridge and Weir.* Blandford Forum L. Town, shops, etc. Line down weir L. Rly. bridge below.
15¾	*Charlton Marshall* R. River narrows.
16¾	River divides into two branches, and the right-hand branch divides again ¼ ml. on. Portages on all three. The **first** leads in ¼ ml. to Keynston Mill, the third to Spettisbury Mill. Take the middle one, on which there is no mill, lining down at weir on L. Shallow below for about 50 yds.
18¼	*Spettisbury* R.
18½	*Crawford Bridge.*
19¾	*Shapwich* L.
21½	*Sturminster Marshall* R. River delightful. Flows through marshland.
22¼	Road bridge.
24¼	*Corfe Mullen* R. Portage at weir ¼ ml. before old mill. Cafe and inn at old mill. Between here and Cowgrove the channel has been dredged out but is winding and fast in places.
26	*Cowgrove.* Ground weir at footbridge—"Ford" on map. Line down either side.
26¾	Road bridge (A.**31**). Wimborne L.
28	*Canford Bridge.* Wimborne Minster L. Town, shops, etc.
29	*Canford Weir.* Portage L. Canford School and Park R. Fine country.
33¾	*Longham Mill and Bridge.* Line down on R of right-hand weir just beyond new sluice. Steel sheet piling makes launch a little awkward.
35	*Ensbury Bridge* (A.**347**). The owner of the fishing rights, approx. 2½ mls. above and below Throop Mill, objects to boating.
38¼	*Throop Weir.* Portage L
42	*Iford Bridge.* Tidal below. Rather built-up below here.
44½	*Christchurch Quay.* Junction with Avon. Stn. Interesting town, Priory Church, etc.

For tides—see Salisbury Avon (Section 99 above).

101. POOLE HARBOUR and RIVER FROME

O.S. 179 ; Barth. 5

Charts : St. 12 ; C.23

Poole Harbour, like other places near the Isle of Wight has double tides and comparatively small rise and fall.

1st H.W.: Dover minus $2\frac{1}{2}$ hours.

2nd H.W.: Dover plus 1 hour.

Rise : springs, $6\frac{1}{2}$ feet ; neaps $4\frac{3}{4}$ feet.

At springs the tide ebbs for about 2 hours after first high water, dropping about 2 feet, then floods for $1\frac{1}{2}$ hours, rising 6 to 9 inches to make the second high water. It then ebbs fast for 3 hours and floods for 6 hours. At neaps, the tide remains at high water for about $2\frac{1}{2}$ hours, then rises another 12 inches at second high water. The ebb is particularly fast at the narrow mouth of the harbour.

There is plenty of water for canoeing at all states of the tide, but the tides must be used to reach the more remote parts.

For those arriving in Poole by rail, the nearest water is in Holes Bay alongside Sterte Road, about 50 yards from the station. However, launching here is only possible near high water. Better, but rather public, is Poole Quay, where there are steps and plenty of water at all states of the tide. More private, but more distant from the station is the fishing boat anchorage near the gas works at the E end of Poole Quay. Those arriving by road can find a pleasant, sandy launching place at Sandbanks, or there is a fairly private spot on the S side of Hamworthy near the premises of the Dorset Yacht Company. Hamworthy Junction station, 1 mile. It is also possible to reach Poole Harbour by using the *River Frome* from Wareham.

Although Poole Harbour is almost completely landlocked, it is of sufficient area to make high winds dangerous to small craft, and due consideration must be given to the weather.

The **Frome** rises in the high ground S of Yeovil and flows E through Dorchester and Wool to Wareham and Poole Harbour. It passes through a pleasant countryside of water meadows with the Purbeck Hills usually in sight. The railway follows it closely all the way to Dorchester. It is never very wide, and in summer has water lilies and other weeds. Anyone who does not object to low footbridges at intervals will enjoy this little river of the Hardy country. But objections from water-bailiffs have been reported.

Dorchester-Wool 9 miles approx.: -Wareham 14 miles approx. Poole Harbour 16 miles approx.

102. EXE

The Exe rises on Exmoor near the coast of the Severn estuary and flows first E then S for most of its course along a beautiful valley. A mountain river, it offers numerous rapids, some shallow, some deep and rocky, and its character varies considerably according to the water level. In spring or summer a start may be possible near Dulverton. The weirs hold up the river for short stretches only. There are objections from fishing interests in the upper parts to canoeing between March and October.

Grading: Rough Water II at medium to low water levels.

O.S. 176 ; Barth. 3, 2 ; Charts : St. 12 ; Y.45.

Miles

0	*Tiverton*. Weir just below bridge holds up the river through the town. If there are shallows here, there will be shallows for 10 mls.
3¼	*Cadeleigh Weir*. Followed by rly. and road bridges. Stn. L. Weir below the bridge. Frequent rapids.
5¼	*Burn* L. Suspension footbridge. Halt. A short distance above is a natural rocky "weir" across river. Try on R. A short distance below the footbridge is a rapid with wire.
5¾	Large island. Keep L then R immediately after. Frequent rapids.
7¼	*Bidwell* R. Long, deep rapid near wood. Keep L.
7¾	*Up Exe*. Short smooth reach followed by a stretch with large boulders.
8	Railway bridge and Weir. Unshootable in low water. (A row of steel stakes project 2 ft. above the concrete at the foot.) Carry at R end of weir.
8¼	Road bridge. Wire across rapid below bridge. Then shallows and a long smooth stretch.
10	*Nether Exe* L. Ford composed of large boulders with no clear channel. Rapids recommence.
10¾	Railway bridge. Rapid under with wire across.
11	*Brampford Speke* R. Rapids frequent.
12¼	Railway bridge. Sunken piles under the bridge. In the next ¼ ml. two branches of the R. Culm join L. In between is a rapid with wire across. After the confl. the river becomes deep and dark (paper works on Culm).
13½	Railway bridge.
13¾	Weir. Shootable in centre in high water. But inspect first on R. Rapid below—keep L. Long, smooth reach to—
14½	Railway bridge. *Keep R along R bank* : immediately above weir *turn R into narrow creek* leading to River Creedy just above Cowley Bridge. This avoids an unshootable weir which cannot be portaged.
15	Weir.
16	Bridge. Exwick R. Exeter St. David's Stn. L. Weirs beyond rly. bridge.
17	Exeter Bridge.

17   Exeter Ship Canal R. Below Exeter the river follows a sluggish
course to the sea, and after Topsham weir it broadens out
into an estuary a mile or more wide between pleasant well
wooded hills and sheltered from the SW by the long sandy
spit of Dawlish Warren. About half of this as shown on the
O.S. map has been washed away.

The **Exeter Ship Canal** runs close to the river for 5½ miles from
Exeter to the estuary at Turf (2 locks ; yearly registration fee 1s.,
payable to Town Clerk, Exeter ; lock fee 2s. 6d. if used).

Railways follow the shore on either side ; stations are Starcross on
the W shore, Topsham and Exmouth on the E shore.

Exeter to Exmouth approx. 9½ miles.

High Water at Exmouth : Dover minus 5 hours.

103.   TEIGN

The Teign is a mountain river and hardly practicable above the tidal
part. The estuary is navigable to Newton Abbot but is muddy at low
tide. From Newton Abbot take S bank to Coombe Cellars landing stage,
then diagonally across to a fisherman's hut on N bank. Current up to
4 knots. Slipway at Shaldon near the "castle." Teignmouth-Newton
Abbot approx. 5 miles.

High Water : Dover minus 5 hours.

O.S. **188**, 176 ; Barth. 2 ; Charts : St. 12 ; Y.46

104.   DART

Rises on Dartmoor and flows SE. The upper reaches are rocky but
very beautiful and the scenery is delightful all the way to Dartmouth.
The highest practicable point for starting is normally Buckfastleigh
(shops, Abbey) below which the river flows swiftly over rocks and
boulders and calls for skill, the difficulties varying with the amount of
water. Lining down may be necessary in some shallow stretches.
Buckfastleigh to Staverton Bridge, 3½ miles : Riberford Bridge and
weir and Staverton Bridge should be inspected before shooting them.
Staverton Bridge to Totnes Weir, 3 miles, below which the river is tidal.

A cruise with the tide from Kingswear or Dartmouth to Totnes is
equally practicable and some think it finer than the cruise down to the
river mouth. Best time for starting from Dartmouth is 3 hours' flood
so as to avoid the mud flats above Dittisham.

O.S. **188** ; Barth. 2 ; Charts : St. 12 ; Y.47

0   *Buckfastleigh*   ⎫ See notes above.
6½   *Totnes Weir*   ⎭

      Portage at Totnes Weir and possibly also at rly. bridge at low tide. At *Totnes Bridge* the steamer landing is immediately below the bridge—caution. Interesting old town, church, castle, High Street. Below, the river gradually widens and deepens.

10¼   *Sharpham* R. Lovely woods, heronry.

11¼   *Duncannon* L.

12¼   *Stoke Point.* Stoke Gabriel up creek L. River widens considerably; heavy seas may be encountered in windy weather. On a falling tide, beware of mud banks.

14½   *Dittisham* R. Pier. River narrows, may be a heavy roll owing to the strong ebb tide.

16¼   *Noss* L.

17   *Dartmouth* R, *Kingswear* L (stn.). Dartmouth is an interesting town—castle, St. Saviour's Church, old houses, etc. Regular ferry service between Kingswear and Dartmouth. The river steamers may throw up a heavy wash and should be avoided.
      High Water Dartmouth : Dover minus 5 hours.
      High Water Totnes : Dover minus 4½ hours.

105. SALCOMBE RIVER

An inlet of the sea, with several side arms, running N for approx. 5 miles from Bolt Head at the S tip of Devon. Good sailing. Access at Kingsbridge at high water, and at Salcombe.

      High Water Salcombe : Dover minus 5¼ hours.
      O.S. 186, 187 ; Barth. 2 ; Charts : St. 13 ; Y.48

106. YEALM

Rises in Dartmoor and flows S through Yealmpton to the sea, a short distance SE of the entrance to Plymouth Sound. Only the tidal part is canoeable ; this is narrow, secluded and very lovely.

Access at Newton Ferrers (hotel and shops).

The whole estuary is not more than 5 miles long and several side arms are worth exploring with the tide.

      High Water : Dover minus 5¼ hours.
      O.S. 187 ; Barth. 2 ; Charts : St. 13 ; Y.50

107. PLYMOUTH SOUND and its RIVERS
including TAMAR

O.S. 186, 187 ; Barth. 2 ; Charts : St. 13 ; C.6

The tide is a very important factor in the navigation of these rivers. The tidal portions are mostly broad (in many places *very* broad at high tide), while above the tidal portions they are, with the exception of the Tamar, not navigable at all.

The wind can raise some very rough water; and the combination of rough water and strong tidal currents can be dangerous if one is ignorant of the conditions. It is very advisable not only to be well acquainted on every occasion with the times of high and low tide at the various spots it is desired to visit, but to consult local boatmen as to the peculiarities of the currents, and the dangers to be avoided.

Sunken stakes and branches of trees, etc., are a danger to a rubber canoe in some of the narrower creeks, especially when one is being carried along by the tide.

The scenery both in the tidal and non-tidal portions is magnificent.

High Water at Plymouth : Dover minus 5½ hours.

Plymouth Sound. An excellent expanse of enclosed sea. To the N is Plymouth and the famous Hoe with its pier, bathing stations, etc. Drake's Island lies in the centre. On the E are fine cliffs crowned by Staddon Heights. Landing can be made at Jennycliff Bay or farther S, after passing outside the breakwater and rounding Staddon Point, in Bovisand Bay. On the W the coast is even finer—some of the finest in England—Mount Edgcumbe, Cawsand Bay, Penlee Point. There are several landing places, notably at Kingsand and Cawsand. One has to be careful to choose a calm day, and a favourable wind, to go outside the breakwater. Plymouth Sound is very popular with sailing boat owners.

From Plymouth Hoe to Bovisand Bay 2½ miles; to Cawsand Bay 3½ miles.

Plym. This very large expanse of tidal water enters the Sound at Plymouth from the NE. The outer part is called the Cattewater—much used by commercial shipping and seaplanes. The inner portion is called the Laira. The Laira looks very fine at high water with Plymouth on one side, and the magnificent wooded estate of Saltram on the other. At low tide it is mostly mud.

Plymouth Hoe to Marsh Mills 4 miles. The upper Plym above Marsh Mills is impracticable, becoming very soon a small rapid rock-strewn moorland stream.

The Hamoaze. The Hamoaze, *i.e.*, the estuary of the three rivers Tamar, Tavy and St. Germans (or Lynher), is a magnificent sheet of water. At Devil's Point, where it joins the Sound (through the "Narrows"), the tidal current is always *very* strong except at slack water. A canoe or small craft can, however, usually creep in or out against the tide by hugging the shore.

The Hamoaze runs N for 3½ miles to the junction of the Tamar and St. Germans rivers at Wearde Quay L. Along the whole of the E bank of the Hamoaze lie Devonport and the Dockyard and other naval establishments. Plenty of naval craft are always to be seen. On the W side, there are first Mount Edgcumbe, and then two large creeks :

MILLBROOK CREEK runs W for 3 miles, with the very beautiful scenery of Mount Edgcumbe on the South. The creek is mostly mud at low tide, but a narrow channel will enable a canoe on the tide to reach the little town of Millbrook. Here, if one lands, one can climb a mile or so and reach the top of the magnificent cliffs overlooking Whitsand Bay and the Channel.

ST. JOHN'S CREEK. Broader than Millbrook Creek ; about 2 miles to the village of St. John. A vast sheet of mud at low tide.

St. Germans or Lynher River. This is a broad estuarial river with Cornwall on both banks, but it is much reduced in width at low tide, revealing large expanses of mud. About 1 mile from Wearde Quay is Antony Passage (ferry slips). About 5 miles from its junction with the Tamar and Hamoaze, it divides into two rivers, the Lynher proper and the Tiddy :

The *TIDDY*, the more westerly branch, after passing St. Germans (stn.)—a very charming and interesting village with a very large church of great historic interest—penetrates inland into Cornwall as a tidal river for about another 4 miles to Tideford. Canoes can go up to this point on the tide, but above Tideford the river is a small unnavigable rapid rocky stream. Tideford (inn) is a pretty Cornish village situated in a charming valley. It once had much commerce and shipped lime and other commodities in barges to Plymouth.

The *LYNHER* penetrates into Cornwall and is practicable on the tide as far as Notter Bridge ($3\frac{1}{2}$ miles from the junction with the Tiddy), where there is a weir. Above the weir the river, which rises in the Bodmin Moors, is unnavigable. Notter Bridge (Inn—"Sportsman's Arms") lies in a very pretty valley. There is a good bus service between Tideford, Notter Bridge and Saltash.
There are also other shorter tidal creeks to explore and the scenery is everywhere beautiful.

Tamar. This, the main river, remains a very wide stream for 5 miles from the point where it merges with the St. Germans into the Hamoaze.
Saltash, a considerable town (stn.) lies on the Cornish side about a mile from the junction with the Hamoaze ; and here Brunel's great bridge, nearly half a mile long, carries the Great Western Railway at a height of 100 feet above high water level from Devon to Cornwall.
The Tamar is navigable to Weir Head, with the tide.

Miles
0	*Wearde Quay.*
$\frac{3}{4}$	*Saltash.* Large town. Brunel's bridge.
$2\frac{1}{2}$	*Kingsmill Creek* (W shore) leading to villages of Landulph and Moditonham.
	Tamerton Foliot Creek (E shore) crossed by S.R. bridge. This pretty creek can be followed on the tide to the village of Tamerton Foliot (2 miles).
4	Junc. with *Tavy* (E shore).
$4\frac{1}{4}$	*Cargreen.* Village and quay (W shore). Ferry slip.
5	*Weirquay* E. River narrows—steep high bank on Devon side.
$7\frac{3}{4}$	*Pentillie Castle* W. Fine castle and beautiful scenery.
$8\frac{1}{2}$	*Halton Quay* W.
$12\frac{1}{4}$	*Calstock* W. Small country town (stn.). Notable rly. viaduct. Favourite spot for steamer excursions.
$15\frac{1}{4}$	*Morwellham Quay* E. Deserted quay, once busy centre of mining industry. River passes large deserted mines.

Miles

16¼   *Morwell Rocks*. Magnificent cliff over 200 ft. high.

17¾   *Weir Head*. Large weir marks the head of the tidal part of the river. Gunnislake ¾ ml. W.

High Water about 1 hour after Plymouth.

Above Weir Head the Tamar Valley is extremely beautiful. The river rises not far from the N coast near Bude and flows almost due S with numerous bends. It was once canalised, but the navigation has long been abandoned. There is enough water except after dry weather from near Whitstone Station (Bude line) but the river is much overgrown and obstructed with trees. Until it has been cleared it is not worth trying above Launceston.

From Greystone Bridge, some 5 miles from Launceston, the river is possible only with favourable water. At low water levels it is little more than a succession of salmon pools ; the fishing is highly preserved and the river private water. The current is fast ; the banks are high and there are a number of V-shaped fishing weirs with an opening at the point at the upstream end. One mile below Latchley (broken weir) there is another partly broken weir (unshootable) and beyond that very difficult, rocky water for 1 mile until shortly above Gunnislake.

Greystone Bridge-Horsebridge 7½ miles.

Horsebridge-Latchley Weir 4 miles.

Latchley-Weir Head, Gunnislake 3½ miles.

Tavy. At the point where it joins the Tamar—4 miles from the junction with the Hamoaze—this river is crossed by a very fine bridge carrying the S.R. main line. For 3 miles beyond the Tavy is tidal, broad at first, and can be entered when the tide is flowing or slack. About a mile and a half from the bridge is the village of Bere Ferrers (ferry slip).

Above the tidal portion, *i.e.*, in the neighbourhood of Buckland Abbey, the river becomes unnavigable for canoes, and is a rapid rocky stream. This upper valley of the Tavy is extremely beautiful, and can be followed on foot, through most of its course, right into the very heart of Dartmoor.

108. FOWEY

Only the estuary is canoeable. Tidal below Lostwithiel. St. Winnow Church can be reached at any state of tide, but the Fowey above here, and the branches of the estuary : Lerryn River, Penpoll Creek, and Pont Pill only at high tide.

Distances from Fowey : Polruan ½ mile ; Pont 1 mile ; Golant 2 ; Penpoll 3½ ; Lerryn 4½ ; St. Winnow 4½.

O.S. 186 ; Barth. 1 ; Charts : St. 13 ; Y.52

109. FAL

The Fal rises in the Goss Moors and is not canoeable above the tidal waters, but the numerous creeks and the Rivers Tresillian and Truro make a good cruising ground, mostly through well wooded country. The most convenient rail access is at Truro.

Cruises may be started from various points, but if staying for more than one night it is suggested that camp should be made above Turnaware Point, as below that the river widens at Carrick Roads to a width varying from 1 to 1½ miles, and the waters here are often rough. Above Turnaware Point, the Fal may be explored as far as Malpas (pronounced Mowpas) at any state of tide, and with a rising tide as far as Ruan Lanihorne, passing through well wooded country with a deer park on the L bank going upstream.

Forking R at Malpas is the Tresillian River, which may be followed as far as the road bridge at Tresillian ; forking L at Malpas is the Truro River, canoeable to Truro.

Truro, Tresillian and Ruan Lanihorne can only be reached with the aid of the tides, and care should be taken not to get stranded on the mudbanks which are very soft (no attempt should be made to walk on the mud unless the canoe is within reach).

At Turnaware Point the river runs very swiftly at the change of tide, and care should always be taken at this point (a wind blowing against the tide makes very heavy water here).

Downstream from Turnaware Point one enters Carrick Roads, and keeping to the eastern side, which has a steep rocky shore, one comes to Messack Point and St. Just-in-Roseland, St. Mawes and its Castle (where Ann Boleyn was imprisoned) is 1¾ miles from St. Just and on the same side of the estuary. Passing St. Mawes pier and keeping to the L bank Percuil (or Porthcuel) is reached after 1¼ miles.

2¾ miles from St. Mawes and across the estuary is Falmouth, with its docks, etc.

Returning from Falmouth towards Turnaware Point and keeping to the western side of the estuary one passes Trefusis Point. From there to Penarrow Point the coast is steep and rocky and landing is not advisable except on a calm day. After passing Penarrow Point one comes to Mylor Creek, which is navigable at high tide for 1 mile to Mylor Bridge. Continuing for 1 mile from the mouth of Mylor Creek, Restronguet Creek forks L and can be followed at high tide to Devoran. On the L side of this creek are woods running down to the water's edge. The stream running at this point into Restronguet Creek may be followed until the main Falmouth-Truro road is reached and is a very pretty trip.

The Carrick Roads and the adjoining creeks make an ideal cruising ground for the experienced canoeist providing the weather is good and the winds not very strong, but after a period of southerly or easterly winds the waters here become rough. During rough or squally weather it is best to keep to the upper reaches.

O.S. 190 ; Barth. 1 ; Charts : St. 13 ; Y.54, 58

110. HELFORD RIVER

A very beautiful sea-inlet on the SE coast of Cornwall between Falmouth and the Lizard. There is a good expanse of water in the lower reaches, which provides good sailing, but the upper parts and side creeks can only be done on the tide. Access at Gweek (which can be reached from Helston) at the head of the inlet. Shop, inn. Side creeks and distances from Gweek are :

Mawgan Creek. (S shore) 1 mile.

Constantine Creek. (N shore) 2½ miles. Navigable on the tide for approx. 1½ miles.

Frenchman's Pill S. 2½ miles.

Porth Navas N. 3 miles. Porth Navas village and quay about ½ mile up creek. Very picturesque.

About ½ mile below Porth Navas is Helford Village (S shore) where there is a ferry slip and stores can be bought. The mouth of the Helford River is about 1 mile beyond. High Water : Dover plus 5¾ hours.

O.S. 190 ; Barth. 1 ; Charts : St. 13 ; Y.57

111. JERSEY COAST

Jersey has no inland waterways, but some 50 miles of interesting coast. This is considered dangerous for boating on account of the numerous rocks and currents. However, a rock which is near enough to the surface to damage a canoe usually reveals itself by disturbing the surface or by floating weed, and sea currents are not very formidable to the canoeist with experience of rapid rivers. The chief danger to the canoeist is inability to land on account of surf, so it is as well to know where the nearest harbour is before setting out, and to remember that surf often increases, even on a calm day, as the tide rises. There are a number of tide races which should be avoided.

The tides are very big round Jersey, and on the SE there is over a mile between spring tide high and low water marks. Most of the harbours are dry at low water with spring tides.

Chart : C.33

112. ISLES OF SCILLY

A canoe will much increase the enjoyment of a holiday in the Isles of Scilly. The islands, some 30 miles out in the Atlantic beyond Land's End are exposed to the full force of Atlantic swell and winds, and shipwrecks there have been frequent during the centuries on the dangerous rocks and shoals.

Canoeing outside the islands is to be avoided. Inside, there is sufficient sheltered water to make canoeing amongst the many islands delightful : the beaches shelve gently and are of shining white sand ; the sea is very clear ; the climate is mild enough to permit sub-tropical plants to grow. A reliable compass is essential.

Only five islands are inhabited and each has its own characteristics. Camping is possible only on private property but owing to the fewness of trees sheltered spots are rare. Camping on common land is prohibited. St. Mary's makes a good centre.

O.S.: Special map of the Isles of Scilly, 2 in. to 1 ml.

113. TORRIDGE

The Torridge rises in the NW corner of Devon, S of Clovelly, and flows in a huge loop to join the *Taw* at Appledore. A mountain river, it rises and falls rapidly, and in low water entails a great deal of wading. The best time is in late autumn or early spring. The valley is deep, winding and beautiful. Shallows and pools alternate and in time of spate the rapids can be exciting. In places the river bed is rocky and serrated, elsewhere there are pools with rocks almost to the surface. The Torridge is tidal from Weare Giffard.

Canoeable in favourable water from Hele Bridge near Hatherleigh, though there is more water after the confluence of the Okement. The railway is never far away from the river all the way from Hatherleigh to Bideford. Objection may be encountered from fishermen.

O.S. 175, 163 ; Barth. 3

Miles
0   *Hele Bridge.* Hatherleigh Stn. (Halwill-Barnstaple branch).
1   Confl. of Okement R.   Meeth Village L.
4   *Huish Bridge.*
7½   *Beaford Bridge.* Village R 1 ml. Look out for wire across river after passing the long wood.
11½ *Weir.* Portage.

12½   *New Bridge.* A short way above is a shallow fall which can be shot.
13½   *Great Torrington* R. Near the factory is a rubble weir, which is always changing shape. Easy, fast run below. Stn.
15½   *Weare Giffard* R. River tidal.
19½   *Bideford Bridge.* Stn. R. H.W.: Dover minus 4¾ hrs.
21½   *Appledore* L.

114. TAW

The Taw rises on Dartmoor near the source of the Teign and the Dart and flows N to Barnstaple. Its estuary joins that of the Torridge at Appledore.

From South Molton Stn. (Exeter–Barnstaple line) the Taw offers fewer difficulties than the Torridge and there is usually a greater depth of water. It is still an upland river, and after dry weather will necessitate some wading. Objection may be encountered from fishermen.

O.S. 163 ; Barth. 3

Miles
0   *Newnham Barton Bridge.* Inn (Fortescue Arms). South Molton Road Stn. Fast, shallow place at junction of the Bray, ¼ ml below, followed by a succession of pools and small rapids along a lovely valley. The rly. follows the valley and Portsmouth Arms Stn. is near the river. Three small falls between Abbots Marsh and Portsmouth Arms Stn.
7   *Umberleigh Bridge.* Stn. Inn. Lovely old mills, portage into weir stream. Fast below the mill.
10   *Chapelton Stn.* L.
12   *New Bridge.* Shortly after this the river becomes tidal, and a little dull.
13½   *Bishop's Tawton* R.
15½   *Barnstaple Bridge.* Town R. Barnstaple Junc. Stn. L. Town stn. R. A good stretch of sand on R bank above bridge for landing.
18½   *Penhill Point* L.
22½   *Appledore* L. Confl. with Torridge estuary L. H.W.: Dover minus 4¾ hrs.

SEVERN BASIN AND SOMERSET RIVERS

115. SEVERN (Newtown to Gloucester)

Of the three rivers, Severn, Wye and Rheidol, that rise on Plynlimon, the Severn takes the most circuitous route to the sea, and by reason of its length and gradual fall from as high up as Newtown gives a canoe run of exceptional duration without anything serious in the way of difficulties.

Though canoeable from Llanidloes in good water, the upper reaches are shallow at other times. Between Newtown, the more usual starting point, and Pool Quay there are several weirs, but after Pool Quay, to which point the Severn was at one time navigable, there is a practically clear run broken only by the weir at Shrewsbury down to the first lock at Lincombe, a distance of 108 miles.

In this stretch there are many minor difficulties, particularly at low water, but in high water most of the rapids are covered over and a fast if not particularly exciting run may be made. About a dozen fences are across the river between Newtown and Buildwas. The long rapid at Ironbridge, where the river enters a narrow gorge, is no longer a serious hazard, though still able to give an exciting run in some states of water.

The Severn is generally a quietly beautiful river, and has little spectacular scenery. Only at Ironbridge has its scenery been marred by industry. None of the towns on the river—Shrewsbury, Bridgnorth, Bewdley, Worcester, Tewkesbury—is of any great size, nor do they detract from the attractions of the river, being worth visiting for themselves.

The Severn is closely connected with the canal system. The Montgomeryshire Branch of the Shropshire Union Canals closely follows the river between Newtown and Pool Quay for several miles but involves portages at bridges and may be overgrown (see Section 148). The Shrewsbury Branch now ends some distance short of Shrewsbury and does not connect with the river. At Stourport the Staffordshire and Worcester Canal connects, and the Worcester and Birmingham Canal joins the Severn a mile below Worcester. Below Gloucester is the junction with the Gloucester and Berkeley Ship Canal.

From Pool Quay to Stourport there is an ancient right of navigation. Between Stourport and Gloucester the Severn is under British Waterways and a charge of 1s. per lock is made at each of the locks in this part of the river, whether portaging or locking through. British Waterways' Inland Cruising Booklet No. 14 will cover this part.

The tidal Severn below Gloucester is not recommended for canoeing. The swift currents, shifting sandbanks and changing channels make its navigation extremely hazardous. If canoed this should be only at or near neap tides and clear of the "bore" or tidal wave. This starts about 2 miles above Sharpness. At Longney it forms a continuous front 4 to 5 feet high, and it moves up the estuary at a rate varying from 4 to 14 knots according to tide and place. Canoeists proceeding beyond

Gloucester are advised to use, as an alternative, the Gloucester and Berkeley Ship Canal to Sharpness whence, with due regard to tides and weather, it is possible to reach Avonmouth and Bristol (see Sections 126 and 128).

Camp sites are easy to find almost everywhere.

The state of the river is very important, and in the dry season the river down to Pool Quay may be very hard on both canoe and canoeist.

Grading :   Rough Water I with occasional stretches II Newtown to Bewdley. Thereafter canalised.

Note.   Between Stourport and Gloucester large barges may sometimes throw up a wash with waves 3 or 4 feet high—*caution.*

Tides :   For High Water at Gloucester subtract 1 hour 45 minutes from Dover times ; at Sharpness subtract 3 hours 35 minutes.

O.S. 128, 117, 118, 119, 130, 143 ; Barth. 22, 23, 18, 13

Miles

0   *Newtown.* Stn. Rapid just below starting point.

½   *Llanllwchaiarn.* Channel centre—watch for old piles. At old water mill weir portage R if necessary. A fall half a mile below by golf course.

2¼   *Penarth Weir.* Canal feeder ; long portage L ; if river low, take feeder for a short distance. The canal is very weedy in summer.

3   *Aberbechan Bridge.* Rocky fall above. Reef under ; let down or portage ; may be shot in high water ; 5 mls. of hazards follow due to confined strong currents, snags in channels, low trees and rocks ; take care, and line down when in doubt.

4½   Confl. of *Mule* R. Rapid and rocks.

4¾   *Brynderwen Bridge, Abermule.* Approach by narrow channel close to L bank ; ¾ ml. below beware tree stump in mid-current R beyond trees.

8¼   *Caerhowel Bridge.* Sharp wooden stakes, exposed in low water. Inn R ; Montgomery 2 mls. R ; tree stumps and fallen trees in the next part.

10½   Confl. of *Rhiw* L.

11¼   Confl. of *Camlad* R.

15   *Kilkewydd Road and Railway Bridges.* Low fall above bridge, shootable in good water ; inn R.

15¼   *Kilkewydd Weir.* Deep sloping weir ; portage, let down or shoot according to water.

17¼   *Leighton Bridge and Weir.* Iron stakes in channel ¼ ml. above bridge. Sloping weir under bridge with stones at foot ; examine ; may be shot in good water ; Welshpool Stn. ½ ml. L and town 1 ml. L.

19   Stakes across river, exposed in low water.

19¾   *Buttington Road and Railway Bridges.* Inn R.

21½   *Abbey Weir* (site of).

22½   *Pool Quay.* Suspension bridge ; Inn ; canal diverges L.

23   Old railway bridge. Breidden Hill R.

30¼   *Llandrinio Bridge.* Take right-hand arch in low water ; beware iron stake in channel ; shallow fall below in low water.

33½   Confl. of *Vyrnwy* L. Rly. bridge below ; the *Vyrnwy* is practicable at least from the Shropshire Union Canal aqueduct (see section 116).

36¼   *Royal Hill.* Inn L.

39¾   *Shrawardine Weir* (site of).

40   Old railway bridge. R arch in low water ; village L.

42¼   *Montford* L. Islands. Inn. Take L of first island, R of second.

44   *Montford Bridge.* Main road (A.5).

45¼   Confl. of *Perry* L. (Canoeable from above Ruyton Eleven Towns in good water—see Section 117.) Rapid below ; begin R, then across to L ; caution.

46½   *Isle Grange.* Severn goes round "The Isle" for nearly 5 mls., but distance overland across neck is only 300 yds. R. Very steep banks. Permission to portage at ref. 456165 should be sought from Isle Grange Farm, near Bicton.

55¼   Shropshire and West Midland Show Ground L.

55¾   *Shrewsbury, Welsh Bridge.* Boathouses ; interesting old town ; river takes a horseshoe course past "The Quarry" L and Shrewsbury School R.

57   *Shrewsbury, English Bridge.*

57¼   Railway bridge. Shrewsbury Stn. overhead. (Islands below.)

57½   *Shrewsbury Weir.* Salmon pass L ; line down or portage R ; keep to L of island below.

60¼   *Uffington.* Inn L ; wire ferry.

61¼   Railway bridge.

62¼   *Preston Bolt.* Stones, stakes across river ; channel extreme R not readily seen from above ; in high water several openings possible ; in low water land and inspect.

63   *Chilton Island.* Keep R.

64¾   *Atcham Bridges* (A.5). Shallows above, channel to L of island above the bridges, then centre arch of bridge and over to L.

67¼   Confl. of *Tern* L. The *Tern* is practicable for canoes for some way (see Section 118).

68   *Wroxeter* (Uriconium) L. L of islands for landing ; Roman remains ; the Wrekin ahead on L.

70¼   *Cound Lodge.* Inn R.

72½   *Cressage Bridge.* Village ½ ml. R ; river enters a narrow valley between hills. Fast water most of way to Bewdley.

77½   *Buildwas Bridge.* Rapid below ; channel L. Abbey ruins R.

78¾   Railway bridge. Beyond electricity generating stn.

79¾   *Ironbridge.* By Telford ; the first iron bridge to be built in England ; town L ; 2 mls. of fast water with two main rapids, the L channel usually carries most water ; in flood the waves run high.

81¾   *Coalport Bridge.* Another early iron bridge. Rapids ½ ml. below: L channel in low water.

84¾   *Apley Bridge.* Apley Park L.

88¾   *Bridgnorth Bridge.* Interesting town ; boathouses, inns.

91¼   *Quatford* L. Inn.

94½   *Hampton Loade.* Rope ferry. Inn R. Shallows in low water ; 2 mls. below take L channel.

97   *Highley.* Inn.

99½   *Arley Ferry* (operated by the current). Inn.

100¼   *Arley Railway Bridge.*

101   *Eymore Rapid.* Channel slightly L of centre. ¼ ml. beyond, to L of island, a low fall usually shootable. At line of stones 200 yds. below island best channel on extreme R.

102½   *Dowles Railway Bridge.* Wyre Forest lies back on R.

103¼   *Bewdley Bridge.* Boathouse above R ; boat club below L; interesting old town ; picturesque quay ; stn. L.

104¼   *Blackstone Rock.* Rapid sets into R bank. Channel extreme R.

107¼   *Stourport Bridge.* Junction with Stour (see Section 118) and *Staffordshire and Worcestershire Canal* (see Section 147); boat club below bridge R.

108¾   *Lincombe Lock.* Weir R—impracticable. The weirs on the Severn are difficult and shooting can be dangerous.

109¾   *Hempstall Ferry.* Inn R.

112¼   *Lenchford Ferry.* Inn R.

113   *Holt Fleet Lock* L ; weir R ; bridge and inn ¼ ml. below.

115¾   *Grimley* R. Entrance of former Droitwich Canal L and River Salwarpe. The *Salwarpe* is canoeable from Impney, 1 ml. above Droitwich, but only with good water levels. Winding course, many obstacles (mills, fallen trees, etc.). About 12 mls. Permission is necessary in several places—advice from B.C.U.

116½   *Bevere Lock* R ; weir L ; inn R.

119   Ferry. Dog and Duck.

119¾   *Worcester Railway Bridge.* Canoe club and racecourse L above bridge.

120   *Worcester Bridge.* Cathedral city ; boathouse near bridge ; Foregate Street Stn. ¼ ml. L ; Shrub Hill Stn. ¾ ml. L.

120½   Junc. of *Worcester and Birmingham Canal* L.

121   *Diglis Lock* L. Weir R.

121¾   Confl. of *River Teme* R (see Section 120). Ketch Inn L ¼ ml. below.

124   *Kempsey* L.

128   *Severn Stoke.* Wharf L. Village and inn ½ ml.

131   *Upton-on-Severn Bridge.* Town R. Landing below bridge.

132½   Railway bridge.

Miles
134½   *Queenhill Bridge* (motorway).
136¾   *The Mythe Bridge.* By Telford ; Tewkesbury ½ ml. L.
137¼   Confl. of *River Avon* L (see Section 121). If weir stream is
           taken it is possible to reach boathouse without portage, in
           order to visit Tewkesbury. Nearest stn. Ashchurch.
137¾   *Upper Lode Lock* R ; weir L.
138½   *Lower Lode.* River becomes tidal about this point. 1 ml. ferry
           and boathouse (Cheltenham College).
141   Inn L.
142¼   *Haw Bridge.*
145½   *Ashleworth Quay* R. Village. Wainlode Hill 1½ mls. below on L.
147¾   *The Upper Parting.* Here the river divides, the two branches
           meeting again at the *Lower Parting*, forming the Isle of
           Alney ; the L arm should be taken for Gloucester.
150¼   *Westgate Bridge, Gloucester* (A.40). Cathedral city ; shops, railway
           stns. L. Land on L in car park before—
150½   Entrance to *Gloucester and Berkeley Ship Canal* (see Section 126).

116. Vyrnwy

Rises in the Berwyn Mountains, where its upper waters are impounded for Liverpool water supply, and flows down a picturesque valley to Llanymynech and then across lowlands to the Severn near Melverley.

It has been canoed from the junction of the *R. Banwy*, above which it is liable to be very dry.

O.S. 117, 118 ; Barth. 23

117. Perry

Rises near Gobowen and flows through NW Shropshire to the Severn about 1 mile below Montford Bridge. Water levels are good until well into the summer, but its upper reaches are liable to be choked later on with reeds. Course narrow and twisting with overhanging trees, barbed-wire, etc. Picturesque, if unexciting, canoeing. Between May and October frequent obstructions and shallows.

The Perry has been canoed from Wykey Bridge, but is probably possible from further upstream. Through Boreatton Park pretty, with high wooded cliffs in places. Footbridge near Ruyton Church (2 miles). Shallows below Ruyton Eleven Towns Bridge (2¾). Milford Mill (4½) is an old corn mill, still working. Weir L can be shot in high water. Road bridge below. Ruins of mill at Adcote (6¼)—difficult ; ½ mile on is the site of another mill. New weir 150 yards below Yeaton road bridge —portage L (7); ¾ mile further on small weir ; difficult portage through undergrowth L, ¼ mile above Grafton Bridge (8½) another ruined mill—

155

difficult (R channel probably best). Mytton Mill (9) portage R ; 8 foot drop at sluice. Confluence with Severn (10).

O.S. 118 ; Barth. 23

118. Tern and Roden

The **Tern** rises NE of Market Drayton and flows SW to Severn at Atcham. Easily canoeable from Longdon on Tern and probably from Stoke upon Tern, 13 miles higher up, in average water conditions. Like the Perry it maintains a good level of water well into the summer, but becomes weedy in places after dry weather.

Portages at Walcot mill (4 miles below Longdon). *R. Roden* joins it at Walcot. Low small bridge at Upton Forge (7¼). The Tern enters Attingham Deer Park (National Trust—Shropshire Education Centre). If there is enough water in the weir stream portage L at Attingham Weir (9). If not, an awkward portage across island to below the sluices. Rather shallow to A.5 road bridge. Confluence with Severn (9½) just beyond.

The **Roden**, a tributary of the *Tern* which rises NW of Wem, has been canoed from Spenford Bridge, 3¾ miles above Wem. It is difficult, shallow and narrow in places, and barbed-wire and fallen trees are to be expected. Small weir at Wem and broken weir below ; ½ mile below Thistleford Bridge is a bridge with a small sill under. After Lee Brockhurst Bridge (A.49) (10¼) shallows for 150 yards, then fine wooded park. Under the second bridge below this is a broken weir (portage R). At Stanton upon Hine Heath Mill (13½) the weir R is in bad condition. Examine to see whether millstream or weir stream is preferable ; both involve portages. At Moreton Mill land R above, carry across road and put in below bridge (trees and 10 foot drop—difficult). No details beyond Shawbury (16¾). The Roden continues past High Ercall to the *Tern* at Walcot (25½).

O.S. 118 ; Barth. 23

119. Worcestershire Stour

The Stour begins inauspiciously on the W side of the central ridge of the Black Country near Cradley Heath, and then flows W past Stourbridge to Amblecote where it leaves the industrial area for the quite pleasant country immediately to the W between Stourbridge and the Severn Valley. It is not further industrialised except at Kidderminster, and near its junction with the Severn at Stourport.

Canoeable from Stourton but it is only advisable to tackle this river with 1 foot of fresh water in. The river bed is very rough with many obstructions ; the banks are generally very soft mud and the water is badly polluted. Low pipes cross the river in several places. The Staffs and Worcs Canal runs close all the way and must be taken instead of the river through Kidderminster, where the river is obstructed by a pipe in the middle of a tunnel. Fast water and quite difficult in places. Not recommended.

O.S. 130 ; Barth. 18
Grading : Rough Water II

120. TEME

The Teme rises on Kerry Hill on the borders of Shropshire, Montgomeryshire and Radnorshire, and flows generally E and SE to the Severn below Worcester. It is a lively and sporting river in all states of water, running through lovely hilly country, well wooded and with hopfields and fruit orchards. The country is thinly populated, Ludlow and Tenbury being the only towns.

Ludlow is the normal starting point, but the river has been canoed after rain from as high as Knighton. Below Leintwardine the river breaks through the hills of Bringewood Chase by the Downton Gorge, and although the scenery on this upper part is very fine this gorge is not to be lightly undertaken. In high water conditions the river through here is often fast and rough, and in places the sides of the ravine are so close that it would be difficult or impossible to pack a boat up and carry it away. To avoid the gorge a 4 mile portage can be made from Burrington Bridge along the road L above the gorge to Bringewood Forge Bridge on the E side of Downton Park, where the valley opens out and the river is quieter.

Ludlow Stn. is a long way from the river at Temeside where a start is usually made.

After Ludlow the Teme is lively all the way. The banks are mostly high ; the course is very winding and there are numerous small rapids and scours and an occasional rocky ledge. Fallen trees and wire across the river should be watched for.

Above Ludlow the river is strictly preserved and prior permission must be obtained. Below Ludlow objections may also be encountered. Advice from B.C.U.

Grading :   Rough Water II ; in spate it can be more difficult.

O.S. 129, 130, 143 ; Barth. 18

Miles
0	*Knighton.* Village R, stn. L. Much barbed-wire before Leintwardine.
$\frac{1}{4}$	Weir. Dam of pumping station.
2	*Milebrook Bridge.* River course diverted—caution.
$5\frac{1}{2}$	*Lingen Bridge and Weirs.* Bucknell Stn. L ; barbed-wire 50 yds. above bridge.
7	Weir. Portage R.
$7\frac{1}{2}$	*Buckton Bridge.*
9	*Leintwardine Bridge.* Village L ; confl. of *R. Clun* ; Roman fortifications.
10	*Leintwardine Fishery.*
11	*Criftonford Bridge.*
$16\frac{1}{4}$	*Burrington Bridge.* Village $\frac{1}{2}$ ml. R ; river enters Downton Gorge.
$17\frac{1}{4}$	*Water Bridge* (Birmingham Aqueduct).
$17\frac{1}{2}$	*Bridge.*
18	*Hay Mill Weir,* long portage R ; get out on R bank about 100 yds. above weir (possibility of being caught between walls of old mill and the cliff); rocks below ; keep R side of island (weir on L of island).

18½   Broken weir. Shoot R.
18¾   *Downton Castle Bridge.* Castle ½ ml. L.
19½   *Bringewood Forge Bridge.* Weir portage R. followed by rapid.
         After ½ ml. another weir, usually shootable with care,
         otherwise portage R on opposite bank to old mill house.
22   *Bromfield Bridge and Weir* below—portage L by old mill house
         and sluices. Ruins of Benedictine Monastery R ; confl. of
         Onny below L. (The *Onny* has been canoed in high water
         from Craven Arms (stn.): much barbed-wire.)
22¼   Weir—portage L. Show-jumping arena L.
24¾   *Ludlow Castle*—dominates the river L. Below castle two weirs
         and *Dinham Bridge* ; portage both L. Rocky ravine round
         foot of castle hill to below Ludford Bridge (A.49).
25¼   *Ludford Bridge.* Inn R, town L. Two V-shaped weirs follow.
         The first weir is partly broken and shootable with great care
         L ; or portage L. The second weir must be portaged L.
         Note. If starting at Ludlow a convenient launching point is
         reached by following the road called Temeside L from
         Ludford Bridge about ½ ml. past the gasworks to a footpath
         on R to and along the river bank. This is below all the
         Ludlow weirs.
26¼   Aqueduct Bridge. Several drops, river faster.
27½   Railway bridge.
28   *Ashford Bridge.* Weir unshootable : long portage L round
         derelict mill, over fence and down steep bank. Ashford
         Carbonell Village L. Ashford Bowdler R. Church on R bank.
30   *Barretts Mill.* Broken weir, clear passage.
31   Demolished canal bridge.
31½   Railway bridge.
31¾   Road bridge.
34¾   Confl. of Ledwyche Brook. Burford House and Church L. At
         end of Burford House garden keep L (pipe on R).
35¼   *Burford Weir.* Shoot extreme L.
35¾   *Tenbury Bridge.* Good shopping R. Shallows under bridge—
         L arch ; many rapids follow.
38¾   Confl. of River Lea L. Beware of rocky shallows in ensuing
         stretch.
41   *Eastham Bridge.* Centre arch.
42½   *Lindridge.* Church on hill L. About ½ ml. further on are some
         awkward rock steps, the top one with a distinct current to L
         They are shootable with care unless blocked by trees ; or
         portage R up steep bank.
44   *Eardiston Mill.* Eardiston Village L back from river. Weir
         broken : shootable R, but beware stakes—some of them
         before the actual weir ; it is possible to portage on L.
46½   *Stanford Bridge.* Shallows under bridge—take L arch—Inn L.
48½   *Shelsley Beauchamp* L. High wooded banks, river deeper.
49½   *Newmill Bridge.*
51   *Ham Bridge.*
51¾   *Site of Ham Mill.* Small drop—easy shoot R.

121.   STRATFORD AVON

The Avon is canoeable from Rugby, but the stretch from that town
to Ashow, near Kenilworth, should be undertaken only when the river
is very full, otherwise there will not be enough water, and before the
reeds have grown. In the first 20 miles or so the water may be dirty or
smelly after dry weather, but it improves as the river gets bigger. It
flows through lovely country, and is accessible easily from Rugby,
Coventry or Birmingham. Such great houses as Stoneleigh, Guy's Cliff,
Warwick Castle, and Charlcote lie close to the river and add interest to
the cruise. A journey down the Avon from Warwick to the Severn
presents some of the most pleasant of English scenery, some fine old
towns and varied water conditions. A century or so ago the Avon was
navigable up to Stratford for vessels of 50 tons, but for many years
several of the locks have been derelict and now the head of the navigation is Evesham. Thus the Avon varies from rocky rapids and shallows
marking the sites of locks and weirs long since broken down, to deep
sluggish reaches where weirs and mills hold up the water. Above
Evesham the views are in general enclosed, although occasional glimpses
may be had of distant hills, and the several hills rising steeply from the
banks offer chances of obtaining more extensive views. Below Evesham
the scenery is more open and is dominated all the time by the isolated
mass of Bredon Hill, which is presented in ever-changing aspects as the
river winds around its foot. For the canoeist interested in history and
architecture the cruise takes one past old market towns like Warwick,
Evesham and Tewkesbury, while the lover of Shakespeare will wish to
visit Stratford.

Camp sites are easy to find all the way down, except near Welford
and Bidford.

The locks are maintained by the Lower Avon Navigation Trust,
Evesham. The charge for canoes is 1s. per lock. Lock keys can be hired.

Permission to pass should be sought in advance by letter (stamped addressed envelope for reply):

Stoneleigh Park : The Estate Office, Stoneleigh Abbey, Warwick.

Warwick Castle Park : H. Godfrey Payton & Son, Warwick Castle Estate Office, Warwick. (Permission may not be given for Sundays or certain other days.)

Charlcote Park (National Trust): The Curator, Charlcote Park, Warwick (or call at house). A fee of 3s. 6d. may be charged. Ask for the deer fence at the end of the park to be opened.

Grading : I-II at rapids, derelict locks, weirs, etc.; long stretches smooth and deep.

Miles

0	*Rugby, Avon Mill.* Inn ; stn. (M.R.) $\frac{1}{2}$ ml.; shallows.
1$\frac{1}{4}$	*Newbold-on-Avon Bridge.* Good starting place—bus from Rugby.
1$\frac{1}{2}$	Low weir. Care needed in low water.
1$\frac{3}{4}$	Weir. Short portage L or R ; shallows below.
2	Railway bridge.
2$\frac{1}{2}$	Island. Keep R of island ; small weir at end, portage R.
3$\frac{1}{4}$	*Little Lawford.* Weir L shootable in most states of water, but no headroom in high water ; footbridge 200 yds. downstream ; little headroom but R arch usually possible ; portage R.
6$\frac{1}{2}$	*King's Newnham Mill* (disused) and footbridge. Weirs gone. Take L branch of river above mill.
6$\frac{3}{4}$	*Church Lawford Bridge.*
8$\frac{1}{4}$	*Bretford Bridge.* Barbed-wire across the arches may be lifted.
9$\frac{1}{4}$	*Marston Mill.* Portage R above mill into side channel.
10$\frac{1}{2}$	*Brandon railway and road bridges.* Just above and below the road bridge are 2 pipes ; unless water very high, portage necessary ; land R cross bridge and enter water L below second pipe.
12	*Brandon Silk Mill.* River forks ; weirs gone ; take R channel.
14	*Ryton Mill.* Portage L at mill, and cross behind wheel. Barbed-wire in two places below.
14$\frac{1}{2}$	*Ryton Bridge.* Ryton Bridge Hotel L close to river ; shallows.
17$\frac{1}{2}$	*Bubbenhall Mill.* Portage R at first weir above mill ; private water near mill.
18$\frac{1}{4}$	*Bubbenhall Bridge.*
19$\frac{1}{4}$	*Cloud Bridge.* River enters Stoneleigh Park. Shallows and. several small bridges.
20$\frac{1}{2}$	*Stare Bridge and Coach Bridge.* Take L arch : stony shallows
21	Confl. of *River Sowe* (see Section 123).
22$\frac{1}{2}$	*Stoneleigh Abbey.* Portage R at weir $\frac{1}{4}$ ml. before the house ; a short distance below the house shoot second weir L.
24	*Ashow.* Footbridge. End of Stoneleigh Park. Shallows.
24$\frac{3}{4}$	*Chesford Bridge.* Take L arch, then cross R.
25$\frac{1}{2}$	Remains of Blackdown Mill. No weirs.

26   Railway Bridge.

29   *Guy's Cliff Mill.* Weir unshootable ; land on sill and line down ; or portage on L at mill. Guy's Cliff House beyond, R.

29¾   *Rock Mill Weir.* Not shootable because of fallen masonry. Portage R above.

30½   *Portobello Bridge, Leamington.* Confl. with *River Leam* (see Section 122).

31   *Aqueduct of Grand Union Canal.* Easy portage from canal to river (see Section 153). Leamington Spa stn. can be reached by canal.

      Railway bridge.

32½   *Warwick Bridge.* Boathouse above and boat club on R below. Town R worth visiting especially Leycester Hospital and Mill Street ; Warwick (W.R.) stn. ½ ml.; spiked chains across old bridge arches.

      Warwick Castle and Park. Weir unshootable. Portage L. Shallows and ferry rope near castle. Submerged trees near castle. If permission to pass through is refused, a long portage of several miles round the Park is required.

35   *Leafield Bridge* (private road). River leaves Park.

37   *Barford Mill.* Mill dismantled. Large house L and river used by a commercial firm for testing. Portage R across island at landing stage to another in lower stream.

37½   *Barford Scours and Bridge.* River shallow and fast to bridge. Channel under bank R.

42   *Hampton Lucy Mill.* Portage R at first weir before mill. Road bridge.

42½   *Charlcote Park.* Fine Tudor house, now National Trust, on L ; river may be blocked by rushes in summer. Deer fence and gates across river at each end of Park. Confl. of *River Dene* above house.

44¼   *Site of Alveston Mill.* Cafe and boathouse ¼ ml. above. Vertical weirs and central sluice under concrete footbridge. Portage R.

48   *Stratford Bridge.* Junc. of Stratford-on-Avon Canal below bridge (see Section 155). Town R ; W.R. stn. ½ ml. through town ; boathouses. Shakespeare Memorial Theatre on R.

48½   *Stratford Mill.* Portage L of weir.

48¾   Railway bridge. Shallows from weir to bridge.

50   Confl. of *River Stour* (see Section 124).

51½   *Luddington.* Site of lock—only remains of masonry.

53¼   *Binton Bridge.* Shallows.

54½   *Welford Mill.* Portage beyond weir by mill. Remains of old lock 200 yds below ; look out for submerged masonry. Small weir round corner to R—examine.

56½   *Bidford Grange.* Islands. Weir gone.

57¾   *Bidford Bridge.* Rocks under all arches—inspect. Probably best on L. Fast water below.

59½   Confl. of *River Arrow* (see Section 125).

60   *Cleeve Prior Mill.* Weir gone.

61½   *Harvington Mill.* Line down on R of weir. In fairly high water, weir can be shot about ⅓ from left bank.

62   *Fish and Anchor Inn.* On L bank ; a ford of the stone causeway type usually makes it necessary to wade and pull canoe over ; may be shootable in centre ; shallows below.

62   *Offenham Ferry.* Inn on L bank.

65½   *Evesham Lock.* In working order ; or line down by broken rollers on R of weir.
    Evesham Bridges. Collins' Boathouse L above first bridge. Town has attractive Tudor houses and is a pleasant country town ; stn. ½ ml. through town.

68½   *Chadbury Weir and Lock.* Broken rollers on R of weir.

71   *Fladbury Weir and Lock.* Weir sometimes shootable on L in high water close to Mill House. William Sandys, who first made the Avon navigable, lived here.

71¼   Road bridge.

75½   *Wyre Mill Lock.* Several weirs ; portage L over grass or across island. First weir may be shootable, L.

76½   *Pershore Lock.* Weir can be portaged L.

77   *Pershore Bridge.*

81¾   *Nafford Lock.* Portage at lock.

83¾   *Eckington Bridge.* River winds round Bredon Hill.

84   Rly. bridge.

85½   *Strensham Lock.* Portage L above weir or R at the weir.

88½   *Twyning Ferry.* Inn on R.

91   *Tewkesbury Lock* R. The upper branch leads through town ; boathouse R before bridge. Town quay on R by flour mill, concrete slipway on L about 200 yds beyond, both with good access. The branch continues to a mill sluice and in about 1 ml. more joins the Severn.

91½   Confl. with *River Severn.* Fine view of Tewkesbury Abbey across flat meadows.

122. Leam

Tributary of the Avon, rising in Northamptonshire and flowing W to join the Warwickshire Avon between Leamington Spa and Warwick.

Written application for permission to pass should be made to : Mr. H. Johnson, Offchurch Bury, Leamington Spa ; Mr. E. Willes, Newbold Comyn, Leamington Spa.

O.S. 132 ; Barth. 19

0   *Marton.* Practicable from higher only in flood. River blocked
      by reeds after July.
1   *Stoneyford Bridge.*
1¾ *Eathorpe Bridge.*
4   *Hunningham Bridge.* Good landing L.
5¼ Ford. Shallow water.
6¼ *Offchurch Bridge.* Good road access R.
8½ *Offchurch Bury* L. Shoot weir R, or portage R in ¼ ml. Second
      weir has underwater spikes, inspect before shooting.
9   *Grand Union Canal.* Above L, difficult portage.
11 *Leamington Spa.* Willes Bridge, footbridge and weir, unshootable.
      Lengthy portage L to slipway L. Victoria Bridge, Royal
      Leamington Spa C.C. on R beyond next road bridge.
12 *Princes Drive.* Rail, road bridges and weir—unshootable—
      portage R.
12½ *Junction with River Avon.*

123. Sowe

Tributary of the Avon. Rises NE of Coventry and joins the Avon
near Stoneleigh. Passes Coventry sewage works. Canoeable in high
water level from Copsewood Grange, Binley near Coventry (7 miles to
the Avon). Permission required to portage round Baginton Mill weir
as in private gardens. River badly polluted.

O.S. 132 ; Barth. 19

124. Warwickshire Stour

Tributary of the Avon. Rises SW of Banbury and flows NE through
Shipston-on-Stour to the Avon a short distance below Stratford.
Canoeable from Shipton only in high water level. Shallow and obstructed in summer. River passes through private grounds, and permission is required to pass. Advice from B.C.U.

O.S. 144 ; Barth. 19

0   *Shipston-on-Stour* road bridge.
1   *Fell Mill* : portage L into weir stream shallows.
2   *Honington Hall.* Weir below house—portage.
2¾   *Tredington.* Weir—portage or line down.
3¼   Broken weir—approach slowly, shootable L ; river becomes **very**
       overgrown and obstructed to—
5   *Halford Mill.* Weir ; road bridge.
6½   *Newbold-on-Stour*, L.
7½   *Ettington Park* R.
7¾   Road bridge ; weir below ; portage R at weir.
11¾ *Preston-on-Stour* ; take L branch ; weirs shootable if sufficient
       water.

12½ *Alscote Park* R. Weir ; portage L. River divides below ; one or both channels often obstructed by fallen trees.

12¾ *Ailstone* ; road bridge.

13¾ *Clifford Mill* ; best to take L channel to where water has broken through the R bank and portage R into weir stream.

14½ *Lower Clifford Mill.* Keep R up to mill and portage L to weir stream by main road bridge where streams rejoin. There is a second weir between the mill and the road bridge which is rarely shootable. Fast water to—

16 *Confl. with Avon.*

125. Alne and Arrow

The Arrow and its tributary the Alne, flow S through Alcester to join the Avon near Salford Priors. In spring the Alne is practicable from Wootton Wawen, and the Arrow from Spernall. The Alne has been canoed at all times of the year from Great Alne.

From Great Alne the river is narrow, with a fair current, numerous small rapids, with many twists and turns. Mills at 1 mile and 2 miles below Great Alne require portages. A small fall ¼ mile before the confluence with the Arrow, above Alcester, is sometimes shootable, otherwise portage L. Alcester is 3½ miles, Wixford 6 miles from Great Alne. Portage either side of weir at Wixford. Portage R at weir 2 miles beyond Wixford. Confluence with *Avon* 10 miles from Great Alne. The whole distance from Great Alne takes 2-2½ hours.

O.S. 131, 144 ; Barth. 19

126. GLOUCESTER and BERKELEY SHIP CANAL

Runs for 16¾ miles from Gloucester to Sharpness, and was built so that the dangerous reaches of the Severn below Gloucester might be avoided by shipping. There is one lock at each end, and a railway station at Sharpness. Permits must be obtained from the Toll Clerk on entry, before using the Canal : monthly and single permits 5s. 6d.; no lock charges. The Canal may be used on Sundays and at night provided the locks and swing bridge are not operated. The Stroudwater Canal crosses it near Whitminster, 8 miles from Gloucester. Always give commercial traffic the towpath side unless signalled otherwise.

O.S. 143, 156 ; Barth. 13

127. STROUDWATER CANAL

This canal and the Thames and Severn Canal formerly connected the tidal part of the Severn Estuary at Framilode with the Thames at Lechlade. It crosses the Gloucester and Berkeley Ship Canal and runs up the Golden Valley to Stroud and is continued by a short stretch of the Thames and Severn Canal, which, however, becomes dry and derelict some way before Sapperton Tunnel is reached. The valley is narrow and steep and the scenery pretty.

The locks are unworkable, and in the late summer weed is very thick. There is water in some stretches, but it is doubtful if it is worthwhile.

There were 12 locks rising from the Ship Canal to Stroud in 7 miles and a further 7 in the 2½ miles to Brimscombe. The canal authorities are : Stroudwater Navigation, 13 Wallbridge, Stroud ; Thames and Severn Canal—Gloucester County Council.

O.S. 156 ; Barth. 13

128. SEVERN ESTUARY (SHARPNESS TO AVONMOUTH)

Navigation of the Severn Estuary is tricky and is best avoided, but the following notes may be of assistance to those who, nevertheless, desire to reach the mouth of the Bristol Avon. Tides in the Bristol Channel have the second highest rise and fall in the world, with a speed during the middle two hours of the ebb of about 6 knots. Prevailing SW wind when blowing against the ebb may lead to a choppy sea. Periods of ebb and flow approx. equal or slightly longer ebb than flood.

The pilots at Sharpness Dock give good advice about weather and tides. The distances to be covered are great and the estuary is exposed to the SW. Sharpness to Beachley approximately 12 miles ; Beachley to "The Shoots" 3 miles ; "The Shoots" to Avonmouth approximately 6 miles. It is therefore necessary to keep to the channel except for a short time after high water because by the time a canoe has reached "The Shoots" the tide will have been ebbing for some hours. The channel is shown by leading marks not indicated on the 1-in. O.S. map, so nautical charts should be used. Chart : St. 14.

Sharpness and Bristol Channel ports tide tables are obtainable from Arrowsmiths, Winterstone Road, Bristol 3.

High water, Sharpness : Dover - 3 hours 35 min.

Beachley or Chepstow to Avonmouth and Bristol via The Shoots. Distance about 16 miles. Because of mud and the great rise and fall of the tides, landing at Avonmouth is unpleasant and difficult. The passage should therefore be timed for arrival off Avonmouth at low water (6½ hours after H.W.), going up the Avon on the first of the flood.

If starting at Chepstow or Tintern it is best to turn up the Severn to Beachley Ferry slipway, rounding Beachley Point inside the lighthouse if the tide is more than half high, or outside if lower. It is possible to land at the slipway at any state of the tide and it is easier to judge conditions there than at Chepstow. Previous permission from the ferry company is desirable.

The passage of The Shoots should not be attempted with a strong wind against the ebb. The best conditions are a light breeze from N or NE, or of course, a calm.

Visibility of 4 to 5 miles is desirable. Leave Beachley 2 hours (or Chepstow 2½ hours if not landing at Beachley) before *low* water, i.e. 4½ or 4 hours respectively after high water. Two courses are possible to the head of The Shoots :

(i) Inside Charston Rock : keep close to the Welsh coast, but not too close to the mud. Make for Black Rock lighthouse on the shore 2 miles from the mouth of the Wye, passing St. Pierre lighthouse on the right about halfway. These are small lighthouses built on top of ironwork. When nearing Black Rock lighthouse, Charston Rock lighthouse, a tall white lighthouse built on rocks, will be passed on the left. Passing between the two lighthouses, set course for a tall mast about 1 mile S of Charston Rock and visible at all states of tide. This marks the beginning of The Shoots.

(ii) Outside Charston Rock : get Beachley Point lighthouse right astern and make for Charston Rock lighthouse, a tall white stone lighthouse built on rocks. Keep checking course to avoid being driven too far out by the ebb from the Wye.

On both courses, when S of Charston Rock lighthouse, get both that and St. Pierre lighthouse in line and dead astern. This is the course through the Shoots, a channel about 50 yards wide between sharp rocks, through which the tide runs at great speed. The water swirls and eddies, but with a good sea-going canoe will be all right (see above as to wind). The course should be parallel to, and about a quarter of a mile west of, an imaginary line joining the two high masts about a mile apart which mark the beginning and end of The Shoots. Then make for the two Avonmouth lighthouses, keeping the shorter behind the taller (nearer) one. This should bring you to the mouth of the Avon at low water, so that you can go up the Avon on the first of the flood. Wait for Bristol City Dock Gates to open—they cannot open before three hours after low water (charge 5s.), or lift out at slipway 100 yards below on the left. Or turn R up "New Cut" passing under a double swing bridge and a swing footbridge to a disused ferry slip on the R under a suspension footbridge. Temple Meads Station ¼ mile.

It is possible to avoid The Shoots by leaving Beachley slipway at high water, crossing to the opposite shore before the stream gathers speed and using the Severn Tunnel pumping station near Redwick as a landmark. Landing easy and clean near this but elsewhere mud is knee deep. Keep about ¼ mile out from the shore. This course takes you over ground that dries out as the tide ebbs and has the disadvantage of necessitating a long wait at Avonmouth for the tide to turn.

Sharpness and Bristol Channel ports tide tables are obtainable from Arrowsmiths, Winterstone Road, Bristol 3.

High water Chepstow and Beachley : Dover - 3 hours 55 min.; Avonmouth : Dover - 4 hours 15 min.

129. BRISTOL AVON

The Avon rises in the Cotswolds near Badminton and flows in a huge semi-circle through Malmesbury, Chippenham and Bath to Bristol and the Severn Estuary. It is, for the most part, a deep river being held up by mills and weirs at intervals. At many of the weirs it is possible to lower the canoe down single-handed, unless there is too much water flowing over, when a short portage has to be made. The Avon flows through some very charming wooded country and the deep valley beyond Bradford is very fine. The Clifton Gorge is famous. There are no real difficulties, except that the higher parts are made laborious by weed in summer.

The Avon has been canoed from road bridge (B.4042) 1 mile SE of Malmesbury. From here frequent easy rapids and meanders ; wading necessary in low water. There is a mill (portage R), four weirs, and some low footbridges before Dauntsey, then fewer rapids and weirs to Chippenham, about 17 miles from Malmesbury.

The Kennet and Avon Canal runs along the valley from just above Bradford and joins it at Bath (see Section 72). There are 6 locks below here before Bristol (lock fee 6d.). Canoes passing by the Feeder Canal between Netham and Cumberland Basin need prior permission from the Dock Master, Dock Master's Office, Welsh Back, Bristol 1, which is not normally refused. The fee is 10s.

Railways follow the river most of the way from Chippenham and access can be gained from a number of stations. Camp sites can be found all the way down.

O.S. 156, 166 ; Barth. 13, 7

Miles

0   *Chippenham Bridge.* Build L bank near Co-op. or go through alley at end of Nestle's factory to river bank (Ivy Fields). Stn. ¼ ml. Shallows and weeds. Diagonal steel and concrete barrier leading to a works water intake, normally covered. Approach carefully, keeping near R bank. Sewage works ¾ ml. followed by fast water between weeds. Some underwater snags.

1¼   Rapid. The river widens and deepens.

2½   *Lackham House* R. Scenery very pretty to Lacock.

3¾   *Rey Mill.* Steep weir R. Portage from mill cut on R across paddock into weir stream. Reybridge Village R about ½ ml. below. Shallows and weeds.

5½   *Lacock.* Village and Abbey R. Worth visiting. At stone road bridge ¼ ml. below take second arch from R. Thick weeds and stones.

7¾   *Melksham Weir.* Boating station ¼ ml. above : access to town. Portage L.

8   *Melksham Bridge.* Take L arch. Stn. ½ ml. R. Town, shops on L. Weeds for ½ ml.

10   *Monkton House* R. Stone packhorse bridge ; old London-Bath route.

10¾   *Whaddon.* Confl. of Semington Brook L—could be used as a link from Kennet and Avon Canal.

11¼   Holt Junc. Stn. R.

12½   *Staverton Weir.* Land at junction of mill cut and weir (L bank) and lift down bank. At stone road bridge ¼ ml. below little clearance if water is high. Railway Halt ¼ ml.

13   *Great Bradford Wood* R. Confl. of R. Biss L ¾ ml. below.

15¼   *Bradford-on-Avon Weir.* Steep weir ; if the river is low lift down R by railway bridge into shallows below. Land at staging upstream of stone pump house, follow footpath across unmade road to river (60 yds.).

15½   *Bradford Bridge* and rly. bridge (stn. ¼ ml. L); landing at stone footbridge beyond. Interesting town. Saxon church. At farm on L of Barton Bridge ½ ml. below, old tithe barn.

17¼   *Avoncliff Weir.* Steep weir. In low water lift down beside mill. If necessary portage to below aqueduct. The L bank above the mill is fenced off and padlocked. Owner at house nearby. Inn L. Railway Halt R. Weedy.

18¼   Confl. of R. Frome. Freshford Village L ¼ ml. below (stn.).

19½   *Lympley Stoke Weir.* Steep weir. Normally land at grassy ledge L just before mill or at other parts if water is low, and lift down over weir. In high water weir not passable and a very long portage is involved, about ½ ml; land R 100 yds. before weir, portage across paddock and along path and canal towpath and canal, where water starts, carrying down steps to river at aqueduct. Stones and shallows below weir. At road bridge take centre arches, fast current. In low water a drop into pool below the bridge, which can be shot except in very low water. Inspect to see if obstructed by masonry below step. Stn. ¼ ml.

20½   *Monkton Combe Aqueduct.* Kennet and Avon Canal.

21¾   *Warleigh* or *Claverton Weir.* Lower down extreme L or carry from mill cut through fields to steps at ferry.

23¾   *Bathford.* Village R. Inn. Halt ¼ ml.

24½   *Batheaston Bridge and Weir.* Land on R of mill cut over boat slip. Bathampton Stn. ½ ml.

25½   *Bath Lido and Boating Station.*

26   *Bath, Pulteney Bridge and Weir.* Land L in backwater below bridge and lower down steps at side. Care required in high water. Many places of interest in Bath. Landing at public slipway on L below weir. River now a navigation.

27   *Junction of Kennet and Avon Canal*, L. Bath Spa Stn. nearby. Access on R upstream of steel footbridge and up steep path through gardens (permission at stn.). River uninteresting through the town.

29   *Weston Lock* : on R branch. Lock fees 6d. per lock.

31   *Kelston Park* R.

32¼   *Saltford Weir and Lock.* Boathouse L. Cafe. Stn. L. Portage over weir R.

33   *Kelston Lock and Weir.* Weir can be shot in high water, after examination, but carrying at lock advised. Inn L.

34   *Swineford Lock and Weir.* Weir unshootable.

Miles

36½   *Keynsham Weir and Lock.* Most convenient finishing point unless going on to Bristol. Stn. ¼ ml. L. Boat hire stn, cafe, etc. Lift down weir R. Confl. of Chew.

38½   *Hanham Ferry, Lock and Weir.* Weir unshootable. Inn and ferry R. Port of Bristol Authority controls river below here.

40½   Ferry. Boathouses and tea gardens.

42   *Netham Weir.* Dangerous ; keep well to R bank to avoid current. Entrance to Feeder Canal R through lock. Permit—fee 10s. —required from Dock Master, Welsh Back, Bristol 1. Water dirty and oily. (River tidal below weir and best avoided. High water 45 min. before Bristol.)

43   Entrance to Bristol upper docks. Landing on L for Temple Meads Stn.

44   *Bristol Bridge.* Bascule Bridge ¼ ml. below.

44½   Swing bridge ; floating harbour.

45½   *Hotwells Locks and Bridges* into tidal river. Clifton Gorge and suspension bridge just below. Very great rise and fall in tides (22 to 33 ft.) and muddy banks. Trips need to be carefully timed.

    High Water Bristol : Dover - 4 hours 20 min.

48½   *Sea Mills Stn.* R.

50   *Pill* L.

52   *Avonmouth.*

130. BRUE

From its source near Bruton the Brue flows generally WNW past Glastonbury and across the levels to Highbridge, below which it flows into the estuary of the Parrett. Reported to be practicable from Alford some 2 miles from Castle Cary Station though the upper parts have many places overgrown with branches and brambles. There are two or three mills and one or two hamlets before the Brue reaches the levels near Glastonbury, an interesting place. Beyond Glastonbury the course of the river has been artificially straightened and is less interesting except to those who like a fenland landscape.

Approx. Distances : Alford-Glastonbury 10 miles.
                 Glastonbury-Highbridge 13 miles.

The **Huntspill River,** an artificial channel from Gold Court (at the corner of "Old Canal" west of former Edington station) across Huntspill Moor to the Parrett Estuary near "The Island," is canoeable and provides good sailing if the wind is in the right quarter. Access from A.38 at West Huntspill, or via "Old Canal."

O.S. 165 ; Barth. 7

131. PARRETT

The Parrett rises on the Dorset border N of Beaminster and flows NNW through Langport to the Bristol Channel at Burnham-on-Sea. With its tributaries, Tone and Yeo, it flows through a district which, in spite of its flatness has a beauty of its own, rich in historical and legendary associations, especially King Arthur and the Monmouth Rebellion.

Starting point at Petherton Bridge on the Fosse Way near South Petherton Village. As far as Langport plenty of water, good current, low banks, a few weirs which involve easy portages. Below Langport strongly tidal, high muddy banks, difficult landings. There is a tidal bore all the year round, varying with tide and wind from a mere ripple to a high, swift wave ; at its maximum at Bridgwater, dies out above Burrow Bridge.

Miles

0	*Petherton Bridge*, on Fosse Way. Shops, inn, etc., at South Petherton, 1 ml. W.
4	*Kingston Episcopi*. Village L, shops, inn.
5½	*Thorney Mill*. Road bridge.
6	Confl. of Isle L.
7	*Muchelney Bridge*. Abbey ruins R, worth visiting.
8	Confl. of Yeo R.
9½	*Langport Bridge*. Market town R.
12½	*Stathe* L.
14	*Burrow Bridge*. Confl. of Tone L just above Inn "King Alfred's Fort."
20	*Bridgwater*. Stn. Landing possible at steps by bridge, or, at certain states of the tide, at slipway. Below here high mud banks for many miles to mouth in Bristol Channel, and this stretch is not recommended.

O.S. 177, 165 ; Barth. 4, 7

132. Yeo and Isle

A tributary of the Parrett, the **Yeo** rises near Sherborne and flows NW through Yeovil and Ilchester to the Parrett at Langport. Attempts have in the past been made to canalize it.

Below Yeovil some pretty stretches, but upper part is narrow, with several mills, and may be choked with weed. At Yeovil both railway stations are near river, but above sewage works. Ilchester, on the Fosse Way, has shops and an inn, and but for the absence of rail access is probably a better starting point (9 miles from Yeovil). Thence 9 miles to Langport across fen country.

The **Isle**, a tributary of the Parrett, is canoeable from Ilminster in winter after rain when there is plenty of water. Fast current at first, later slower and meandering ; always narrow. Not very pretty. Four mills or weirs. Ilminster—junction with Parrett 12¼ miles.

O.S. 177 ; Barth. 4

133. Tone

The Tone rises in Brendon Hills and flows S to Wellington, then NE through Taunton to the Parrett at Burrow Bridge.

Practicable in good water from Wellington; many small rapids. Obstructions, such as fallen trees, brambles, wire, may make the stretch above Bishop's Hull very awkward, and some wading will be necessary in low water. Below Taunton a number of weirs necessitate portages until tidal influence is felt below Creech St. Michael.

O.S. 164, 177, 165 ; Barth. 4, 7

Miles

0	*Wellington (Som.).* Stn. $\frac{1}{2}$ ml. from river.
4	*Bradford.* Mills.
6	*Hele.* Several weirs.
6$\frac{3}{4}$	*Norton Fitzwarren.* Stn. close to river.
7$\frac{3}{4}$	*Bishops Hull Bridge.* Rapid under : hidden rock R at low water. Line down.
9	*Taunton : French Weir.* Portage through recreation ground.
9$\frac{1}{2}$	*Taunton Bridge.* Landing R up side creek. County town, shops. If starting at Taunton, go down hill from rly. stn., turn L after second rly. bridge and L again to swing gate leading to footpath near goods stn.
10	*Firepool Lock and Weir.* Stay in R channel and portage L just above sluices, before footbridge. Stumps below sluices.
11$\frac{1}{2}$	Weir. Portage L above weir. Bathpool Bridge.
13	*Creech St. Michael Weir.* Portage R near sluices. A second weir just below ; lower down L and use slipway. Tidal influence below here.
14$\frac{1}{2}$	*Ham Half Lock.* In medium and low water gate levers visible. In high water keep in centre.
15$\frac{3}{4}$	*Knapp Bridge.* Banks very muddy below here.
20	*Isle of Athelney.* Monument.
21	*Burrow Bridge.* Junction with Parrett.

134. TAUNTON CANAL

A pleasant alternative to the Tone and Parrett. Runs from Taunton to Bridgwater and can be used to make a round trip.

Five locks which must be portaged : 15 miles long : starting point near Taunton goods station (see Tone). Railway stations adjoin at Creech St. Michael and Durston. (S.W. Division.)

O.S. 177, 165 ; Barth. 4, 7

WALES (including Wye and Dee)

135. WYE

The Wye rises on Plynlimon Fawr near the source of the Severn, and flows SW through Builth to Glasbury then NE and E to Hereford and finally S, with numerous turns ending with a magnificent 40 mile stretch between wooded hills and cliffs to the Severn Estuary near Chepstow. Apart from the Thames it is probably the most popular and satisfying river in England and Wales for the average canoeist.

Most of the railways shown on the map are now closed or abandoned. Bus services between Hereford, Ross, Monmouth and Chepstow. Also from Hereford Bus Stn. near rly. stn. to Whitney, Hay and Glasbury.

As with all mountain rivers the upper reaches of the Wye are only navigable in favourable water. From Glasbury, one is fairly certain, at any time of the year, to find enough water to take a canoe, though in a dry season even this starting point may involve some wading.

Above the confluence of the Elan near Rhayader the river is only for the very experienced and is only possible on a few days each year. From Pant Mawr past Llangurig to Dernol (all adjoining A.44) the river bed is mostly pebbly, with an occasional rocky fall and many gravelly rapids. Between Dernol and Rhayader the Wye has cut a deep rocky gorge, which is usually impracticable, but in times of spate gives Rough Water III-IV conditions with some impracticable places.

Between the Elan and Glasbury there are a number of heavy rapids the difficulties of which change quickly with changes in water level, and this stretch should only be attempted by those with previous rough water experience. In high water spray covers essential. (Grading— Rough Water II-III.)

Below Glasbury there are few difficulties (Grading I with long stretches of smooth water). This is the normal starting point for a Wye cruise and with a total fall of 300 feet gives 100 miles of enjoyable canoeing without a portage.

It would be useless, if not impossible, to mention all the minor rapids of the Wye below Glasbury, for the river rises and falls quickly, and a foot of water, more or less, makes an enormous difference. In low water much shallow "white water" will be seen, but in times of even moderate flood the river below Glasbury flows black and heavy, with all the small rapids covered over, and with only the larger rapids as Monnington Falls, Lydbrook and Symonds Yat to give a change from the fast but smooth going.

Far from all industrial areas, the Wye Valley is quite unspoiled and shows a variety of scenery along its course, the most outstanding parts being below Kerne Bridge where the river flows between high wooded cliffs, and in the final reaches between Tintern and Chepstow. If the Wye has any fault at all it is that the tidal part is so very muddy that any landing is extremely uncomfortable, but this may be reduced to a minimum by running through from Tintern at high tide, in order to arrive at Chepstow before the tide has fallen far. This tidal part should not be missed, for the beauty of the river reaches its culmination in this stretch. The estuary below Chepstow is not recommended, though it is possible to make a crossing of the Severn to reach the Bristol Avon and return to London via the Avon, Kennet and Avon Canal and River Thames.

Above Glasbury prior permission should be sought for a number of places. Advice from B.C.U. Below Hay the Wye is an open navigation.

High Tide at Chepstow : Dover − 3 hours 55 min.

O.S. 128, 141, 142, 155 ; Barth. 17, 13

Miles

0   *Rhayader Bridge.*

1   Awkward fall : inspect.

2   *Confl. of R. Elan* R. River now wide and shallow with no definite channel for 4 miles.

4   *Doldowlod.*

8¾   *Newbridge on Wye.*

10¼   *Confl. of R. Eithon* L. (Has been canoed from Cross Gates on A.44 above Llandrindod Wells in good water.).

14½   *Builth Road Railway Bridge.* Builth Road Stn. L. (Shrewsbury - Craven Arms-Swansea Line).

14¾   River is very rocky and there is a rapid that should be inspected. The first part is a narrow fall with exposed rocks on L and in centre in low water. The second, 50 yds. below, is a five-foot drop on an S bend, narrow, channel on R. Heavy in high water. Portage R available. After that no difficulty to Builth Wells Bridge, except line of stakes ½ ml. before the bridge. Keep extreme R.

16   *Builth Wells.* Recreation ground on R bank above bridge. Shallows under bridge followed by deep rapid. Take second arch from L. Staff gauge on upstream side of bridge near R bank. If gauge shows less than 1 ft. much wading necessary.

16¾   Rocky shallows, channel R.

18   *Llanfaredd.*

18¼   *Llanfaredd Rapids* (½ ml. long). The first of three stretches where the river breaks through outcrops of rock forming reefs extending across the whole river bed. The reefs slope upwards and in a downstream direction. River confined mainly to a very deep, narrow channel usually on right-hand side of river bed. Halfway down is a ledge *which should be inspected.* At the end of the rapid is a "weir" made of an iron girder held in place by stakes—unshootable ; there are shallows to the L.

174

Miles

18¾   *Boatside Farm.* On L bank at pool at end of rapids.

20½   *Aberedw.* Inn L.

20¾   *Alltmawr.* On main road R.

21½   Fishing weir runs out obliquely from L bank. Shoot at extreme R.

22   *Erwood Rapids* (¾ ml. long). Fishing lodge (L bank) of corrugated iron painted red, marks beginning of second stretch of reefs. Rocks are horizontal. Long, narrow, straight channel with ledge a quarter of way through, *which should be inspected.* After a wide pool channel starts again in centre then round to L with a fall between two large rocks, then long, narrow channel between rocks.

23¼   *Erwood Bridge.* Inn L "Caban Twm Bach".

23½   *Erwood.* Village and inn on main road R.

24½   Rocky rapid without defined channel. *Inspect.*

24¾   *Llanstephan Rapids* (¾ ml. long). Third, and most difficult of three stretches of reefs. Reefs slope upwards and upstream, so that the water breaks against the edge of the reefs. Begins as Llanstephan (suspension) Bridge comes into sight. The second part of this rapid *must always be inspected*, and a *portage is essential* at most states of water. At first a long, narrow, clear channel on R. Second part is a very narrow, rocky channel on extreme R (4 to 5 ft. wide) down a ledge, forming a heavy rapid which breaks on to a point of rock. If the bow of the canoe is carried to the R of this rock the boat could not be prevented from jamming between the rocks and would probably be smashed. Portage over rocks on R bank round this place (40 yds.) not difficult.

25¾   *Llanstephan Bridge.* Ledge under bridge—channel in centre.

26¾   *Llangoed Rapid.* River flows over rocky step. Channel on R of island near bank—*inspect.*

28   *Boughrood Bridge.*

28¼   *Llyswen.* Village and inn on main road R.

28½   River doubles back and forms a rocky rapid with at first undefined channel past a mill and abutments of old rly bridge. After two or three small "runs" the character of the river changes completely. From this point the main obstacles are shingle banks and shallows. Navigation easy. (Difficulty I with long stretches of smooth water.)

32   *Glasbury Bridge.* Launch near bridge on L bank. Shops, Inn.

36¾   *Wyecliffe Weir.* Caution. Passage at extreme R.

37½   *Hay Bridge.* Good shops in town. Launch near bridge on L bank. Rocky rapids below.

40   *Clifford Castle.* Inn R.

41   *Rhydspence.* Inn L.

42   *Whitney Bridges.* Inn and shop L. Launch near bridge R bank.

Miles

47¼   *"Turner's Boat."* Channel on R of island impracticable. Fallen trees where river narrows just beyond.

50½   *Bredwardine Bridge.* Inn R. Notices prohibit landing.

53½   *Moccas Court* R.

54½   *Bycross Ferry.*

54¾   *Monnington Falls.* River divided by island. Narrow L channel falls over rocky ledge. Shallow descent on R. Land on L bank to inspect channel before taking the fall as passage may be obstructed by fallen trees.

57½   *Bridge Sollers.*

61½   *Lower Eaton* R. Ferry and inn.

66½   *Hereford Bridge.* Stn. ¾ ml. through town. Shops. Cathedral. Boathouses above bridge. Numerous places for launching on R bank near bridge.

70   "Bunch of Carrots" Inn L.

73   *Holme Lacy.* R.

74   *Confl. of Lugg* L. ½ ml. upstream to Mordiford Bridge. (See Section 136.)

74½   Road bridge. Inn L.

81   *Carey Bridge.* River divided by island ½ ml. above the bridge. Keep to R channel.

82¾   *Hoarwithy Bridge.* Inn and shop in the village R.

84   *Sellack Bridge.* Suspension footbridge.

86   *Strangford Railway Bridge.*

90   *Hole-in-the-Wall.* Islands with small rapids between.

90½   *Foy Bridge.* Suspension footbridge.

92   *Backney Railway Bridge.* Rapid above bridge.

93   Motorway bridge.

94   *Ross-on-Wye.* Shops. Interesting town.

94½   *Wilton Bridge.* Shallow below. Centre arch then over to R.

98½   *Goodrich Court and Goodrich Castle* R. The castle is worth a visit. Ancient monument.

99½   *Kerne Bridge.* Inns L.

102   *Lydbrook.* Welsh Bicknor R (youth hostel). Rapid. Channel leads from L to R.

102¾   *Welsh Bicknor Railway Bridge.*

104   *Huntsham Cliff* L.

106¼   *Huntsham Bridge.*

108¾   *Symonds Yat.* Straight running rapid. Quite deep water.

111   Shallows and island.

113   *Dixton Church.* R bank close to river.

114   *Monmouth Bridge.* Landing at boathouse before bridge. Shops. Monnow Bridge worth a visit.

114½   *Confl. of Monnow* (see Section 137) and two railway bridges. Confused series of rapids below Monnow. Keep L at first. then take rapid below first bridge on R. Beware hidden rocks.

116¾   *Redbrook.* Railway bridge and inn. Straight running rapid. Rocks in river.

120   *Bigsweir Bridge.* Limit of tides (approx.).

120½   *Bigs Weir.* Rapid to L round island. At high water channel to R of island may be possible. Between this point and Chepstow are ground weirs which may be covered at high tide but form rapids at low water. None are difficult but care is necessary.

121¼   *Llandogo.* Next good landing at Tintern except at high water. *Ridingstream Weir.*

122   *Coed Ithel Weir.*

123½   *Brockweir Bridge.*

124   *Tintern Railway Bridge.*
    Lyn Weir immediately below.

124½   *Tintern Parva.*

125   *Tintern Abbey.* Inn R. Rapid at low water under bridge. Land either bank 100 yds. below bridge near abbey. Small wooden landing stage on R bank : on L bank the masonry of old ferry slipway is covered at high tide. This is the last good landing before Chepstow. From this point the river should only be attempted at high water. For several hours at low water only the natural flow of the river passes at Tintern. The rise and fall of the tide on the Wye at Chepstow may exceed 30 ft. At low water between Tintern and Chepstow a succession of weirs is exposed and they may be awkward. At high water the run is easy and safe and the scenery magnificent. The best time to leave Tintern is between ½ and 1 hr. before the time of high water at Chepstow, i.e. about 1 hr. or so before the tide turns at Tintern.

132   *Chepstow Bridge.* Land on R at the steps below the road bridge or at stone slipway a few yards lower downstream R. If the tide is too low there will be a stretch of mud to cross over to reach steps or slipway. Do not go below the railway bridge.

The navigation of the Severn Estuary is not recommended, but for those who, nevertheless, desire to cross to the Avon, see Section 128.

136. Lugg

The Lugg rises in the hills of Radnor Forest, but is not so rapid as the Wye, which it joins at Mordiford, a few miles below Hereford. It has a winding course through lovely country with low wooded hills, at times between very high banks. It passes through the park of Hampton Court, a historic mansion belonging to Lord Hereford.

The Lugg is usually canoeable from Leominster, above which it is strictly preserved. At one time in the 18th century it was made navigable up to Leominster.

Grading : Rough Water I.

Rail access at Leominster.

O.S. 129, 142 ; Barth. 18, 13

Miles

0	*Leominster.* Several bridges. River divides—use Kenwater channel if starting in the town.
1¼	*Eaton Bridge* (A.44). A convenient starting point.
1¾	Weir with arch over : may be shootable, or portage R.
2¾	Confl. of River Arrow R.
4½	*Ford Bridge.*
6	*Hampton Bridge.*
7½	*Hampton Court* L. The weir is unshootable—line down or portage L.
8½	*Bodenham Bridge.* Village R.
10½	*Dinmore Rly. Bridge.*
13	Rly. Bridge.
14½	*Laystone Bridge.*
16	*Moreton Bridge.*
17½	*Wergins Bridge.* Old Hereford and Gloucester Canal aqueduct below—now demolished.
19¼	Rly. bridge.
20	*Lugg Bridge* (A.465). Hereford 2 mls. R. Mill channel just below bridge may be shot.
22	*Lugwardine Bridge* (A.438).
22½	*Site of Tidnor Weir,* now completely washed away.
25½	*Mordiford Bridge.* Fast water through old mill channel ; keep L ; caution.
26	*Confl. with Wye.*

137. Monnow

The Monnow rises in the Black Mountains and flows SE to the Hereford at Monmouth. A very lovely river flowing through quite remote country, it is very sporting when it carries sufficient water. Probably spring and late autumn are the best times. This is not a river for the beginner, and it is turbulent when in spate.

There is convenient access at Monmouth Cap Bridge, near Pontrilas. There are weirs at Kentchurch, Garway, Skenfrith, 3 between there and Rockfield, and 3 more to the junction with the Wye at Monmouth : some of these are in process of being washed away. A long stretch of rocky rapids below Kentchurch Bridge. Grosmont and Skenfrith both have ruined castles and interesting churches. Distance from Monmouth Cap Bridge to the Wye—approx. 19 miles.

N.B. In recent years there have been objections to canoeing on the Monnow. Advice from B.C.U.

Grading : Rough Water II.

O.S. 142 ; Barth. 13

138. USK and BRECON CANAL

The **Usk** rises on the borders of Carmarthen and Brecknock, flows E to Brecon, then SE through Abergavenny and Usk, and then sweeps round SW to the Severn Estuary S of Newport. An upland river all the way, it flows along a beautiful valley—at first bounded by mountains, then more open—all the way to Caerleon. Being usually broad, it is often very shallow and rockstrewn after dry weather and is then not usually worth attempting ; it is subject to sudden spates after rain in the hills.

Some parts above Crickhowell are really tricky, wild water and should only be attempted by experienced canoeists in single-seaters ; when the river is in flood these become really difficult. But the difficult stretches between Brecon and Crickhowell can be avoided by taking the Brecon Canal to Llangattock (short portage to Crickhowell); this is just as beautiful as the river and follows it closely. Even in low water the Usk is not easy, and fast water continues all the way down. Fallen trees should be watched for along the wooded stretches, and for this reason all corners should be taken with circumspection.

The tide reaches to Tredunnock at springs, and all authorities speak with great respect of the mud below this point—it is like that on the Wye below Tintern, only more so. As with the Wye the tidal rise and fall is very great.

Grading (low to medium water):

        Senny Bridge-Crickhowell—Rough Water III.

        Crickhowell-Tredunnock—Rough Water II.

        Below Tredunnock—Tidal.

The Usk is canoeable from Senny Bridge. Rail access only at Abergavenny.

The Usk is private water with important fishing interests. It should not be attempted without (or against) advice from the B.C.U. Between Abergavenny and Usk there are notices in a number of places prohibiting canoeing.

O.S. 141, 142, 155 ; Barth. 17, 13, 12

Miles

0	*Senny Bridge.* Village, cafe. Shallow below.
½	Road bridge. River is canoeable when boulder below centre pier of bridge shows approx. 1 ft., though shallows will be met with. River very lively, passing through a wooded valley.
1	River bends sharply to R, with high bank on L and an island ; just round the corner is a 3 ft. drop, shootable near R bank ; 200 yds. further on is a weir (unshootable); portage R.
1¾	Rocky fall—line down on R.
3	Rly. bridge. Awkward rapids and heavy water.
3½	Fall. Line down on R ; shootable in favourable water. River remains lively and interesting.
5½	*Penpont.* Weir, shallows below.
5¾	*Aberbran Bridge.*
7¼	*Aberyscir* L. Confl. of Yscir L. Slow, deep stretches alternating with difficult rapids.

Miles

9   *Llanspyddyd* R. Woods, heavy rapid : the river runs against a large rock which turns it through 90 deg. to L ; then placid.

11   *Brecon Weir and Bridge.* Town, shops L. The weir is above the town and in good water can be shot on L of centre island. In low water line down. There is a ledge under the bridge. On the downstream side of the bridge there is a gauge ; *from this point the directions describe conditions at a reading of 3 inches or a little more. In spate the difficulties to Crickhowell would be much greater.* End of Brecon Canal L (see below).
    Below Brecon the river is fairly easy for some way.

12¾   *Dinas* R.

13¼   Confl. of Cynrig R.

14   *Abercynrig Bridge and Canal Aqueduct.* Broken water and rocks continue to—

14¾   *Millbrook Mill.* In good water the weir can be shot at the notch to the R of the centre ; 150 yds. of rocks below.

15¼   *Llanhamlach* L.

16   *Penkelly* R. Castle.

18¼   At bend to the R where river is close to A.40 a tree blocks the whole channel (1959).

18½   Island.

19   *Talybont-on-Usk Bridges* (*Llansantffread*). Excellent view, well worth the climb, from NW end of the hill called Allt-yr-esgair on L bank. River deep and slow for about 1½ mls. and then, after a small diagonal weir (composed of stakes), it is consistently difficult all the way to Glan Usk. (The canal is available as an alternative from Talybont to Llangattock.)

21   *Mill House Weir* (recognisable by the fish weathervane on the house which has a balcony above the river and belongs to Sir Roy Fedden). In low and medium water the weir is shootable on the L of the big rock in centre. In the rocks and broken water below, cross to the R and then to L. ½ ml. further on there is a tricky stretch through rocks which demands skill. River rocky and fairly fast to Llangynidr.

22   *Llandetty Hall* R.

24   *Llangynidr Bridge.* Above the bridge a rapid starts : go L of island, cross R, under the bridge, then keep R for 200 yds. to a diagonal step to the L, then R again to a heavy rapid.

26   *Gliffaes* (*near*). River bends to L between steep woods. Heavy fall, unshootable in low water. In favourable water it can be shot, *after inspection*, by crossing the stream nearly to L bank, then turning R about 6 ft. from the drop, and bearing L with the force of the water whilst actually going over. (*Do not try this without being quite sure what you are going to do.*) After some quiet water comes the *"Hundred Yard Straight"*, a confused stretch with rocks.

180

27   Island. Keep L.

29   *Glan Usk Bridge and Park.* Quieter water.

30½   *Crickhowell Bridge.* Village, shops, inns L.   Llangattock R.
       Below here the river is fairly easy but rather shallow.

34½   *Glangrwyney Bridge.* Rapid below, with trees about ½ ml. along—
       caution : line down in low water.

36   *Tymawr.* Rapid. Broken down weir on a corner is troublesome
       in low water. Trees on the corners should be watched for,
       and also stakes anywhere between here and Abergavenny.

39   *Abergavenny Railway and Road Bridges.* Town, shops, inns L.
       Row of steel piles across river below road bridge.   At
       moderate levels about 8 in. of water over the top and a drop
       of 9 in.—portage advisable. For Abergavenny Monmouth
       Road Stn. (main line), continue ½ ml. beyond road bridge
       and land L bank just beyond a stream which flows in on L.
       Go up path and turn R into main road and follow this till
       station road is reached. At Abergavenny the valley opens
       out ; the river remains fast but less difficult ; rapids are
       usually fast runs over a pebbly bed. The scenery remains
       good.

40½   Motorway bridge.

42   *Llanelen Bridge.* Village R.

44   *Llanover* R.

45   Railway bridge. Island and shallows.

47   Rapid.

47¾   *Llanvihangel-nigh-Usk Bridge.*

49½   *Trostrey Lodge.* Weirs.

50   *Brynderwen.* Rapids.

51¼   *Chain Bridge, Nantyderry.* Kemeys Commander ½ ml. L. Several
       rapids below bridge.

54   *Trostrey* L. Weir. Several rapids follow.

56   *Rhadyr Mill.*

57½   *Usk Bridge.* Town L. Stn. closed.

63½   *Newbridge, Tredunnock.* Tide flows to here at springs. Wait for
       high water as the mud is worse than on the Wye at Chepstow
       further down.

69½   *Caerleon Bridge.* Town and stn. R. Roman remains. Landing is
       difficult beyond here until Newport, owing to the mud,
       except at high water.

High Water : Dover—4 hours 9 min. (Newport).

The **Brecon Canal** is, for most of its length, scenically one of the
finest canals in England and Wales. Connecting Newport and Brecon,
it rises by 31 locks in its first 7 miles from Newport, after which it runs
level without any more locks for 25 miles to Llangynidr, mostly along
the side of the hills a couple of hundred feet above the Usk. The canal
is now disused as a commercial waterway, but is now in good order
between Pontymoyle and Talybont, and canoes can easily get to Brecon
in spite of 5 disused lifting bridges. The views are extensive, the water
clear. There are five locks at Llangynidr, and another between there

and Brecon. A trip along the canal to Brecon would make a first-class preliminary (given road transport for the 12 miles from Brecon to Glasbury) to a trip down the Wye, and it can be used to avoid the worst places on the Usk (see Section 138). The canal is weedy in the latter part of the summer.

The best points of access are at Pontymoyle aqueduct (Pontypool Road Stn. Newport-Hereford-Shrewsbury line), Talybont and Brecon. It is not worth starting nearer to Newport than Griffithstown, owing to the frequency of locks and the bad state of the canal. British Waterways, Govilon, near Abergavenny, issue an itinerary and permits.

O.S. 141, 142, 155 ; Barth. 17, 12

Miles

0	*Newport.* **31** locks in **7** mls. to Pontnewydd.
8¼	*Griffithstown.* Panteg Stn. nearby R.
9	*Pontymoyle Aqueduct.* Pontypool Road Stn. R.
20¼	*Llanfoist.* Abergavenny 1½ mls. R.
21¾	*Govilon.*
27	*Llangattock.* Crickhowell R. 1 ml.
32	*Llangynidr.* 5 locks.
34	Tunnel.
35½	*Talybont.*
40¼	Aqueduct over Usk. Brynich lock.
42¼	*Brecon.*

139. TAFF

Rises in the Brecon Beacons and flows through Merthyr Tydfil and Pontypridd to Llandaff and Cardiff. Like all mountain streams water levels are very variable. For about 8 miles about halfway between Merthyr and Pontypridd it flows through a narrow defile, which is impracticable in low water, and gives very heavy and severe rapids in flood (Grading III-IV). There are impracticable falls at Quaker's Yard, followed by a 7 foot weir. At the outskirts of Pontypridd is another impracticable fall. Below the bridge at Treforest is a sheer 14 foot weir, after which rapids are easier. Two more weirs before Llandaff, and another two to Cardiff. The distance from Merthyr Vale is about 23 miles. Anyone considering an attempt to canoe the Taff is advised to consult the Llandaff Canoe Club beforehand.

140. TOWY

The Towy (or Tywi) rises near the source of the Teifi and flows S and SW through Llandovery and Carmarthen to Carmarthen Bay. No weirs or portages from Rhandir-mwyn to Carmarthen and the scenery is fine. Above Llandovery the character of the river is quite difficult ; there are rock-walls, gorges and falls ; below it flows through a wide valley between hills and mountains with fine views all the way. There are a number of castle ruins close by. This stretch is fairly consistent : a fast current with shingly shallows and rapids ; wide and winding after Llandilo, with moderate current and few shallows.

There have recently been objections to canoeing on parts of the Towy. Advice from the BCU.

Grading : Above Llandovery—Rough Water III.
       Below Llandovery—Rough Water I.

Coracles are still in use on the Towy.

The **Gwili,** a tributary of the Towy just above Carmarthen is canoeable for a short distance. The Shrewsbury-Builth Road-Swansea line follows the Towy from Llandovery to Llandilo; thereafter the Carmarthen branch. Above Llandovery access only by road.

O.S. 140, 152 ; Barth. 17, 11

Miles

0	*Bron-y-cwrt Bridge.* Rocks below.
1	*Rhandir-mwyn Bridge.* Fast, shallow. $\frac{1}{2}$ ml. below barbed-wire across river.
2	Rapids into gorge and within gorge.
$2\frac{1}{4}$	*Dol-achddu Falls* and rapids. At the fall the stream banks up against a rock wall and an eddy goes round pool, while to the L the separated flow goes into rapids on L of elbow. In heavy water some difficulty in keeping away from the rock face. But in heavy water fall may be shot on extreme L. Mainly gorge to—
$4\frac{1}{4}$	*Cilycwm Bridge.* (Y.H. near Cilycwm Village R.)
$5\frac{1}{2}$	*R. Gwenlas* R. Falls into gorge and rapids at Danant and at—
$5\frac{3}{4}$	*Pont Newydd.* Gorge widens out.
$6\frac{1}{4}$	Rapid as river leaves road, goes towards road on other side of valley.
$7\frac{1}{4}$	Rapid under Troed-y-rhiw. Rock shelves R, keep close to gorge wall R. Restricted channel.
$7\frac{3}{4}$	*Dolau-hirion Rapids and Bridge.* Three short drops. Wide and confused entry into rapid, first fall 70 yds. above Dolau-hirion, last fall under bridge. Keep close L 10 yds. above, then quick R to avoid rock below fall almost dead centre. Passage is very narrow and usually tumultuous. The river quietens gradually till it assumes its new character.
$8\frac{1}{2}$	*Llandovery Bridge.* Stn. and town L. Wide valley, shallow, shingly rapids with numerous channels. Grading : Rough Water I.
$9\frac{1}{2}$	Rly. bridge.
$13\frac{1}{2}$	*Llanwrda.* Stn. and village R.
$14\frac{1}{2}$	Rly. bridge.
$15\frac{1}{2}$	*Llangadock Bridge.* Stn. and village L.
$17\frac{1}{2}$	Rly. bridge.
23	*Llandilo.* Stn. and town R.
$23\frac{1}{2}$	Rly. bridge.
$23\frac{3}{4}$	*Llandilo Bridge.*
$26\frac{3}{4}$	*Cilsan Bridge.*
$30\frac{1}{4}$	*Dryslwyn Bridge.* Castle ruins R.
32	*Llanarthney.*
$33\frac{1}{2}$	Rly. bridge.
35	Road bridge. Confl. of Cothi $\frac{1}{4}$ ml. before.
$39\frac{3}{4}$	Confl. of Gwili.
$41\frac{1}{2}$	*Carmarthen Bridge.* Town R, stn. L. River now tidal. The estuary continues for 9 mls. to Ferryside (stn. L). The coast can be followed westward to Saundersfoot; the estuary of the *Taf* can be explored to Laugharne.

141. MILFORD HAVEN

A long, winding inlet of the sea in the SW corner of Wales, with a number of side branches. Rail access at Haverfordwest, at the head of the Western Cleddau branch, at Pembroke Dock, Pembroke Town, and Milford Haven. The tides run fairly strongly, except in Dale Roads. High water at Pembroke : Dover - 5 hours.

O.S. 151 ; Barth. 11

Miles   *Distances from Haverfordwest—*
 5¾ *Junction with Eastern Cleddau.* Picton Castle L ; the Eastern Cleddau can be followed to Canaston Bridge, 4¾ mls. from the junction.
 7   *Blacktar Quay* R. This part is called the Daucleddau.
 9½ *Lawrenny Ferry.* On L the branch leads—
         (i) *Cresswell River*—to Cresswell Quay 2½ mls.
         (ii) *Carew River*—to Carew Castle (ruins) 3 mls.
         The whole of this upper part of the Haven has very charming scenery.
11¾ *Cosheston Creek* L. 1¾ mls. long.
12¾ *Hobbs Point Ferry, Pembroke Dock* L. Neyland on R. Best landing for Pembroke Dock Town—good for supplies.
14½ *Pennar Creek* (*Pembroke River*) L. 3 mls. up this to Pembroke town ; fine castle.
17½ *Milford Haven* R. Below here the Haven widens considerably, and there are a number of bays, roads and creeks (*Sandy Haven, Angle Bay, Dale Roads*). Angle and Dale villages both interesting. Fine rocky coast nearby. Oil tanker jetty and installations.
23   *St. Anne's Head.*

142. TEIFI

Unlike many rivers the Teifi (or Tivy) starts free from hazard and becomes more difficult as it approaches the sea. It rises in the hills of Cardiganshire, near Strata Florida, and runs by Tregaron and Lampeter to the sea near Cardigan.

The Teifi has been canoed from Strata Florida. It is, however, apt to be very shallow all the way through Pontrhydfendigaid as far as the railway bridge about ¼ mile from Strata Florida station, and for the next 8 miles runs across a great marsh, with some sharp twists, and low footbridges, but always a good current. The Teifi Bridge at Tregaron is some ¾ mile from the station, so if coming by rail a start is more conveniently made at Pont Llanio, where the station adjoins the river. The river flows for the next 15 miles through an open valley, and the real rapids do not begin until Llanllwni is reached. A portage is probably necessary at Llandyssul and absolutely imperative at Henllan and Cenarth.

The Teifi offers some of the most sporting wild water in the British Isles, and the scenery is good all the way.

Bus services: Aberystwyth-Tregaron; Tregaron-Lampeter (Crosville, Crane Wharf, Chester); Lampeter-Newcastle Emlyn (Gwalia, Llanybyther); Llandyssul-Cardigan (Western Welsh, Cowbridge Road, Cardiff).

Four to five days are not too much to allow for the Teifi.

Grading : Generally—Rough Water II. Llandyssul Rapids III, except last two, IV. Henllan Falls impossible. Newcastle Emlyn Rapid III. Cenarth Falls impossible.

O.S. 139, 140 ; Barth. 17

Miles

0　　*Tregaron.* Shops. River placid but barbed-wire may be encountered in the next 6 mls.

5　　*Pont Llanio* (bridge). Inn L.

5¾　*Felin Llanio* (mill). Weir—portage (shootable in high water). Loventium (Roman remains) R.

7½　*Pont Gogoyan* (bridge).

7¾　*Felin Gogoyan* (mill). Small weir ; portage may be necessary. The country here is open, and there are few houses ; river deep, sometimes weedy. It follows a rather lonely valley away from road and rly., and with good views of the hills.

10　　*Llanfair-Clydogau Bridge.* Inn and shop R. Village L. Swift run 300 yds., with tree in middle of main stream, followed by barbed wire.

10½　Small weir.

12　　*Cellan.* On L above footbridge. Barbed wire may be encountered below here.

14　　*Lampeter.* Rly. and road bridge (Pont Stephen). Landing R below bridge. Town R. River now widens, banks become higher, and scenery less pretty for a while. Many windings.

19　　*Confl. of Afon Grannell* R. Two or three easy rapids before—

21　　*Llanybyther.* Shallow rapid under bridge. Inn (Black Lion) and stn. L. Village. Scenery becomes more wooded.

25¾　*Llanllwni Rapids and Fall.* River turns sharply R towards a high wooded cliff, then L ; two rapids as Llanllwni Church—square tower—comes into view on L lead to the fall between two big rocks. Rocks in the stream below the fall make it awkward to shoot, especially at low water. Inspect before deciding whether to shoot or portage.

26　　*Llanllwni Bridge.* Village L ; shop 100 yds. R.

28　　*Llanfihangel-ar-Arth Bridge.*

31　　River makes a big loop to the N, with fast stream between high wooded banks. Road runs close to the river R and Llandyssul Church comes into view. *Land* near church R and walk down through village to inspect Llandyssul rapids (½ ml. long). If in any doubt portage the whole way to beyond the last rapid.

Llandyssul Rapids. After passing Llandyssul Church there are two heavy rapids above the bridge (Pont Tyweli) and four below, all between rocks. Broken water leads to the first two heavy rapids on a bend. Both are awkward and the correct channel is not readily discernible. It is just possible to land R or L underneath the bridge, for inspection of the last four rapids, immediately below the bridge. These are heavy rapids, or falls between rocks, and the last is the most difficult. The tail-race of the first leads straight to the second. There is a little bay R before the third rapid where a landing can be made. The third and fourth, especially the fourth, are difficult owing to oblique currents and rocks, and require considerable skill in wild water technique. The fourth requires a central approach with a sharp turn to the R as the boat goes over the sill, in order to avoid rocks L. It is possible to land on R bank and line down or portage. Below the rapids the river is quieter and the scenery very fine.

35½ *Pont Allt-y-Cafan.* Weir just below bridge shootable through V-notch in middle. Inspect rapids before shooting weir. In high water shoot on extreme R as the V-notch is difficult to see from above. Four heavy rapids below weir, with ill-defined channel. The first of the four rapids is the heaviest. Cross L after the weir. Take second and third rapids in centre, and fourth on left.

38½ *Henllan Rapids and Falls.* Rapids start gradually ½ ml. above Henllan Bridge after 300 yards of calm water parallel to road L. Although Henllan Falls have been shot in medium-high water, there are severe stoppers and portage is advised. There is a footpath in the woods R. Land well above falls and portage on road L to a point about 100 yds. beyond the bridge. Inns R. After this the river runs deep and more peaceful.

43 *Newcastle Emlyn.* River above town doubles back on itself, the second loop winding round the castle ruins L. Round the second corner is a weir with salmon ladder followed by a fall, both of which may, with care and skill, be shot. Watch for cross-currents and for eddies from the waterfall where stream enters L. At Newcastle Emlyn Bridge, town L.

44½ *Cwm Coy* R. Confl. of Ceri R. Coracles may be seen between here and Cardigan.

46 *Cenarth Falls and Bridge.* Although the falls have been shot in medium-high water, there are severe stoppers, and damage to the boat is probable. Portage strongly advised. Inn and village L.

52 *Llechryd Bridge.* Fine 6-arch bridge. Village R. The scenery becomes more striking as each corner is turned.

52¼ *Castle Malgwyn* L.

53½ *Cilgerran.* Village L. Cilgerran Castle L. Quarries. Tidal from about here.

55 *Cardigan Bridge.* Town R. Quaint town. High water : Dover —4 hours. The estuary continues for another mile or two.

143. RIVERS OF CARDIGAN BAY

The Dovey, the Mawddach and the Glaslyn all have short canoeable stretches leading into fine mountain-girt estuaries. Generally speaking, the short stretches of river are pebbly and inclined to be shallow in dry weather, and the estuaries have narrow, winding channels at low tide between extensive sandbanks. High water at the mouth of all three estuaries—approx. Dover − 3 hours.

The **Dovey** (or **Dyfi**) is practicable from a little above Machynlleth but there have been objections from fishing interests. In the estuary the channel mainly follows the N shore. Machynlleth to Aberdovey approx. 9 miles.

The **Mawddach** (Barmouth Estuary). The spring tide flows up to Llanelltyd Bridge and the round trip from Barmouth (8 miles each way) can be accomplished on one tide. When enough fresh water is coming down the 2 miles of the Wnion from Dolgelley can be added to the down trip. The estuary is said to have the closest resemblance to a Scottish sea loch of any waters south of the Border. At low water the flat sandy bottom of the estuary is exposed. The sand in places is uncomfortably "quick" and consequently tiring to carry a canoe on. It is advisable therefore to start or finish a trip where the low water channel comes near to the shore. The bridges at Penmaenpool and Barmouth are pile bridges and at full flood of spring tides must be shot square. This beautiful piece of water is little used by boats of any sort but is well suited to canoes.

The **Glaslyn** is practicable from a little below Aberglaslyn Bridge, below which it runs through reclaimed estuarial flats (Traeth Mawr). Approx. distance to Portmadoc, 7 miles ; the mouth of the estuary is some two miles further on opposite Morfa Harlech.

The **Dwyryd**, which joins the Glaslyn opposite Borth-y-gest, gives a fine round trip at spring tides from Morfa Harlech up Traeth Bach into the Vale of Ffestiniog as far as Maentwrog and back (10 miles each way). At the start of the flow the tide enters the dry sand-estuary at good speed, causing overflows reminiscent of a rapid river. After the toll bridge at Penrhyndeudraeth the hills close in and the only resemblance to a normal tidal river is the flatness of the water.

O.S. 127, 116 ; Barth. 22, 27

144. CONWAY

Normally not practicable from above Llanrwst but in high water in winter would be worth trying from Bettws-y-coed or from the stream junction ½ mile below that town. Above Trefriw the river is private ; permission is not given for canoeing in spring or summer. (Advice from B.C.U. Headquarters about any trips above Trefriw.)

From Llanrwst the Conway is rather shallow but quite practicable under normal summer conditions and several minor rapids will provide interest.

It is tidal from Trefriw and it will only be possible to make headway with a favourable tide. At low tide further rapids will be met. Under certain conditions sea-like waves are likely some distance above Conway.

A branch rail line follows the river but there is no Sunday service. There are, however, Sunday buses. A better main line service will be found from Llandudno Junction than from Conway.

Llanrwst is a fair-sized shopping centre and accommodation can be secured there. Youth hostel. No camp sites are known in this valley.

Grading : Llanrwst-Trefriw : Rough Water I.

Trefriw downwards : Tidal.

A round trip using the tides from Conway to Trefriw and back is well worth while.

High Water at Conway : Dover—26 min. The tide takes some time to run up the river and may be an hour later at Trefriw. It flows $4\frac{1}{2}$ hours, ebbs $7\frac{1}{2}$ hours and reaches 3-5 knots.

Miles

0 *Bettws-y-coed.* Only practicable in high water.

$\frac{1}{2}$ Another stream joins L.

4 *Llanrwst.* Convenient starting point 50 yds. below bridge.

$4\frac{1}{2}$ *Gower Bridge.* Llanrwst and Trefriw Stn. R.

6 *Trefriw* L. Tidal from here. Starting point on B.5106 (west bank)

8 *Dolgarrog* L. Stn. R.

$10\frac{1}{2}$ At about 4 hours after high tide a rock-strewn bed is exposed.

11 *Tal-y-cafn Bridge.* Stn. R. Approaching Conway the river widens considerably. The right dries out in low water and at all times is the scene of shifting sandbanks. The channel well to the L should be taken.

15 *Conway Bridge.* There is a good landing for boats on the L shortly below the suspension bridge. Alternatively for privacy a landing may be made under the R buttresses of the bridge, there being steps leading to the road to Llandudno Junction Stn. Conway Castle and town are interesting.

16 *Deganwy* R. The trip may be continued down the estuary and a landing made on the beach below the level-crossing near Deganwy Stn. It is also possible, with due regard to weather and tides, to round the Great Orme.

O.S. 107 ; Barth. 27

145. CLWYD

This is practicable from Bodfari to Rhyl, quite pleasant but not exciting. It can be done in one day. It is a salmon river and advice about the necessary permissions should be sought from B.C.U. Headquarters. Distance—13 miles.

O.S. 108 ; Barth. 27

146. WELSH (or Cheshire) DEE (Dyfrdwy)

Three mountain streams, the Dyfrdwy, the Lliw and the Twrch unite near Llanuwchllyn a short distance above Llyn Tegid or Bala Lake.

Bala itself is situated $\frac{1}{2}$ mile from the lake. The scenery is of a high order all the way to Overton, particularly below Corwen.

While the Dee has the reputation of being a difficult river, it is not until Glyndyfrdwy is reached that difficulties of any serious moment are encountered. The best stretch, from the ordinary sporting canoeist's point of view, is that from Glyndyfrdwy to the Horseshoe Falls. From there to Llangollen is generally regarded as too difficult and is best avoided by transferring to the canal. There are more rapids between Llangollen and Overton (particularly between Trevor Rocks and New-bridge) but after Overton the river becomes uninteresting, and the section between Bangor and Farndon monotonous. After Farndon the country is pleasant and the river passes the wooded estate of the Duke of Westminster. This section is well frequented by pleasure craft from Chester.

Whilst other British rivers have individually more exciting rapids and falls, for consistent interest and fast water the stretch from Bala to Overton is undoubtedly one of our finest rough water rivers. Between June and September water levels may be too low. The late autumn is preferable to the spring on account of the fishing which is valuable. Some land-owners do not permit canoeing during the spring and summer. Do not attempt this river above Overton without, or against, advice from B.C.U.

Four days should be allowed for the trip from Bala to Chester.

Grading :   Bala-Glyndyfrdwy—Rough Water II.

Glyndyfrdwy-Horseshoe Falls—Rough Water III.

Horseshoe Falls-Llangollen—Rough Water IV by **river** (by canal 0).

Llangollen-Erbistock—Rough Water II (Trevor Rocks and Tymaen III).

Erbistock-Bangor-is-y-coed—Rough Water I.

Bangor-Chester—0.

O.S. 117, 118, 109 ; Barth. 22, 23, 28

Transport—

Buses (Crosville, Crane Wharf, Chester):

Llangollen, Corwen, Bala—Not on Sundays.

Llangollen, Ruabon, Wrexham, Chester—Good Sunday service.

Overton, Wrexham—Not on Sundays.

Bangor, Wrexham—Not on Sundays.

Farndon, Chester—Fair Sunday service.

Miles

Bala Lake (Llyn Tegid)—3 miles long.

0   Outfall from Bala Lake, beneath road bridge. A few yards lower a plank crosses the river and may be covered in flood. Wire may be encountered across the river in several places in first 15 mls. or so.

Miles

¼	Old railway bridge. Confl. of Tryweryn just below L.
¾	Low weir with two gaps, shootable. Drop about 1 ft.
1½	*Berth-lafar Ferry.* Ropes across river. Normally 3 ft. above river but may be dangerous in high water.
2	Footbridge.
3	*Bodweni.* Farm with wall close to river L heralds approach to double bend, sharp L then R, fast water, keep L but be prepared to cut to R around large rock after second bend.
4½	*Llandderfel Bridge.* Ledge underneath. May scrape in low water. Inn (Trust House) on R.
6	*Dol-y-gadfa Railway Bridge.*
9	*Pont Cilan.* Road bridge.
9¼	*Llandrillo Railway Bridge.*
12	*Cynwyd Bridge.* (Owner of both banks for several miles below here does not permit canoeing from March through spring and most of the summer. Advice from B.C.U.)
13½	Confl. of *R. Alwen* L. Fast water, channel R.
14	*Corwen Bridge.* Take centre arch or second from L. Good shopping facilities.
15	Road bridge and railway bridge. Between these bridges is a pier of a derelict bridge. Water is fast.
17¾	Sharp bend to L. Just after this bend is a heavy rapid which presents no particular difficulty.
18	*Carrog Bridge.* Fast water continues under the bridge.
20¼	*Glyndyfrdwy Bridge.* ½ ml. after the bridge is a sharp bend to the L. From here there is a succession of rapids and pools for the next 3 mls. One of the most exciting and also most beautiful sections of the river, which takes a horseshoe-shaped course to the N between steep hills. Difficulty III.
22¾	Old footbridge.
23¼	*Upper Plas Berwyn Rapid.*
25	*Gwyfelia Farm.*
25¼	*Lower Plas Berwyn Rapid.* Land and examine. This rapid may be identified as being nearly opposite Pendre Farm, visible ¼ ml. to the R. Best passage is usually on L but conditions vary greatly according to height of water. Slack water from here to the Horseshoe Falls.
26	*Horseshoe Falls, Llantysilio.* A low, horseshoe-shaped weir. Sheer drop. Valle Crucis Abbey ruins ½ ml. L.
	From here it is best to transfer to the canal feeder, which leaves the pool above the weir on the L, as the next 2 mls. of river are extremely difficult—the fall is about 30 ft. per mile. Incidentally, the 10 mls. along the canal over Pontcysyllte aqueduct and along to Chirk (aqueduct over Ceiriog, and stn.), is a very rewarding trip. By going further the Vyrnwy and the Severn may be reached (see Section 148).
	If the river is attempted, over three hours should be allowed for the 2 mls. as several sections require inspection. Difficulty IV.

Land on L above the weir and inspect the rapid under the Chain Bridge and also the Serpent's Tail. Ferry canoe across to R bank and portage the weir.

26¼ *Chain Bridge and Hotel.* Heavy rapids above and under the bridge. Channel L.

The Serpent's Tail (100 yds. below bridge). River narrows to about 5 ft. and falls through a twisting chasm. Portage over rocks on L. *Do not attempt to shoot unless you are sure of your techniques.*

27 *Island and broken weir.* White mill on L. It is best to approach via L of island and land on concrete on L of weir. Canoes can be slid down from here, or if conditions are suitable for shooting on R paddle upstream again and approach via R of island.

27¼ *Railway Bridge.* Just above the bridge is a fair rapid. Keep L as close to rock as possible. 100 yds. below bridge is a ledge— shoot on L in medium water. In low water land on rocks in centre.

27½ *Weir.* Vertical drop. Land on L. Awkward portage over barbed-wire fence. May be possible to line down the salmon pass on R.

Island. Before re-embarking after weir portage, inspect next rapid. Good run on L but top ledge is rather shallow.

27¾ *Reefs.* As first church of Llangollen town comes into sight there is a confused series of reefs continuing to the bridge. The first can usually be negotiated but land on R just below church to examine the others. These have been shot on R and a landing made on L of weir below bridge. *If this is attempted be sure beforehand that the landing point is not covered by high water, as the retaining walls will prevent a landing elsewhere.* If a portage around these reefs is made, access to the river again can be made below the bridge and weir via the alley in Bridge Street at the side of the Home-land Cafe. In high water this is not suitable.

28 *Llangollen Bridge.* The water below Llangollen is lively and there are several minor rapids in the next few miles.

29¾ Footbridge. Sun Trevor Hotel. The river can be reached from the canal (with permission) across one meadow.

32 *Trevor Rocks, Mill, Road Bridge and Pontcysyllte Aqueduct.* At the mill around a bend to the R is a very good rapid known as Trevor Rocks, the river running over a confused series of reefs. Land on R bank and examine. Generally the course is to the R of a large rock near bank and then L almost across the stream to shoot the second fall. Fast and heavy water continues below the rapids and through the road bridge (middle arch). 200 yds. below the bridge is the aqueduct beneath which is another rapid. Middle arch is probably the best. (These rapids were the scene of the first British National Canoe Slalom in 1938.)

32½ *Island.* Channel to R. Fast water close to L bank.

33½   *Cefn Railway Viaduct.* Heavy rapid just above. Below here there have been objections. Advice from B.C.U.

34   *Tymaen Island.* Land above on L and examine. The narrow channel to L should be taken, as the wider one to the R is usually too shallow. At the foot of L channel is a large rock which should be taken as close as possible on the L. There is a tendency for the stream to force one too far to the L and the foliage of an overhanging tree may cause trouble, particularly in summer. (This was the scene of the second Slalom in 1948.)

34½   *Newbridge.* As the bridge comes into sight there is a heavy rapid. Rebound from retaining wall on R usually keeps one in the correct course.

      From here to Overton are many more rapids the difficulty of which depend on the state of the water. May involve wading in a dry summer.

37½   *Confl. of Ceiriog* R.

38½   Island. Keep to R.

38¾   Footbridge.

40   *Erbistock Ferry.* Inn.

42   *Overton Weir.* High weir. Land on R. Portage usually necessary but has been shot in high water through the salmon cut.

42½   *Overton Bridge.*

48   *Bangor-is-y-coed.* From here river bends and twists to Farndon with high banks ; most monotonous.

49¼   Railway bridge.

50½   *Confl. of Clywedog* L.

55½   Footbridge.

59¼   *Holt Castle.* Ruins L.

61   *Farndon Bridge.* England R, Wales L.

62¾   *Confl. of Alyn* L.

63¾   *Almere Ferry.*

65¼   *Confl. of Pulford Brook* L.

67¼   *Ironbridge, Eaton Park and Hall.* Aldford R. Estate of Duke of Westminster.

68¾   *Crook of Dee.*

69¾   *Eccleston Ferry.*

73   *Chester, Queen's Bridge.*

73¼   *Chester Weir. Old Dee Bridge.* Portage R bank if it is desired to proceed further. This is not recommended. This weir normally marks the limit of the tide, though the high spring tides are felt as high up as Farndon. Canoeists proceeding below this point should remember that the Dee has a bore. High Water : Dover plus 1 hour 9 min.

73¾   *Grosvenor Bridge.*

74   Railway bridge.

74¾   *Entrance to Shropshire Union Canals.* From this point to Connah's Quay the river is confined between high banks, one stretch of 5 mls. in straight line.

Miles
80¼   *Queensferry Bridge.*
81   Railway bridge.
82   *Connah's Quay* L. The river widens out into the Dee Estuary.

Dee Estuary. This estuary is very dangerous as the shallow water which covers the mud only for a short while at high water, quickly runs out and the whole expanse is very exposed to the wind, making very short steep waves. Timing of the tides must be very accurate and consideration of the wind strength and direction is even more critical. Many lives have been lost in this estuary.

The downstream cruise. A good starting point is at the bottom of Marshlands Road, off Burton Road, ¾ mile S of Neston Cross. Water runs back up this gutter and a start must be made as soon as it appears (1 hour before High Water at Liverpool). The Admiralty chart of Liverpool Bay covers the estuary only from Dawpool North ; sailing directions as far as here are entirely commonsense.

There are many sandbanks but there is a channel ¾ to 1 mile out from the shore from Dawpool to Thurstaston. When the anchored yachts off Thurstaston are abaft of beam bear in towards the Caldy Cliffs, turning then to follow the line of the beach a fair distance out until West Kirby is reached. A landing may be made here or continue on to Hilbre.

Crossing the estuary. This trip must only be done with very calm and settled weather conditions. Allow 1½ hours each way for the crossing : West Kirby to Mostyn and back.

Start 2 hours before High Water and leave for the return not later than 1½ hours after High Water. The cross-current runs at about 2 knots but is considerably more with spring tides.

CANALS OF THE MIDLANDS

147. STAFFORDSHIRE and WORCESTERSHIRE CANAL
Connects the *Severn* at Stourport with the *Trent* or the *Trent and Mersey Canal* at Great Haywood. Runs via Kidderminster, Tettenhall, near Wolverhampton, and Penkridge.   30 locks rising to Tettenhall (23½ miles from Stourport), then 10 miles level, followed by 12 locks, falling, to Great Haywood (46¼).   Scenery pleasant.   At Aldersley Junction (25 miles) the main line of the Birmingham Canal Navigations leaves R. At Autherley Junction (25½ miles) the Shropshire Union Canal leaves L.

British Waterways Inland Cruising Booklets Nos. 4 and 13.

O.S. 130, 119 ; Barth. 18, 23

148. SHROPSHIRE UNION CANALS
(*a*) **Birmingham and Liverpool Junction Canal.**   From Autherley (junction with *Staffs. and Worcs. Canal*) through the heart of Shropshire to Market Drayton (26¾ miles—8 locks, falling), Audlem (33 miles) and Nantwich (39 miles). 23 locks, falling, between Market Drayton and Nantwich, 15 together at Audlem. (British Waterways Inland Cruising Booklet No. 5.) At Norbury Junction (15½ miles from Autherley) the **Newport and Shrewsbury Canal** leaves L. (26 locks,

falling, to Shrewsbury—25 miles). This canal is officially abandoned but it is usable by canoes between Newport and Rodington. The last few miles are quite derelict and impassable. At several places nearby, the canal is close to the Severn but never joins it.

O.S. 118, 119, 110 ; Barth. 18, 23

(b) **Chester Canal** continues from Nantwich. Two miles N of Nantwich the *Ellesmere Canal* joins (see below) and 3¾ miles N of Nantwich the **Middlewich Branch** leaves on R. This crosses the *R. Weaver* 3½ miles from the junction (see Section 10) and joins the *Trent and Mersey Canal* at Middlewich : 11 miles, 3 locks.

British Waterways Inland Cruising Booklet No. 5.

The Chester Canal continues via Beeston and Tarvin to the *R. Dee* at Chester : 19 miles from Nantwich 12 locks, and then to Ellesmere Port, 8 miles further.

O.S. 109, 110 ; Barth. 23, 28

(c) **Ellesmere and Montgomeryshire Canals.** Perhaps the best known to canoeists. The **Ellesmere Canal** runs from Hurlestone Junction near Nantwich SW near Whitchurch to Frankton, 29 miles from the junction with the Chester Canal ; 19 locks, rising in 13 miles to a point near Whitchurch, then 16 miles level. At Frankton the *Llangollen Canal* continues R, through Chirk to Llangollen and Llantisilio (*R. Dee*). This passes through beautiful country, and over two famous aqueducts : Chirk Aqueduct over the Ceiriog, and Pontcysyllte Aqueduct over the Dee. Only two locks in 17 miles. Two short tunnels.

British Waterways Inland Cruising Booklet No. 1.

From Frankton the Ellesmere Canal once continued to Llanymynech and Carreghofa, 6 locks, falling, in 11 miles. But immediately beyond Frankton there is a break and the canal is dry or impossible for most of the way to a point ½ mile S of Pant. From Carreghofa the canal continues as the **Montgomeryshire Canal** (now isolated from the rest of the system) over the *Vyrnwy* Aqueduct (see Section 116) to Pool Quay (5¾ miles from Carreghofa), Welshpool (10 miles), and Newtown (24 miles). From Pool Quay the canal is close to the *R. Severn*. 19 locks rising. This, too, runs through lovely country up the valley of the Severn. A number of bridges have been lowered and the water piped, making a portage necessary. The locks cannot be used, and the canal is overgrown in summer.

The Llangollen Canal and the Montgomeryshire Canal make a good approach to a cruise down the Severn, by the Vyrnwy, or direct from any point above Pool Quay, but land transport is necessary from near Gobowen to Pant or Llanymynech.

O.S. 108, 117, 128 ; Barth. 23, 18, 22

149. WORCESTER and BIRMINGHAM CANAL

From Birmingham via King's Norton (*Stratford-on-Avon Canal*—see Section 155) (5¾ miles), Tardebigge (14½ miles), near Bromsgrove and Droitwich (20¾ miles) to the Severn at Worcester (30 miles). 58 locks, all falling, from Tardebigge, 30 of them in a ladder at Tardebigge. A long tunnel, over $1\frac{1}{4}$ miles long, $\frac{1}{2}$ mile beyond King's Norton, and two short ones. Scenery not striking, but remains pleasant to within a mile of the centre of Birmingham.

British Waterways Inland Cruising Booklet No. 14.

150.   MACCLESFIELD and PEAK FOREST CANALS

The **Macclesfield Canal** runs from the *Trent and Mersey Canal* at Hardings Wood, 7 miles N of Stoke, through Macclesfield to Marple and the *Peak Forest Canal*. This canal runs half way up the westernmost ridge of the Peak, from near Bollington to Marple, and provides some extensive views over the Cheshire Plain. A pleasant canal for canoeing. 28 miles, 12 locks rising, all together at Bosley, 10 miles from Hardings Wood. The *Peak Forest Canal* continues at the same level.

British Waterways Inland Cruising Booklet No. 11.

The **Peak Forest Canal.** Runs from Ashton-under-Lyne via Marple to Whaley Bridge or Buxworth. From Woodley (stn.) it runs through very pleasant hills on the outskirts of the Peak, following the Etherow and Goyt Valleys, to Whaley Bridge or Buxworth. The railway is never far away, and there are some very fine views. From Woodley to Marple (junction with *Macclesfield Canal*) 4 miles, 16 locks, all together, rising, at Marple. The Etherow aqueduct at the foot of the locks is dry (1962). From Marple to Whaley Bridge or Buxworth (6 miles) level.

These two canals provide many miles of waterway free from locks and with extensive views.

O.S. 101, 110, 111 ; Barth. 28

151.   OXFORD CANAL

Runs from the Thames at Oxford via Banbury, Napton and Braunston to the Coventry Canal at Hawkesbury Junction. It provides an alternative route to the Grand Union Canal from the Thames to many Midland rivers. The scenery apart from the lower parts of the Cherwell Valley, which are pleasant, is not notable.

Entrance from the Thames at *Oxford* at Tumbling Bay $\frac{1}{2}$ mile above Osney Lock. A pleasanter approach is to continue up the Thames (Isis) to *Duke's Cut* which leaves on R above King's Lock. For a short distance the canal uses the R. Cherwell. The railway is never far away from the canal all the way from Oxford to Fenny Compton.

30 locks rising from the Thames to the summit level at *Claydon* in $34\frac{3}{4}$ miles. Summit level 11 miles ; then 10 locks falling in 2 miles to *Napton Bottom Lock*. At $49\frac{3}{4}$ miles from Oxford the Napton and Warwick section of the Grand Union Canal leaves L ; from here to *Braunston* ($54\frac{3}{4}$) the Grand Union uses the Oxford Canal, leaving it R for Leighton Buzzard, Tring, Watford and Brentford. From Braunston the Oxford

Canal continues, with 4 locks, falling, at *Hillmorton*, past *Rugby* and *Newbold-on-Avon* (see Stratford Avon, Section 121), to *Hawkesbury Junction* (77½) where it joins the *Coventry Canal* a few miles N of Coventry.

British Waterways Inland Cruising Booklet Nos. 6 and 9.

O.S. 145, 132 ; Barth. 14, 19

152. COVENTRY CANAL

Runs from Coventry via Hawkesbury (Junction with Oxford Canal), Nuneaton, Atherstone and Tamworth to Fradley where it joins the *Trent and Mersey Canal* (see Section 156). At Fazeley Aqueduct near Tamworth it crosses the *Tame* (see Section 25). From Hawkesbury Junction to Fazeley 21½ miles ; (13 locks, descending, 11 in 2 miles between Atherstone and Grendon, and 2 at Glascote); to Fradley 32 miles. From Marston, 3 miles S of Nuneaton the **Ashby de la Zouch Canal** leaves R : 24 miles, no locks, to Measham. Very pleasant scenery.

Although the Coventry Canal passes close to the Warwickshire coalfield, the scenery is not uniformly dull.

British Waterways Inland Cruising Booklet Nos. 9 and 12.

O.S. 120, 131, 132 ; Barth. 19, 24

153. GRAND UNION CANAL

Connects the Thames at Limehouse and at Brentford with the canal system of the Midlands. The canal runs via Hanwell, Watford, Tring, Leighton Buzzard, to Braunston, where it joins the Oxford Canal (see Section 151) for a few miles and then diverges again R as the Napton and Warwick Canal, which leads into the Warwick and Birmingham Canal. Very busy with commercial traffic.

From the Thames at *Brentford* there are 54 locks, rising, to the summit level at *Tring*. West Drayton Stn. is close to the canal, but it is preferable not to start much below *Rickmansworth*. From there up through the Chilterns the scenery is pleasant. From *Tring* (36¾ miles from Brentford) 15 locks, falling to *Leighton Buzzard* (47 miles). From here the canal follows the valley of the *Ouzel* (see Section 40) with 6 locks, falling, to *Fenny Stratford* (55 miles) followed by a level of 11 miles through *Wolverton* to the aqueduct over the *Bedford Ouse* (66¼ miles) (see Section 38). From here 9 locks, rising, to *Blisworth Tunnel* (73¾ miles). This is 1¾ miles long and has two bends in it. Keep *right*. Just beyond Blisworth Stn. (77 miles) at *Gayton* the **Northampton Branch** leaves R connecting with the *Nene Navigation* (see Section 37). The canal continues through *Weedon* with 7 locks, rising in succession, to *Norton Junction* (89½ miles) (where the **Leicester Canal** leaves R (see Section 154)—41 miles to Leicester and the *R. Soar*). Then follows *Braunston Tunnel* (91¼ miles)—1¼ miles long, straight. Keep *right*. Then 7 locks, falling, to *Braunston Junction* with the **Oxford Canal** (93¾ miles). The scenery for most of the way is pleasant, particularly just after Leighton Buzzard. The canal is not far from the M.R. main line all the way from near Watford to Weedon, and there are stations nearby at Berkhamsted, Tring, Leighton Buzzard, Fenny Stratford, Wolverton, Blisworth and Weedon.

From *Braunston* the canal uses 5 miles of the Oxford Canal (turn L) to *Napton*, then leaves it R. 21 locks, falling, to *Leamington* (15¾ miles from Braunston) (stns.). The canal crosses the *Stratford Avon* (see Section 121) by an aqueduct and runs wide of *Warwick* (2 more locks) to *Hatton* (21 locks, rising, in 2¼ miles). At *Kingswood Junction* (26½ miles) after a short tunnel at Shrewley, the **Stratford Canal** leaves on L (see Section 155). Then the canal passes through *Knowle and Solihull*—11 locks falling—to *Birmingham*. The W.R. main line is close to the canal at Leamington, Hatton, Kingswood (Lapworth Stn.), and *Olton* (37 miles), beyond which the canal is not recommended.

British Waterways Inland Cruising Booklets Nos. 8 and 9.

O.S. 160, 146, 132, 131 ; Barth. 14, 15, 19

154. LEICESTER CANAL

This is part of the Grand Union Canal and leaves the latter at Norton Junction. After this there are 7 locks, rising, to Crick Tunnel (3¾ miles from Norton Junction), nearly a mile long. This is followed by a long summit level with Bosworth Tunnel, nearly ¾ mile long, to Foxton Locks (22 miles from Norton Junction), 10 locks, falling. Inclined plane. Saddington Tunnel (½ mile long) is followed by 24 locks, falling, in 17 miles to Leicester (41¼ miles from Norton). The last three miles are part of the *R. Soar*, and the canal continues using that river to the Trent (see Section 21). There is a short branch from the bottom of Foxton Locks to Market Harborough (5¾ miles).

Scenery on the summit level is open but not exciting. Here the canal crosses the watershed dividing the Severn Basin from the Nene, Welland and Trent Basins.

British Waterways Inland Cruising Booklet No. 10.

O.S. 133 ; Barth. 19

155. STRATFORD-ON-AVON CANAL

Connects the Worcester and Birmingham Canal (see Section 149) at King's Norton, the Grand Union Canal at Kingswood Junction and the Avon at Stratford. Scenery good all the way. Level from King's Norton to Lapworth, then a chain of 18 locks, falling, to the connecting canal at Kingswood (12½ miles from King's Norton). 19 locks, falling from here through the former Forest of Arden country, to Bearley Aqueduct (20 miles), in the valley of the Alne. Then 16 locks, falling, to the Avon by Stratford Bridge (25½ miles). Between Lapworth and Stratford this canal has recently been put in order by the Stratford on Avon Canal Society. This stretch now vests in the National Trust, not British Waterways.

British Waterways Inland Cruising Booklet No. 14 (King's Norton to Lapworth).

O.S. 131 ; Barth. 19

156.   TRENT and MERSEY CANAL

From the Bridgewater Canal near Runcorn via Middlewich (junction with *Shropshire Union* system) and Stoke-on-Trent, along the *Trent* Valley to Derwentmouth, where it joins the *Trent*.

36 locks, rising in 36 miles from Preston Brook to the summit at Kidsgrove ; 40 falling to Derwentmouth in 58 miles. Scenery down the Trent Valley from Trentham, near Stoke, quite pleasant. At Great Haywood, 18 miles from Stoke, the *Staffs. and Worcs. Canal* enters R ; at Fradley, 31 miles from Stoke, the *Coventry Canal* enters R. At Hardings Wood, ½ mile before Kidsgrove, the *Macclesfield Canal* leaves R. Long tunnels at Preston Brook and Harecastle.
British Waterways Inland Cruising Booklets Nos. 12 and 13.

Caldon Branch Canal

See under *Churnet* (Section 26)

O.S. 109, 110, 119, 120, 121 ; Barth. 28, 23, 24

157.   BRIDGEWATER CANAL

This canal was a very early one. It now belongs to the Manchester Ship Canal—not to British Waterways—and connects Manchester and Runcorn. Pleasure craft are not normally permitted, but may be allowed on special application to the Manager, Bridgewater Canal Offices, Chester Road, Manchester 15. From the *Bollin* aqueduct (see Section 12) to Preston Brook (junction with the *Trent and Mersey Canal*—Section 156), 13 miles.

O.S. 101 ; Barth. 28

198

SCOTLAND

To the canoeist Scotland offers a wide variety of cruising waterways, leading through unspoiled country and magnificent scenery. Its principal rivers, Spey, Tay and Tweed, though not of great length, are usually exciting. The Caledonian Canal and Loch Lomond have been popular with canoeists for over 50 years, and there are many other inland waters of great charm and interest. But perhaps most attractive to the cruising canoeist is the western sea coast, from Greenock to Skye. This coast gives wonderful opportunities for exploration, amid the finest scenery, of lochs and narrow channels, as well as the open sea and its islands. Coastal cruising has long been the most popular form of canoeing in Scotland, and the Scottish Canoe Association usually organises at least one summer cruise annually on these waters, which visitors are welcome to join.

Youth Hostels. Hostels of the Scottish Youth Hostels Association are available to members of English and foreign Y.H.A. These hostels are mentioned in the text only where they lie close to the waterway described. Some hostels are closed and new ones opened every year, and canoeists who wish to use them are advised to consult the current S.Y.H.A. Handbook, obtainable through other Y.H.A. or from S.Y.H.A. 7 Bruntsfield Crescent, Edinburgh.

Midges. These biting flies are often a nuisance to canoeists and campers in Scotland. They appear mostly in the morning and evening, dislike strong sunshine and winds, and are most common among bracken, bushes and long grass, and near fresh water. Camp sites on bare ground and in exposed positions are often free of them. Slacks and sleeves give good protection, and should be worn in the evening, and a chiffon scarf over the head is often useful. A recently produced repellent (D.M.P.) is incorporated in a number of satisfactory preparations which have the approval of the Scottish Tourist Board, and are sold by most chemists in Scotland.

Acknowledgments. A large part of the material which follows is based on the information collected by the late E. L. Carmichael. The editor wishes to acknowledge the considerable help he has had from Mr. J. H. Cuthill, formerly Hon. Secretary of the S.C.A., from Mr. Jack Henderson, and from the many other canoeists, in both Scotland and England, who have helped with information and advice.

Arrangement of the Sections. These fall into four groups : coastal waters, starting with the Solway Firth and following the West, North and East coasts ; canals ; inland lochs ; and river basins.

COASTAL WATERS

GENERAL

The Northern and Eastern coasts of Scotland are described only briefly, as they are not, on the whole, suitable for extended cruises.

The West coast of Scotland offers the canoeist an extensive cruising area with some incomparable scenery. The waters are largely sheltered, and the numerous sea lochs and islands made good refuges in bad weather. There are not many dangerous places on the usual routes, and while, from the text, it may appear that there are many difficulties, it must be remembered that these are mostly influences of tide and wind, and that, given good weather, and using ordinary caution and care, the cruising canoeist is not likely to run into serious danger.

Weather. The summer months are the most suitable for West Coast cruising, June often being considered the best. Rain may be expected at any time, though it is far from being as frequent as many believe.

The prevailing wind, being SW, generally sets on-shore, which makes for safety. It also makes it most advisable to cruise as much as possible from S to N.

Strong winds may be encountered, and can make some parts very unpleasant, especially on promontories such as Ardlamont Point or the Mull of Kintyre. For this reason it is advisable not to have too rigid a time-table, but to allow for the possibility of being held up by weather. A strong wind which makes a crossing difficult, *e.g.*, that from Oban to Mull, will often be found to drop almost to a calm at dawn or sunset, especially if the tide changes at these times. Strong gusts or squalls are often met when passing a glen or the mouth of a loch.

Tides. Tidal streams are of great importance to the cruising canoeist. The general direction of the flood stream on the West Coast is N, and the ebb sets S, but N of Skye the direction is reversed. Where tidal streams run at 3 knots or over it is not worth trying to make headway against them, and over any distance 2 knots makes progress very slow.

The configuration of the land has a considerable effect on tidal streams. Strong tides are met in narrow channels, as between islands and in the entrances to some lochs, and it is especially necessary in such places to time a journey so that the tide is not against the canoeist. There is usually a period of one or two hours slack water at high and low tide. In some bays there are eddies running in the opposite direction to the main tide, and the canoeist who finds it necessary to work against the tide can make use of these by keeping close inshore, though he generally has to fight the main stream round every point.

In many lochs it is found that, after heavy rain, the flow of fresh water from the rivers neutralises the flood tide entering and increases the strength of the ebb stream leaving the loch.

Spring tides occur at the full and new moons, and at these times the range between high and low water is greatest, and the tidal streams strongest. Neap tides occur in between springs and usually run at about half their speed.

A strong tide running against the wind raises a short, steep sea which is very uncomfortable for a canoe and should be avoided when possible. Overfalls, the effect of a strong tide running over an uneven sea bottom, are sometimes encountered, and are aggravated by a strong wind. They may be avoided by waiting for slack tide. Advantage should be taken whenever possible of local information from fishermen and boatmen.

Equipment. In coastal cruising portages are not common, and kit may be increased rather above river standards. A full change of warm clothing should always be carried, and this, and the bedding, must be in waterproof kitbags. A good spray cover and a waterproof jacket are essential for comfort.

A good map is required, and the 1-in. Ordnance Survey is to be preferred as it gives most accurately details such as the distance to which bays dry out at low tide, and the position of burns which may serve as a water supply. Admiralty charts are useful and give a lot of details but they are rather cumbersome to carry. A compass is also necessary, as mist descends very rapidly.

A foot controlled rudder should generally be used on both single and double seaters as it greatly eases the strain when a following sea or a cross-wind is encountered.

Camping. Except on the more inhabited coasts of Renfrewshire and Ayrshire camp sites are easy to obtain, and on the more secluded parts no permission is necessary unless there is a house nearby. On the more rocky northern coasts flat ground is often difficult to find, and search for a site should not be left until dark. Sites are mentioned in the text only where difficulty has been experienced. Milk and eggs are often obtainable in the more isolated areas, though not in large quantities. Shopping centres are often far apart, and it may be necessary to carry stores for several days.

It should be noted that some bays which make good landing places at high tide show a considerable area of mud or sand at low tide. If it should be necessary to launch when the tide is out a steep-to shore is to be preferred.

Fishing. Canoeists will find a simple fishing tackle useful in keeping the larder stocked. Bottom fishing for codling and flat fish, with bait, is best learnt from the locals, as only certain times, places and baits are suitable. In the summer months a line for mackerel, lythe (pollack) and saith (coal fish) may be trailed while travelling. The fish take best between sunset and dark, and the last two especially are found among rocks. The tackle is simple, being about 20 yards of strong hand line with two or three large white flies attached by 6 inches of gut. The flies may be made by tying a white feather to a 1-inch hook. A 2-ounce weight is added about 6 feet above the flies, and a swivel above this keeps the line from tangling. Refinements such as extra flies or spinners may be added. When mackerel are shoaling a fly trailed on the surface without a weight is sufficient.

Sharks. Basking sharks may be encountered on the West Coast, particularly in Loch Fyne, and while there is no record of mishap to canoeists on their account they have been known to overturn boats and so should be avoided. They will not attack persons.

Acknowledgments. Very full details of the whole West Coast, with descriptions of the tides and other dangers, may be found in "Sailing Directions, West Coast of Scotland," published for the Clyde Cruising Club by Gilmour & Lawrence, Ltd., 2 West Regent Street, Glasgow, and obtainable through booksellers. Acknowledgment is hereby made of the very considerable help which has been obtained from the Sailing Directions in the preparation of this guide, and also from the Admiralty publications "West Coast Pilot" and "North Sea Pilot, Part II."

TIDAL INFORMATION

In the text which follows the times of change in the tidal streams are related to the time of high water at Dover. Similarly, all tidal constants show the time of high water in relation to high water Dover on that day. The time of high water at any place can be found from the Dover tide-table, by adding or subtracting the figure given, as indicated by the sign before the constant. On an average low water is 6 hours 12 minutes before and after high water, and one day's tide is about 48 minutes later than the previous day's.

Constants for the principal ports in Scotland are as follows :

Greenock + 1 hr. 17 min.—Dover
Leith + 3 hr. 47 min.—Dover
Oban + 5 hr. 31 min.—Dover
Aberdeen + 2 hr. 14 min.—Dover

Rates of tidal streams are given in knots (k) at springs (sps.). One knot is slightly more than 1 m.p.h. Rates at neaps (nps.) may be expected to be about half those at springs.

A copy of the appropriate Dover Tide Tables should be obtained when planning a cruise, and a note of the times when favouring tides can be expected on the route should be prepared beforehand.

GALLOWAY COAST

201. Solway Firth
O.S. 75 ; Barth. 38

This firth is noted for its extensive sands and fast tides. At low tide there is a narrow channel with as much as two miles of sand on either side and the channel is liable to shift. Navigation should be done as far as possible on the flood tide, to avoid the danger of being left high and dry. The tidal streams themselves are so fast as to be dangerous. This area is not advised as a cruising ground.

202. Urr Estuary to Mull of Galloway
O.S. 79, 80, 81 ; Barth. 37

This is a little known but interesting and picturesque coast, with few dangers but exposed to the SW. The estuaries and bays dry out, and the tides are high, rising as much as 25 feet springs, and 15 feet neaps. Estuaries should only be entered on the flood. (*Const.*+ 0 hr. 25 min.) The flood stream is westerly, and sets into estuaries and large bays.

There is a bad race round Burrow Head, which should be avoided by keeping close inshore. An even worse race round the Mull of Galloway must be avoided in the same way and is best taken at slack tide. It is especially dangerous in an onshore wind, and on the ebb extends into Luce Bay, while on the flood it lies NW of the Mull.

203. Mull of Galloway to Loch Ryan
O.S. 79 ; Barth. 37

This coastline is bold, rocky and exposed. The tide runs at a maximum of 5 k. with small races off the headlands, setting N 1½ hours before, and S 4½ hours after H.W. Dover.

From Portpatrick Harbour (now disused) the crossing to Ireland is 18 miles of exposed water. It should only be attempted in settled weather.

204. Loch Ryan
O.S. 79 ; Barth. 37

This loch, seven miles long, offers good shelter, but has considerable commercial shipping. Stranraer is the best rail-head on this part of the coast.

LOWER FIRTH OF CLYDE
(Loch Ryan and Mull of Kintyre to the Cumbraes)

205. Ayrshire Coast
O.S. 59, 67, 72 ; Barth. 37, 40

This coast, from Loch Ryan to the Cumbraes, a distance of about 50 miles, is not an attractive cruising ground, as it is populated, has no natural harbours, and is an exposed lee shore in the prevailing westerly winds. Tide runs 2½ k. sps. N from 5½ hrs. after, and S from ½ hr. before H.W. Dover.

Corraith Y.H. lies 3 miles inland from Troon and can be reached by bus. Crosbie Y.H. lies about 4 miles inland near West Kilbride, and canoeists should land in the Sea Mill region.

206. Kintyre, East Coast
O.S. 58, 65 ; Barth. 43

This rocky coast is not of great interest to canoeists, though fairly sheltered. In Kilbrannan Sound tide runs 2½ k. sps. N from 4½ hrs. before, S from 1½ hrs. after H.W. Dover. It is best to start from Campbeltown, reached by steamer or bus from Glasgow, and cruise N to Bute or Loch Fyne.

207. Mull of Kintyre
O.S. 65 ; Barth. 43

This dangerous and exposed point should be avoided by canoeists. Heavy seas are common, and may rise very quickly, especially in the tide race off Deas Point (Sron Uamha) when tide and wind are opposed. The passage round the point should not be attempted except in quite settled weather. The flood tide sets W one hour before L.W. and runs 5 hrs. and the ebb sets E 2 hrs. before H.W. and runs 7 hrs. (*Const.* − 0 hr. 21 min.) The race is worse in the last quarter of the ebb.

A crossing has been made from the Mull of Kintyre to Ireland (12½ miles between the nearest points of land) but it is definitely not advisable. The nearest Irish coast is steep and rocky, with strong tides, overfalls, and rips extended about a mile off-shore. In mid-channel the tide flows 4 k. sps. SE from 5 hrs. before until H.W. Dover and NW from 1 hr. after to 6 hrs. after H.W. Dover.

208. Island of Arran
O.S. 66 ; Barth. 44

This island lies between the Ayrshire coast and Kintyre, and is 17 miles long with a circumference of 60 miles. The best approach is from the Kyles of Bute or Loch Fyne, or by steamer from Greenock, Glasgow or Wemyss Bay. The crossing from the S end of Bute is often rough.

Camping should not be difficult except in populated areas. The N shore is steep and bare, and fierce squalls are met in strong winds. The Youth Hostel at Loch Ranza is near the head of the Loch on the S side. The E shore is pleasant and free from dangers, and there are a number of popular holiday resorts. The Y.H. at Whiting Bay is near the shore ½ mile S of the pier, but that at Brodick is about 1½ miles from the shore, up Glen Cloy.

The S and W shores are more barren and exposed and there are tide rips off some of the points which are bad in strong winds. On most of the coast the flood tide starts 5 hrs. before H.W. Dover flowing E along the southern shore and N up the east and west shores.

UPPER FIRTH OF CLYDE
(*Bowling to the Cumbraes, with adjacent lochs*)

209. Bowling to Gourock
O.S. 59, 60 ; Barth. 44

This stretch is a busy commercial waterway, with a narrow dredged channel and extensive mud-banks on either hand at low water so that, if stuck in the mud, it is necessary to wait for high tide. It is not a good canoeing area and the shores are largely populated so that camping is difficult. However, it makes a good starting place for Loch Long. The Y.H. at Cove (Section 212) is accessible.

Bowling is the entrance to the Forth and Clyde Canal (Section 268), and 2 miles below is Dumbarton where the River Leven enters from Loch Lomond (Section 271). It is necessary to have a favouring tide (*Const.* Bowling + 1 hr. 17 min.) so that, coming down the river on a falling tide, the buoyed channel must be used and care must be taken to keep clear of shipping. Craigendoran (Section 211) makes the best point of access by rail.

210. Gourock to the Cumbraes
O.S. 59 ; Barth. 44

This area connects the upper reaches with the Kyles of Bute. There are no dangers and the tides are not strong. Wemyss Bay and Largs (railway and bus) make good points of access.

Camping is generally prohibited both on the mainland and on the Cowal and Bute shores, and canoeists are advised to make for the Kyles of Bute (Section 215). Skelmorlie Y.H. lies $2\frac{1}{2}$ miles S of the village and $\frac{1}{4}$ mile N of small private jetty.

211. Gareloch
O.S. 53, 59 ; Barth. 44

Access by Craigendoran (railway and bus) or from River Clyde. The Loch is 7 miles long and has largely been spoilt by industrialisation. Tide in narrows 5 k. sps. (*Const.* + 1 hr. 17 min.).

212. Loch Long
O.S. 53, 59 ; Barth. 44

This interesting Loch, 16 miles long, runs through very fine mountainous country and is useful as a connection between Loch Lomond and the Firth of Clyde. Access from the S by Firth of Clyde or from Craigendoran. A ferry and steamer run from Gourock to Kilcreggan on the E shore (Cove Castle Y.H. 1 mile) and to Strone on the W shore (Strone Y.H. $\frac{1}{4}$ mile). Access from the N by portage from Tarbert, Loch Lomond (2 miles) or from Arrochar Station (1 mile) (Section 271).

Navigation offers no difficulty, though fierce squalls are sometimes met. There is a torpedo testing station in the upper reaches of the Loch, but warning is given when it is being used ; a red flag is shown on the raft and a siren is blown when torpedoes are running. In addition, there is a prohibited zone 200 yards wide extending 1,000 yards along the E shore at Coulport.

Camp sites are few, especially in the lower part, as the shores are very steep. There are three accessible Y.H's as follows : Cove Castle, 1 mile from Kilcreggan, near Cove Pier ; Strone, between Loch Long and the Holy Loch on Strone Point ; Ardgartan, on W shore, 2 miles from the head of the loch (land at jetty S of promontory).

There is a C.C. of G.B. & I. Permanent Site beside Ardgartan Y.H. Note that the head of the loch dries out $\frac{1}{2}$ mile at low water (*Const.* +0 hr. 53 min.) and that the promontory at Ardgartan is very shoaly and should be avoided by keeping outside the beacon. Stores : Cove and Arrochar. Distances : Cove to Mouth of Loch Goil $6\frac{1}{2}$ miles, to Ardgartan 14 miles, to Arrochar 16. Tides run at less than 1 k., flooding $4\frac{1}{2}$ hrs. after H.W. Dover.

The portage to Tarbert, Loch Lomond, is on 2 miles of first-class road rising to only 100 feet. Land near Arrochar Pier. Buses pass at intervals.

213. Loch Goil
O.S. 53 ; Barth. 44

This loch, 6 miles long, is a branch of Loch Long, which it resembles. There are camp sites near the mouth. It may often be closed by the Admiralty, except at night and at week-ends.

214. Holy Loch and Loch Eck
O.S. 53, 59 ; Barth. 44

Holy Loch is 2 miles long, and its shores are heavily populated. A portage of 4 miles leads to Loch Eck, 6 miles long, where there is a Y.H. just N of Whistlefield Hotel. From the N end of Loch Eck a portage of 5 miles leads to Loch Fyne at Strachur. Apart from its scenic value this route may be useful as a short-cut, or when bad weather makes it unwise to go round Ardlamont Point. The roads are good.

ISLAND OF BUTE
(With adjacent lochs)

215. Kyles of Bute
O.S. 59 ; Barth. 44

This pleasant waterway makes a good route to the W. Access : Wemyss Bay or Largs. Steamer may be taken from Wemyss Bay to Rothesay (7 miles) if weather is bad.

From Toward Point to Ardlamont Point through the Kyles is 18 miles. Winds are often squally. The flood tide setting through from the W reaches as far S in the East Kyle as Strone Point, and is felt throughout. In the narrows at the Burnt Islands the flood sets SE and the ebb NW at 3-4 k. sps. (*Const.* + 0 hr. 52 min.) Camping on Bute is not encouraged, but there is a pleasant site at Balnakailly Bay just S of the Burnt Islands. Tighnabruaich Y.H. lies up the hill half way between Tighnabruaich and Auchenlochan Piers (land at slipway).

Stores : Rothesay, Colintraive, Tighnabruaich, Kames.

Distances from Wemyss Bay : Toward Point 3½, Ardbeg 7, Burnt Islands 14, Tighnabruaich 17, Ardlamont Point 23 miles.

216. Adjacent Lochs

Loch Striven (8 miles), is a very secluded loch with steep sides, which is sometimes closed by the Admiralty (warnings being displayed).

Loch Riddon (3 miles), is a pretty loch with wooded shores, which dries out for nearly half its length.

217. West Coast of Bute
O.S. 59 ; Barth. 44

This 10 miles of coast from the West Kyle to Garroch Head is an exposed shore, with the Island of Inchmarnock lying 1 mile off. It makes an approach to Arran. The tide runs at 1½ k. sps. N from 5 hrs. before to 1 hr. after H.W. Dover, and S otherwise. There is a tide race off the W side of Garroch Head which is bad in strong winds, and should be taken at slack tide.

218. LOCH FYNE
O.S. 52, 53, 58 ; Barth. 44, 48

The lower part of this loch, which is 42 miles long, gives access to the Crinan Canal and thence to the W coast of Argyll. The upper part is well worth exploring on its own. A portage can be made from Strachur to Loch Eck and thence to Holy Loch (Section 214).

Basking sharks are to be met with more often in Loch Fyne than in any other part of the West Coast—see General Introduction.

Access : From Kyles of Bute or Kilbrannan Sound, or by bus or steamer to Tarbert, Ardrishaig or Inveraray.

On the E side camp sites are easy to obtain, but there are none on the W side in the lower reaches ; note that many of the bays dry out for some distance. Tides run 2 k. sps. except at narrows, flooding 5 hrs. before, to 1 hr. after, H.W. Dover.

Miles

0	*Ardlamont Point.*	Can be tricky in S winds. Do not keep too close to shore.
8	*Tarbert.*	Bus, steamer, stores, hotel. A portage of 1½ mls. leads to West Loch Tarbert and the W coast of Kintyre.
18	*Ardrishaig.*	Stores, bus, hotel. Entrance to Crinan Canal (Section 219).
18	*Otter Spit.*	Leave beacon to E. Through narrows flood tide (3 k.) runs N from 5 hrs. before until H.W. Dover, and ebb (5 k.) runs S from H.W. Dover for 7 hrs.
26	*Minard Narrows*	and Islands. Flood 3 k., ebb 4 k.
30	*Furnace.*	Bus, stores.
36	*Inveraray.*	Bus, stores, hotel. An historic and attractive town, seat of the Duke of Argyll.
42		Head of Loch dries out almost 1 mile.

219. CRINAN CANAL
O.S. 52 ; Barth. 44 or 43

This pleasant canal, 9 miles long, connects Loch Fyne with the W coast of Argyll. The canal is run by British Waterways. It usually takes four or five hours to go through using the locks.

There are 15 locks, in four groups, so that only four portages are necessary if locks are not used.

At Ardrishaig, land on the shore about 200 yards N of the pier, opposite the Royal Hotel, and portage up to the canal above the first four locks. There is a stretch of 4 miles from here to the four locks at Cairnban, then a mile on the summit, and five locks descending at Dunardry. In the middle of the last reach (2 miles) is Bellanoch Hotel. where a camp site is available on the roadside. The two locks at Crinan may be avoided by a short but steep portage to the sea just beyond the bridge ½ mile short of Crinan. (Hotel, stores.) Trout fishing on the canal is free. Midges are often troublesome, especially during a portage.

WEST ARGYLL COAST
220. Mull of Kintyre to Crinan
O.S. 52, 58, 65 ; Barth. 43

This coast is pleasant but exposed, the best part being N of Gigha.

Access :	(i)	Crinan Canal.
	(ii)	Portage (1½ mls.) from Tarbert to West Loch Tarbert.
	(iii)	Portage (10 mls.) by bus from Campbeltown to Machrihanish.
	(iv)	Bus from Glasgow to West Loch Tarbert or the coast S of it.
	(v)	By rounding the Mull of Kintyre, though this is not advised.

In general tide runs at 2½ k. sps. N from 1 hr. before to 5 hrs. after H.W. Dover. In Gigha Sound there are many rocks and the tide sets at 2-3 k. Approaching Loch Crinan from the S, keep fairly near the E shore as NNW of Ruadh Sgeir, which lies in mid-channel, the flood tide runs at 4 k. sps. towards the Gulf of Corryvreckan and causes bad tide rips over the ledges.

221. Adjacent Lochs

West Loch Tarbert, Loch Caolisport, and Loch Sween, present no difficulty and are worthy of exploration.

222. Crinan to Oban
O.S. 52 ; Barth. 44, 47

This is a fine stretch of sheltered coast, and forms part of the regular route to the N. With a favouring tide the trip takes two days.

Access : By sea from the S (Section 220), by Crinan Canal (Section 219), or by portage from Loch Awe (Section 272).

If storm-bound at Crinan it is possible to portage to Loch Awe (Section 272), and portage again from Dalmally to Taynuilt, reaching Oban by Loch Etive.

Warning. Canoeists must be careful to keep clear of the Gulf of Coirebhreacain (Corryvreckan) between Jura and Scarba. This Gulf is considered the worst in the West Highlands and strangers are warned against it. The tide sets through at 8 k. sps., and the overfalls caused by the uneven bottom make it extremely dangerous. The flood sets through from E to W and causes a whirlpool near the Scarba shore. The Gulf can often be heard roaring many miles away.

Miles

0   *Crinan*. Course NW to Craignish Point. Except for a few hours during the ebb there are many currents and tide rips in this area which are very uncomfortable. It is best to keep well into Loch Craignish, passing N of Liath-sgeir Mhor and then to Craignish Point.

4   *Dorus Mor* ("The Big Door"), the passage between Craignish Point and the island of Garbh Reisa. The tides here are variable and attain a rate of 4-5 k. sps., with strong eddies, the flood running from about 1 hr. before, and the ebb from about 5 hrs. after H.W. Dover with little slack water. The flood sets NW through most of the channel, with a reverse stream close to Craignish shore, and strong tide rips between the two streams. The ebb sets SE mostly through the S part of the channel, and there is usually slack water between mid-channel and the Craignish shore.

Travelling N, it is best to pass Dorus Mor near low slack water, and take the flood tide which flows northward into Shuna Sound at 2 k. sps. There is an eddy on the flood close to the shore N of Craignish Point. Be careful not to go to the W of the two small islands lying westwards of Craignish Point, as a branch of the flood tide sets straight over to the

Gulf of Corryvreckan. Shuna Sound, W of Shuna, is the best passage, but if it becomes necessary to work against the tide the E side of Shuna should be taken as the tides here are very weak.

10   *Toberonochy.* Pleasant village on Luing. Camp site ¼ ml. S of village. Stores, milk and lobsters.

Keep N into Seil Sound. This must be taken with a favouring tide, and is almost dry at L.W. Ebb sets S 1¾ hrs. before H.W. (*Const.* - 6 hrs. 7 min.)

17   *Clachan Bridge.* Hotel, no stores. Bus to Oban. Continue N along coast into Sound of Kerrera. Here tide sets N at 1-2 k. from 1 hr. before to 5 hrs. after H.W. Dover, and S otherwise.

25   *Ardantrive Bay.* On Kerrera, opposite Oban, is the best camp site. Land beside ruins of wooden jetty and ask permission at farm 100 yds. inland.

25   *Oban.* Stores, railway, bus, hotels, etc. (*Const.* - 5 hrs. 31 min.) There is a municipal camp site in Ganavan Bay, 2 mls. N of Oban.

223.   Adjacent Lochs

Loch Craignish, 5 miles long, gives access by portage to Loch Awe (Section 272). Tide at entrance runs 2 k. sps.

Loch Melfort, 3¼ miles long, offers no difficulties.

Loch Feochan, has a narrow entrance where the flood runs at 5 k. sps. for 4 hours, while the ebb runs for 8 hours. The flood runs from 3 hours after to 7 hours after H.W. Dover.

224.   Inner Hebrides
O.S. 51, 52, 57, 58 ; Barth. 43

The adventurous canoeist may explore the islands of Islay, Jura, Scarba and Colonsay. Tidal streams are very complicated, rocks and overfalls abound, and local advice should be sought whenever possible. Be careful to keep clear of the Gulf of Corryvreckan at the N end of Jura. The channel to the N of Scarba is also highly dangerous, and should not be attempted. The Clyde Cruising Club Sailing Directions should be consulted. Shuna, Luing, Lunga, Seil and Kerrera may also be explored and are not so exposed.

Oban. This town is a good centre from which to explore the West. The canoeist may go NE up Loch Linnhe and on to the Caledonian Canal, or branch off at Fort William up Loch Eil and portage to Loch Sheil. Or he may go NW up the Sound of Mull and into Loch Sunart, gaining Loch Sheil by a portage to Acharacle. Loch Sheil leads to the W coast and the route to Skye and the N.

LOCH LINNHE AND ADJACENT LOCHS

225. Loch Linnhe
(Oban to Fort William)
O.S. 46 ; Barth. 47, 50

This is a fine sheltered arm of the sea 32 miles long. The usual wind is SW and the tide sets 1-2 k. sps. except in the narrows, the flood setting NE from 1 hr. before to 5 hrs. after H.W. Dover. Camp sites can be found by asking on the NW shore in the upper reaches, and on the SE shore S of Corran.

Miles
- 0   *Oban (Const. – 5 hrs. 31 min. Dover).*   Through N entrance of Oban Bay and along the coast.
- 2   *Ganavan Bay.* Public camp site.
- 4   *Dunstaffnage Castle.* Entrance to Loch Etive. Cut across Ardmucknish Bay into Lynn of Lorn between Lismore and Appin.
- 10   *Entrance to Loch Creran.*
- 11   *Port Appin.* Stores. Narrow channel with rocks. Tide 1½ hrs. later than above.
- 17   *Eilean Balnagowan.* Camp site in Cuil Bay. Railway at Duror.
- 22   *Entrance to Loch Leven.* Railway and stores Ballachulish. Bus and stores Onich.
- 24   *Corran Narrows.* Tide runs 6 k. sps. 2 k. nps. NE from 1 hr. after to 7 hrs. after H.W. Dover though there is a variable period of slack water at the turn. Go through with a favouring tide, and keep near the centre, as there is a strong eddy on either shore. Rough water may be expected when the wind is against the tide. At neaps it may be possible to work through against the tide by keeping close to the NW shore.
- 30   Camp sites on SE shore 2 mls. short of Fort William (on payment), or on opposite shore near Treslaig.
- 32   *Fort William.* Railway, bus, stores, hotels, etc. Glen Nevis Y.H. is up the glen 3 mls. from the shore. From Fort William one may cross to Corpach and go up the Caledonian Canal (Section 267), or go up Loch Eil (Section 230) into Loch Sheil.

226. Island of Lismore
O.S. 46 ; Barth. 47

This island is well worth visiting. Camp sites are obtainable and there is a store near the pier at Achnacroish. The S shore has been described. The Lynn of Morvern has a tide rip, especially at springs, from ½ mile NW of Bernera Island to near the Morvern Shore, for two or three hours from the beginning of the ebb. Flood NE from 1¼ hrs. to 7 hrs. after, ebb SW from 4¾ hrs. before to 1 hr. after H.W. Dover.

The currents at the SW end of Lismore are strong and complicated and are described below (Section 231).

210

227. Loch Etive
O.S. 46 ; Barth. 47

This is a beautiful loch, 19 miles long, and well worth exploring.

Miles

0   *Dunstaffnage Castle.*

2   *Connel Bridge.* The narrows here are called the Falls of Lora ; a ledge of rock above the bridge produces a heavy fall on the N side and a tide race on the S side after half ebb, and the flood does not enter the loch until this ledge is covered. Tides are irregular, but generally the ebb runs for 7 hrs., from $3\frac{1}{2}$ hrs. before to $3\frac{1}{2}$ hrs. after H.W. Dover and the flood the remaining 5 hrs.

The best place to pass the narrows is a few yards off the S pier of the bridge. Entering the loch is easy after the flood has covered the ledge, provided the rocks and eddies near the shore are avoided. The best time to start is $4\frac{1}{2}$ hrs. after H.W. Dover. Leaving the loch after half ebb is generally dangerous owing to the very heavy water and fierce eddies at the bottom of the ebb race, and the first three or four hours of the ebb should be taken. It is advisable to inspect the run from the S shore.

4   *Kilmaronaig.* Camp site on S shore.

9   *Bonawe.* Camp site on S shore. Land at E side of pier. Taynuilt 1 ml. inland has railway, bus, stores, hotel. Bus or railway from here to Loch Awe or Loch Lomond (Sections 272, 271).

$9\frac{1}{2}$ *Bonawe Narrows.* Tide $2\frac{1}{2}$ k. sps. (*Const.* − 3 hrs. 4 min. Dover). From here, for the 10 mls. to the head of the Loch, there are no dangers and practically no habitation.

228. Loch Creran
O.S. 46 ; Barth. 47

Eight miles long, this is a small loch between high hills. In the narrows at the entrance tide runs 6 k. sps. (*Const.* − 5 hrs. 35 min. Dover). At Creagan, 6 miles up, a railway bridge crosses, with station near the N shore and bus connection.

229. Loch Leven
O.S. 46, 47 ; Barth. 47, 50

This narrow and rather gloomy loch runs for 10 miles between very high hills, and gives access to Glencoe.

Miles

0   *Entrance.* 1 ml. *Ballachulish Pier* (stores).

2   *Ferry* (railway, bus, hotel). Tide runs 6 k. sps. ebbing for 7 hrs., from 5 hrs. before until 2 hrs. after H.W. Dover and flooding the remaining 5 with little slack water.

$4\frac{1}{2}$ *Carnoch* and *Glencoe.* Stores, bus, hotel. The Y.H. is 2 mls. up the Glen.

The rest of the loch, to the Aluminium Works at *Kinlochleven*, is very narrow and the shores are steep. Camp sites may be obtainable on the N shore.

230. Loch Eil
O.S. 35 ; Barth. 50

This loch, 8 miles long, runs W from Corpach, near Fort William, and a portage of 4 miles at its head gives access to Loch Sheil and the West Coast (Section 238). The tide is only strong at Annat narrows, where it sets at 5 k. sps., flooding from 2½ hours after H.W. Dover to 3½ hours before the next H.W. If portaging land on N shore at head of loch.

ISLAND OF MULL
(and adjacent lochs and coasts)

231. Sound of Mull
O.S. 45, 46 ; Barth 47

This waterway leads to the W, and to Loch Sunart, whence, by a portage of 3 miles to Loch Sheil, the canoeist reaches the route to Skye. Camping should be easy in all parts. The crossing from Oban to Duart Point by the Lady Rock (6 miles) is dangerous, especially in strong wind, and is not advised. The tide runs 4 k. sps., flooding up each side of Lismore and into the Sound of Mull. On both flood and ebb the currents are very confused, with tide rips, and the race near the Lady Rock is sometimes very bad. It is best to keep SW along the coast of Kerrera, and cross from Eilean nan Gamhna to the Mull shore N of Loch Don (4 miles). But note that off the mouth of Loch Don there are overfalls about ½ mile off shore on the flood, which runs N into the Sound of Mull at 3 k. sps. from ½ hr. to 6½ hrs. after H.W. Dover.

Miles
- 0   *Oban.* Leave Bay by N entrance and cross (as above) to the Mull shore.
- 9   *Duart Point.* From here tides set at 1-2 k. sps. flooding NW from 1 hr. after H.W. Dover for 6 hrs., though towards the western end of the Sound the flood starts 1 hr. earlier and runs for 7 hrs.
- 11   *Craignure.* Stores, hotel, steamer. Ferry from Oban.
- 22   *Salen.* Stores, hotel, steamer.
- 30   *Tobermory.* Stores, hotel, steamer. A good centre for excursions in Mull. (*Const.* – 5 hrs. 19 min.)

232. Loch Sunart
O.S. 45, 46 ; Barth. 47

A beautiful loch, 21 miles long, opposite Tobermory, giving access by portage to Loch Sheil.

Miles
- 0   *Tobermory.* N across Sound of Mull to loch entrance.
- 3   *Auliston Point.* Keep between point and Stirk Rocks lying ½ ml. W. Tide will be felt from here, flooding 1¼ hrs. after to 4¾ hrs. before H.W. Dover. Keep to the N shore, as the channels between the islands and the S shore are rocky and some dry out.

14   *Salen.* Stores, hotel. Land at W side of Salen Bay at the very
         head. Camp by burn side behind whitewashed cottage.
         Portage from here to Acharacle (Section 238).
22   *Strontian.* Stores, hotel, bus.

233. Mull, S.E. Coast, Duart to Iona
O.S. 51 ; Barth. 47

The Firth of Lorne Coast from Duart to Loch Buie is fairly sheltered, but the coast of the Ross of Mull is exposed to the S. In the western part, and especially round Iona, tides are strong and there are many dangerous overfalls and rocks.

Iona is connected with Fionphort on the Ross of Mull by a ferry and, from here, a bus runs to Salen and Tobermory. Camping on the island is difficult because of lack of water, and the W side is advised if a long stay is intended.

234. Mull, West Coast
O.S. 45 ; Barth. 47

This coast is very exposed and deeply indented with lochs, and the cliffs make many parts unapproachable except in calm weather. It is studded with rocks and tides are very strong, causing overfalls in many places. Off Caliach Point, the extreme NW point of Mull, there is a dangerous tide rip extending about 2 miles off shore. There is a good chance of the canoeist being stormbound on this coast, in which case he would have to pack up and take a bus to some more sheltered part, or portage from Loch na Keal to Salen. The off-lying Treshnish Isles are interesting bird haunts, but should only be visited in very settled weather, as the tide races are strong and the surf heavy.

235. Coll and Tiree
O.S. 44 ; Barth. 47

These islands, lying 7 miles W of Mull, are surrounded by dangers, both rocks and overfalls. They are very exposed and should be avoided.

236. Ardnamurchan
O.S. 45 ; Barth. 50

This rocky point of land, the most westerly in Britain, is completely exposed to the S and W, and a very considerable sea rises in even moderate winds. In southerly winds it is necessary to keep about a mile off-shore, as the seas are much wilder within this radius. Except in very settled weather it is much better for the canoeist to avoid Ardnamurchan altogether by going up Loch Sunart and portaging into Loch Sheil.

237. Small Isles and North Shore of Ardnamurchan
O.S. 33, 34, 45 ; Barth. 50

This area, comprising the islands of Rhum, Eigg, Muck and Canna, is not a good cruising ground, as it is exposed and the canoeist may easily become stormbound. Tide floods NW from 1 hr. to 7 hrs. after H.W. Dover. The N coast of Ardnamurchan is more sheltered and offers some camp sites. It is accessible from Loch Moidart (Section 239).

238.   Loch Shiel and River Shiel
O.S. 35, 45, 46 ; Barth. 50

Though this is a freshwater loch it is described here as it is a link in the W coast route to the N.

Access : (*i*) By rail or bus to Glenfinnan (Mallaig Line).

(*ii*) By portage from Loch Eil (Section 230) over 4½ miles of good road with only slight hills. After rain the last ¾ mile of the River Callop may be used to shorten the portage. A short lorry, which has taken double-seaters, may be hired from Mr. Blyth, Carrier, Glenfinnan (Tel.: Stage House Inn, Glenfinnan 203). Buses pass along this road twice daily. Launch at boathouse on L just before Glenfinnan. Trains run twice daily from Kinlocheil to Glenfinnan.

(*iii*) By portage from Salen, Loch Sunart (Section 232) to Acharacle at the W end of Loch Shiel. This 3 miles portage is rather hilly. Buses pass twice daily and a transport lorry is available about 5 p.m. on Tuesdays, Thursdays and Saturdays.

The loch is 17 miles long and camp sites are obtainable, though there is not much flat ground on the shores. The water is safe if boiled. Camping at Glenfinnan beside boathouse or on SW shore behind island. Shop at station.

Eilean Fhianain, an old burial island with chapel, 12 miles from Glenfinnan, is worth visiting. At Acharacle, 5 miles further on, see Mr. Campbell, Ardshealach (large white house ¼ mile inshore among trees on L) for camp site.

The River Shiel, starting at Acharacle (P.O., no stores) is 3 miles long and may be shallow in summer. Where it enters Loch Moidart (Section 239) there is a tidal fall, which can only be run near H.W. (*Const.* ‑5 hrs. 15 min.) At any other time there is a short but very difficult portage.

WEST INVERNESS COAST
(*Ardnamurchan to Kyle of Lochalsh and adjacent lochs*)

Access.   By road or rail at any point between Loch Ailort and Mallaig or by Loch Sheil (Section 238). The approach by Ardnamurchan Point is not advised.

239.   Coast, Loch Moidart to Mallaig
O.S. 34, 45 ; Barth. 50

This 21 miles of coast is very broken and rocky and camp sites are not easy to find. The lochs offer good shelter in bad weather and are worth exploring for themselves. On the open coast the tide is little felt but it runs into all lochs flooding from 1 hr. after to 7 hrs. after H.W. Dover.

Miles

  0   *Dorlin*, Loch Moidart. Leave Loch Moidart by S channel and turn N to Arisaig Peninsula. Camp site may be found at Glenuig, 2 mls. inside the Sound of Arisaig. The coast N of the Sound of Arisaig is very foul with rocks and a good look-out must be kept, especially if a sea is running.

14   *Arisaig*, lies in Loch nan Cilltean. It is not worth putting in here unless stores are urgently needed. Good camp sites with white sand beaches may be found 2 or 3 mls. further N at Bunacaimb or Traigh.

17   *Morar*. The bay offers some shelter from SW winds, but at low tide there is only a narrow channel and a large expanse of sand.

20   *Mallaig*. Stores, Railway Hotel. (*Const.* -- 5 hrs. 9 min. Dover.) Nearest camp site 2 mls. E at Mallaigvaig or Mallaigmore.

240. Adjacent Lochs
O.S. 34, 45 ; Barth. 50

Loch Moidart, 5 miles long, is divided in two at its entrance by Eilean Shona. The N channel dries out at low tide, as does the upper part of the loch. The tide runs strongly (see above).

Loch Ailort, 6 miles long, has a hotel at its head. Westerly winds against the ebb tide cause breaking seas right across the entrance. Small camp sites may be found on N shore near head of loch.

Sound of Arisaig and Loch nan Uamh. Much broken by rocks but tide is weak. Shores are rocky and camp sites difficult to find.

Loch nan Cilltean, is 2 miles long, and, at Arisaig at its head, are stores, hotel, railway. Tide runs strongly until near L.W.

241. Loch Morar
O.S. 34, 35 ; Barth. 50

This beautiful freshwater loch, 12 miles long, offers a refuge in heavy weather, and good camp sites. It is reached by a portage of ¼ mile from the road at the river mouth to above the dam. A further portage of less than a mile from South Tarbet Bay, in the middle of the N shore, leads to the sea at Loch Nevis (Section 243) but this is very difficult as there is only a rough, steep track, unsuitable for trolleys.

242. Sound of Sleat, Mallaig to Kyle of Lochalsh
O.S. 26, 34, 35 ; Barth 50, 54

This passage lies between Sleat (pronounced Slate), the southern part of Skye and the mainland. Tides run at 1-2 k. except in the narrows, flooding NE from 1½ hrs. to 7½ hrs. after H.W. Dover. There are three lochs which offer shelter and are worth exploring.

Miles
0   *Mallaig*. Course N across mouth of Loch Nevis.

6   *Airor*. Camp site in sheltered bay with houses.

12   *Sandaig Islands*. Good camp site in Bay, or on islands.

17   *Glenelg*. Stores, camp sites may be obtainable. Glenelg Y.H. on E shore at entrance to narrows. Land at ferry slip.

17   *Kyle Rhea* (pronounced Ray). In the narrows, 2 mls. long, the tide is fast, the flood setting N at 6 k. sps. from 1½ hrs. after to 7½ hrs. after H.W. Dover, and the ebb S at 8 k. sps. from 4½ hrs. before to 1½ hrs. after H.W. Dover. Neap tides are usually ½ hr. later. There is no slack water, but usually 40 min. at each turn during which the rate is less than 2 k.

It is best to start up the Kyle at this time, as the water may be rough when the stream is strong, especially if the wind is against the tide. In southerly winds there is a very heavy overfall on the ebb of the E side of the entrance.

19   *Loch Alsh.* Turn W. Tides weak and confused. A camp site may be obtained near Balmacara Hotel, directly across Loch Alsh.

22½   *Kyle of Lochalsh.* Good shopping centre, hotel, Y.H. Railway to Inverness, steamer to Mallaig. Land at steps on railway pier.

Camping is not easy, but a site may be found on Plock of Kyle. There is a good site on the Skye shore ¼ ml. past the lighthouse on Eilean Ban 1¼ mls. from Kyle. (Water obtainable from stream.)

243.   Adjacent Lochs
O.S. 26, 34, 35 ; Barth. 50, 54

These lochs offer no difficulties but tides run strongly in places, flooding from 1 hr. to 7 hrs. after H.W. Dover. *Loch Nevis* (12 mls.) has a tide of 5 k. sps. in the narrows, and a portage from Tarbet leads to Loch Morar (Section 241). *Loch Hourn* (13 mls.) is noted for its scenery. *Loch Alsh and Loch Duich* are together, 14 miles long, and *Loch Long* is a narrow branch running 5 miles to the N. Ratagan Y.H. lies at the head of Loch Alsh, on the S shore.

INNER SOUND and SOUND OF RAASAY

This stretch of water, lying between Skye and the mainland, is fairly sheltered and makes an attractive cruising ground. It contains several islands, of which Raasay is the largest.

244.   Kyle of Lochalsh to Portree
O.S. 25 ; Barth. 54

The tide in the narrows at Kyle Akin runs at a maximum of 3 k. sps., but its direction is liable to variation at different heights of tide. At springs it usually runs E from 4 hrs. before until 3 hrs. after H.W. Dover, but at neaps it is 3 or 4 hrs. later. The usual route from Kyle to Portree leads between Scalpay and Raasay and is 22 miles. There are no difficulties, and both between Scalpay and Longay, and in the narrows between Skye and Raasay, the flood runs S at 2 k. sps. from 2 hrs. after until 5 hrs. before H.W. Dover, and the ebb N. There is a camp site beside the lighthouse at Eyre Point at the S end of Raasay.

The inshore route, S of Scalpay, may be used in bad weather, though it is 2 miles longer. It passes Broadford where there are stores and bus. In Caolas Scalpay, the narrows between Scalpay and Skye, there is only 1 foot of water at low tide, and the flood sets SE at 1 k. sps. from 1 hr. after until 7 hrs. after H.W. Dover, and the ebb NW.

Portree. Stores, bus, steamer to Mallaig. Camp sites are hard to obtain as the head of the bay near the burn is very muddy. The best found so far is Camus Ban, a clean, sheltered bay with a firm sand beach, on the S just before reaching the pier. There is no water, and this must be brought across from the pier, or from the burn over the hill behind the bay.

245.   Inner Sound
O.S. 25 ; Barth. 54

This sound lies between Raasay and Applecross.   Applecross has stores and steamer connections. Tides are weak, flooding S at 1 k. sps. from 2 hrs. after until 5 hrs. before H.W. Dover (see Section 249).

246.   Sound of Raasay
O.S. 25 ; Barth. 54

This sound lies between the islands of Skye and Raasay and is well sheltered.   The Skye coast is steep and rocky and offers little facility for camping, but the Raasay shore is more hospitable.   The tide is weak except in the narrows (Section 244).

247.   Loch Carron and Loch Kishorn
O.S. 25, 26 ; Barth. 54

These two beautiful and sheltered lochs run eastward between Applecross and Kyle.   There are many rocks and reefs but tides are weak except at the narrows where they run 2-3 k. sps., flooding from 2 hrs. after to 4 hrs. before H.W. Dover.   They make a good refuge in bad weather and stores and hotel are available at Plockton and Jeantown. North Strome Y.H. lies at the entrance to Upper Loch Carron.   The railway station at Strome Ferry is a convenient finishing point for a tour.   Good camp site 1 mile NW of Strome Ferry.

248.   ISLAND OF SKYE
O.S. 24, 33 ; Barth. 54

The eastern coast of this island has been described (Sections 242, 244).   The western and northern coasts consist of a series of deep lochs and would make a very fine cruising ground, but they are considerably exposed, and the canoeist runs the risk of being stormbound on a rugged coast, parts of which are uninhabited.

WEST COAST OF ROSS and SUTHERLAND

These coasts are broken into a series of lochs and promontories with many small islands.   Their scenery is exceptionally fine and, though exposed, especially to the quick rising north-westerly winds, they offer great scope to the cruising canoeist.   Land transport is mostly by local buses and these are not reliable.   Villages are few and are not to be depended upon for provisioning.

Tidal streams on the whole are not strong.   The general direction of the flood stream is southward, and into all bays and lochs, and it runs from 1½ hrs. after H.W. Dover to 4½ hrs. before the next H.W.   Even in the narrow parts of lochs the tide does not exceed a rate of 1 k. sps.

249. Applecross
O.S. 25, 26 ; Barth. 54

The Applecross promontory is mainly rocky with several inlets for shelter such as at Toscaig, Poll Creadha and Sand. The village of Applecross is one of the least accessible as the road winds over hills of exceptional gradient. In the event of high winds blocking a passage N, it is possible to portage over the track from Loch Kishorn to Shieldaig. It is, however, heavy going on a bad surface which rises to a height of 320 feet. There is no public service and passing transport is seldom seen.

250. Loch Torridon
O.S. 25, 26 ; Barth. 54

This loch is worth seeing and its mountains are popular with climbers. Inver Alligin Y.H. lies on the N shore near the head of the loch. Shores are stony. The coast from here N is rocky and full advantage should be made of good weather to cover it quickly. Milk and eggs can sometimes be had at the village of Diabeg. Except as a standby in bad weather, the Y.H. at Craig should be passed, as it offers little for the canoeist. There are fine sands both before and after Red Point and again at Opinan where there is yet another Y.H. Red Point offers no difficulty, except in westerly winds. It cannot be emphasised too often that canoeists should make the most of calm periods to travel the unbroken coastlines, resting in the shelter of the deeper bays during bad weather.

251. Gairloch
O.S. 19 ; Barth. 54.

Gairloch is noted for its sands and has an excellent Y.H. at Carn Dearg. This can be regarded as a junction point by the canoeist for he has now the choice of three routes. He can proceed N by the headland of Rudha Reidh, or he can portage either direct to Poolewe or to Loch Maree by Kerrysdale. A bus runs the former route, but the latter has no public service and is a long pull over a 400 foot summit. Rudha Reidh should be avoided. It has dangerous races and no landings in rough weather.

252. Loch Maree
O.S. 19 ; Barth. 54

Loch Maree is a worthwhile diversion and can be reached from Poolewe. The connecting River Ewe is navigable only for half its length and a 1 mile portage is the alternative to wading the lower part of the river. Loch Maree is famed for its lovely little islets, grouped in inter-linking channels which make it ideal for the canoeist. Camp sites are available.

253. Loch Ewe
O.S. 19 ; Barth. 58

This sea loch presents no problems, but Aultbea at its further end has been spoiled by naval occupation during the war and should be regarded only as a provisioning quarter.

254. Gruinard Bay
O.S. 19 ; Barth. 58

Reached by portage of 3 miles to Laide. Greenstone Point is not advised except in settled weather. The sands of Little Gruinard are noted for their beauty.

255. Loch Broom and the Summer Isles
O.S. 19, 20 ; Barth. 58

Loch Broom can be reached without difficulty, and from Ullapool connections S can be made by bus to Garve and then train to Inverness, joining there with the main line. There is a Y.H. at Ullapool. Badcaul Y.H. lies on the S shore of Little Loch Broom, and Achininver Y.H. at Achiltibuie N of the entrance to Loch Broom.

The **Summer Isles** are a group of small islands off Loch Broom, all uninhabited, and accessible in quiet weather by canoe. Fresh water can be found on the larger ones. Landing places are mostly difficult.

The inner isles, Tanera Mor and Tanera Beg and their satellites, could be used in most types of weather but the more isolated ones like Priest Isle and Bottle Isle require really settled weather as one might be marooned there for the duration of bad weather. Fish can be caught to eke out supplies.

Priest Isle, the most westerly, has 6 miles of coast but only two good landings, both on the E side, facing NE. The cliffs of Bottle Island contain splendid caves.

Glas Leac Mor has only one landing place, on E side of island, and that is rough. Tanera Mor has several possible landing places, the best being at the quay in the Anchorage on the E. Tanera Beg has only two landing places, both difficult, on the N and S sides. Eilean Fada More has a coral sand beach at low tide. Difficult landing (boulders) on N of Eilean Dubh.

256. Far North West: Cape Wrath District
O.S. 9, 13 ; Barth. 58

Journeys N of Ullapool should be made in the understanding that the coast has little habitation, few roads and conveyances, no railway. Possible connections may be made at villages such as Lochinver, Unapool and Scourie. The coastline is very broken ; reefs and races many and conditions notoriously changeable. The headlands of Rhu Coigach and Stoer should be attempted only in settled weather. Provisions are not easy to obtain and the basic needs should be carried.

OUTER HEBRIDES
O.S. 8, 12, 17, 18, 23, 32 ; Barth. 53, 57

257. These islands, known collectively as "Long Island," are a group 113 miles long, lying off the W coast of Skye. Access by steamer. The Minch should not be crossed by canoe. The land is mostly low-lying and the E coast is steep and rocky, with many small islands, and deeply indented with innumerable lochs. Tidal streams on the whole are not strong, though in places they form dangerous overfalls. Being scenically attractive parts of this coast would form an interesting cruising area in good weather, but canoeists should consult the Clyde Cruising Club Sailing Directions for details of tidal streams and dangers.

NORTH and EAST COASTS OF SCOTLAND

258. North Coast

This coast which extends from Cape Wrath to Duncansby Head is rugged and stormy, and cannot be recommended to canoeists. Details of tidal streams and dangers are to be found in the North Sea Pilot, Part II, published by the Admiralty.

259. East Coast

This offers no particularly attractive cruising areas, and is seldom used by canoeists other than local residents. The estuaries are described below but the rest of the coast is exposed and affords little refuge in bad weather.

Details of tidal streams and dangers will be found in the North Sea Pilot, Part II, published by the Admiralty.

260. Dornoch Firth
O.S. 22 ; Barth. 59

This narrow firth runs 23 miles W from Tarbat Ness. In its lower part tidal streams are weak, seldom exceeding 1 k., and the flood runs from 5 hrs. before until 1 hr. after H.W. Dover. Both shores dry out exposing up to 1 mile of sand at low tide. The upper part of the firth is much encumbered by shifting sandbanks, and the tidal streams are irregular and may reach a speed of 6 k.

A main road follows the coast for most of its length on either shore and the railway runs along the S shore.

261. Cromarty Firth
O.S. 22, 28 ; Barth. 55

This sheltered estuary extends 20 miles W and SW from its narrow entrance at Invergordon on the Moray Firth, and the town of Dingwall lies near its head. A main road runs along its northern shore. There are some extensive sandbanks and tidal streams run at 1-2 k., flooding from ½ hr. to 6½ hrs. after H.W. Dover. The Firth is a naval base and considerable traffic may be expected.

262. Moray Firth
O.S. 28, 29 ; Barth. 55, 56

The southern coast of the Moray Firth has a pleasant sandy shore on which lie the towns of Lossiemouth, Burghead and Nairn. In many parts there are extensive sands at low tide. This coast connects the mouth of the River Spey (Section 286) with the Inverness Firth and thus with Inverness and the Caledonian Canal (Section 267).

The tidal streams run at 2 k. sps., the flood setting eastwards along the coast from 1 hr. after H.W. Dover until 4 hrs. before the next H.W.

263. Inverness (Inner Moray) Firth
O.S. 28 ; Barth. 55

The NW shore of the Inverness Firth is fairly steep, but the SE shore is flat and many sandbanks are exposed at low water. Tides are not much felt, except at the entrance between Fort George and Chanonry Point, where they run at 2-3 k. sps.

The River Ness is navigable upstream into the centre of the town of Inverness.

264. Beauly Firth
O.S. 28 ; Barth. 55

In the Beauly Firth there are 4 miles of open water about 1 mile wide. The remainder of the firth is almost entirely occupied by drying sands through which the River Beauly maintains an irregular, shifting channel. The tide at the entrance runs 3 k. sps., flooding 4 hrs. before to 2 hrs. after H.W. Dover. The streams are strongest in the narrows abreast Craigton Point, and heavy rips and swirls are experienced between Inverness Beacon and Kessock Ferry during both streams. The entrance to the Caledonian Canal (Section 267) lies at Clachnaharry, 1 mile along the southern shore from Kessock Ferry.

265. Firth of Tay
O.S. 52, 56, 50 ; Barth. 49

This estuary forms a continuation of the River Tay (Section 277), and the River Earn (Section 283) also runs into it. The extensive sandbanks must be avoided on a falling tide, and also make landing difficult in many parts. It will be described eastwards from Perth. The Tay Canoe Club has its H.Q. near Perth Harbour on the S shore.

Miles

0 *Perth Bridge.* Shallows above central pier. Arch to R of centre is best in low water.

¼ *Victoria Bridge.* At Moncrieff Island, immediately below, keep R.

½ Railway bridge. Take third arch from R and turn L immediately afterwards to take a rapid. From here on the river is tidal, and at low water there is a slow current with no rapids, and the banks are muddy. (*Const.* + 4 hrs. 30 min.)

4½ *Elcho Castle* R is worth visiting, and there is a camp site nearby.

7 *River Earn* joins on R (Section 283). Camp site on E bank just inside mouth.

From here tide runs at 2-3 k. sps. The water can be rough if the tide is against the wind.

8½ *Mugdrum Island.* Keep R.

9½ *Newburgh.* Bus, stores. Camp site on shore E of town. (*Const.* + 4 hrs. 19 min.)

From here to Dundee keep to S shore, as on N there is a mudbank which stretches nearly 2 mls. out at low tide.

17 *Balmerino.* Bank extends ½ ml. out from R. Cut over narrow part of bank. Abbey R may be visited.

20½ *Tay Bridge.*

22 *Dundee.* Railway, bus, stores, hotel. Land at Boat Club Slip, W of Ferry Pier. (*Const.* + 3 hrs. 50 min.)

25½ *Broughty Ferry.*

32 *Buddon Ness.*

266. Firth of Forth
O.S. 54, 55, 61, 62 ; Barth. 45 (West of Edinburgh)
O.S. 56, 62 ; Barth. 46 (East of Edinburgh)

This estuary makes a pleasant small cruising ground, and is accessible to Edinburgh, and to the Forth and Clyde Canal at Grangemouth (Section 268). It is rather exposed to easterly winds, and there is not much shelter. (Granton Harbour, Edinburgh—*Const.* + 3 hrs. 50 min.)

Of the larger islands Inchkeith, which has a lighthouse, Inchmickery and Cramond Islands are fortified and landing is not permitted at present. Inchcolm, lying near the northern shore at Aberdour, has a 12th century monastery and is well worth visiting.

East of the Forth Bridge the estuary is 31 miles long and gradually widens to its mouth, being 5 miles wide at Granton. The N shore is generally deep, and the S shore shallow, with some extensive sand and mud flats at low water. Tides run at 1 to 3 k. sps. except in the narrows under Forth Bridge, and between Inchcolm and the shore, where they reach 5 to 6 k. sps. The flood sets W from $2\frac{1}{4}$ hrs. before H.W. Dover for 6 hrs. and the ebb E.

Camping in this area is very difficult, though small sites may be found near Kinghorn or Longniddry. In most places where sites could be found camping is prohibited. There is a civic camping site at Edinburgh between Granton and Cramond.

W of the Forth Bridge the waterway is more sheltered and does not exceed $2\frac{1}{2}$ miles in width, with as much as $\frac{1}{2}$ mile of mud exposed on each shore at low tide. Some camp sites are obtainable, especially on the N shore. Tide runs 2 to 3 k. sps., flooding from $\frac{1}{2}$ hr. before to $5\frac{1}{2}$ hrs. after H.W. Dover. 13 miles W of the Forth Bridge is Grange-mouth (*Const.* + 4 hrs. 16 min.), and the entrance to the Forth and Clyde Canal (Section 268). 8 miles further up is Alloa, and from here to Stirling, where the Forth becomes a river (Section 275) is 15 miles by water though only 6 miles by road. The tides in this reach are $\frac{1}{2}$ hr. later than those given above.

CANALS

Of Scotland's five canals only two, the Crinan and the Caledonian, are of real interest to the canoeist. The Crinan Canal has already been described (Section 219).

The rule of the road on these canals is as follows : when meeting a vessel keep to starboard, when being overtaken keep to port ; when meeting a vessel being tracked keep clear of the tow-path side. These rules should be interpreted with commonsense, and if one bank is obviously shallow canoes should hold to that side and leave the deep water for larger vessels.

Power vessels passing through the canals make a considerable wash, and it is not advisable to hold canoes close alongside the banks when being passed. Similarly canoes should not be left in the water un-attended unless it is certain that no boats will be passing.

Canals are normally open for traffic from dawn to sunset, with a maximum of 6 a.m. to 9 p.m., and are closed on Sundays, but canoes not using locks can of course pass any time.

Owing to the many portages necessary it is advisable to carry a trolley, and to have kit stowed for easy unloading. Precautions should be taken against midges.

British Waterways period licences are applicable to the Scottish canals, including the Caledonian and Crinan Canals.

267. CALEDONIAN CANAL
O.S. 27, 28, 35, 36 ; Barth. 51, 55, 50

The Caledonian Canal, which runs from Loch Linnhe (Section 225) on the West coast, to the Beauly Firth (Section 254) on the East coast, is 60½ miles long, and the scenery throughout is magnificent. The through passage by canoe generally takes 5 days and makes a good finish to a trip on the Firth of Lorne. Because of the prevailing wind it is advisable to start from the SW end. Stores are available at several places, and though the shores are generally steep, many camp sites will be found if permission is asked. There are three accessible Youth Hostels.

The canal is controlled by British Waterways—Canal Offices at Corpach and Clachnaharry. There is a good tow-path, and a trolley is of great value in portaging.

The waterway consists of three lochs, Lochy, Oich and Ness, totalling 38½ miles, connected by stretches of canal which total 22 miles. There are 29 locks, 15 in the SW part in four groups, and 14 in the NE part in six groups, so that ten portages are required from sea to sea. The nine swing bridges do not hinder the canoeist, as they are well clear of the water.

The River Ness is navigable downstream and may be used in preference to the canal. The Rivers Oich and Lochy are of doubtful value. These will be mentioned later.

Access. At SW end : (1) Corpach or Fort William by railway or bus. (A portage is saved by leaving train or bus at Banavie Station and launching above Banavie Locks, but if a licence has not been obtained beforehand it will be necessary to get one from Corpach, 1½ miles further on.) (2) From Loch Linnhe (Section 225) or Loch Sheil and Loch Eil (Sections 236, 230).

At NE end : (1) Inverness by railway or bus. (Launching at Muirtown, but obtaining a permit, if a period licence is not already held, from Clachnaharry, 1½ miles distant.) (2) From Inverness and Beauly Firth (Sections 263, 264).

The bus route between Inverness and Fort William is accessible throughout the canal. The railway to Fort Augustus is now disused.

The canal is here described from SW to NE, i.e. from Fort William to Inverness.

Miles

0	*Corpach.* Rly. Bus, stores, hotel. Obtain permit from Canal Office. There are 3 locks here, and coming from the sea it is best to land on the shore E of the canal entrance, and portage to the canal above the locks.
1	*Banavie.* Rly. Bus, stores. The 8 locks here ("Neptune's Staircase") cover nearly half a mile. The next 6 mls. of canal are free of obstructions.
7½	*Gairlochy Locks* (2). P.O. Shop.
8	*Loch Lochy.* 10 mls. long, surface level 90 ft. above O.D.
18	*Laggan Locks* (2). Stores. The summit is reached here.
19	Loch Lochy Y.H., R. Land on tow-path where burn enters over fall and under iron bridge, leave canoes in wood and take path to main road. Hostel ¼ ml. SW, R at South Laggan.

Miles
19½ *Loch Oich.* 3¾ mls. long, surface level 100 ft. above O.D.
22   R. Garry, L. Hotel ½ ml. up.
23¾ *Bridge of Oich.*
     River Oich. Just before the bridge the river runs off L over
     a weir. This river is not well known but it is fast (fall 52 ft.
     in 5½ mls.) and shallow in many parts except at winter levels.
     There is a rapid in the last ½ ml. which is dangerous and
     probably impassable. The river by-passes 7 locks and is
     probably worth running in high water conditions, i.e. if
     there is plenty of water in the first ¼ ml.
24¼ *Cullochy Lock* (1).
26¼ *Kytra Lock* (1).
28½ *Fort Augustus* (5 locks). Bus, stores, hotel.
29   *Loch Ness,* with Loch Dochfour, extends 24¼ mls. This loch must
     be treated with respect in bad weather as a sea rises quickly
     and squalls are fierce. The shores are steep but a few camp
     sites are available.
33½ *Invermoriston* L. Stores, hotel.
36¼ Alltsaigh Y.H., L, overlooking loch.
39   Foyers, R. Stores. The falls are worth seeing after rain.
44½ *Urquhart Bay,* L. Stores, hotel.
52   Bona Ferry. Entrance to Loch Dochfour.
53½ *River Ness* runs off R over weir. This is described below and
     should be used by canoeists wishing to reach Inverness.
55½ *Dochgarroch Lock* (1).
59   *Muirtown Locks* (4). Canoeists going to Inverness should leave
     the canal above these locks and portage by road (2 mls.).
     Bus to town. Rly. lorries collect gear.
60½ *Clachnaharry.* Lock and Sea Loch. Entrance to Beauly Firth
     (Section 264). *Inverness* : rly., bus, stores, hotel, etc. Y.H.
     at 1 Old Edinburgh Road, above the river near the Castle.

River Ness. This river leads into the town of Inverness and to the
Inverness Firth (Section 263). It is worth using in most conditions and
falls 40 feet in 7 miles.

Miles
0   *Dochfour Weir.* Shoot on R or portage L.
1   Island. Either channel.
1½   *Broken Weir.* Inspect—run centre or L.
4½   *Holm Mills Weir.* Lift over on L.
5   *Bucht.* The Islands. All channels are obstructed by shallows and
     may be dangerous. Land L above bridge or R in entrance
     to lade and inspect.
6   *Inverness.* Rly., bus, stores, hotel. River is navigable a further
     mile to the sea, but the run beneath the bridges requires
     great care and should be inspected. To reach Inverness Y.H.
     land at church R between suspension footbridges and road
     bridges and keep uphill to the top of Culduthel Road.
     Canoes should be taken up to hostel.

224

When travelling in the reverse direction from NE to SW canoeists should enter the canal at Muirtown though a permit will have to be obtained from the Canal Office at Clachnaharry, if a period licence is not already held. The directions given above apply except that L and R must be interchanged. The Rivers Ness and Oich are not navigable upstream, and so are of no use.

River Lochy. When leaving Loch Lochy it is possible to take either the canal, which leaves at the west (R) corner, or the River Lochy which leaves at the south (L) corner, and flows into the sea at Loch Linnhe. This river is shallow in many parts in summer and at least two difficult portages are necessary. The first at Muccomer Falls can generally be done through the R arch of the bridge. The second, below Tor Castle Hotel, should be done on R. The bar at the mouth of the river is not passable except near high water. (*Const.* — 3 hrs. 30 min. Dover.)

268. FORTH AND CLYDE CANAL

O.S. 60, 61 ; Barth. 44, 45

This canal, 35 miles long, runs from Grangemouth on the Firth of Forth (Section 266) to Bowling on the Firth of Clyde (Section 209). It has little to recommend it as a canoeing waterway as it has no great scenic attraction, and a large part of its course is through industrial suburbs. There are 39 locks, 20 on the E, and 19 on the W, and the summit stretch of 15½ miles is the most attractive part. The locks are rather scattered, and about 12 portages of lengths up to a mile are necessary.

The canal is run by British Waterways and has recently been closed.

The Union Canal (Section 269) can be reached by a portage from Camelon, and the Monkland Canal (Section 270) joins at Glasgow.

Miles

    0   *Grangemouth.* Rly. Bus, stores, hotel. The mile long tidal stretch of the River Carron which gives access from the Firth of Forth to the sea lock is very muddy, and approach should not be made in low water. (*Const.* + 4 hrs. 16 min. Dover.) There are 2 locks here.

  1½ *Lock No.* 3.

    2 *Lock No.* 4, followed by 11 locks in the next 2 mls.

    4 *Lock No.* 16, near Camelon. Access to Union Canal.

    7 *Bonnybridge.* Rly., bus, stores.

    8 *Greenhill,* 3 locks in next mile.

  10½ *Windford Lock.* Beginning of summit level reach.

  14 *Kilsyth Bridge.* Kilsyth (bus, stores) 1 ml. N.

  19 *Kirkintilloch.* Rly., bus, stores.

  25½ Junction of Glasgow Branch to Monkland Canal.

26   *Maryhill.* Rly., bus, stores. Summit level ends with 5 locks.

26¼   *Kelvin Aqueduct.* 400 ft. long and 83 ft. high—11 locks follow in the next 3 mls.

34½   *Old Kilpatrick Lock.*

35¼   *Bowling.* Lock and sea lock. (*Const.* + 1 hr. 54 min. Dover.) It is best to leave the canal above these locks and portage to the sea. Rly., bus, stores.

269. UNION CANAL
O.S. 61, 62 ; Barth. 45

This canal runs for 31 miles, from near Tollcross, Edinburgh, about 4 miles from Granton (Section 266) to near the Forth and Clyde Canal (Section 268) at Camelon. There are 11 locks, all within ½ mile of the Camelon end, but these are not now used. There is a tunnel nearly half a mile long 2 miles from Camelon. Much of the country through which the canal passes is pleasant though not very interesting. Linlithgow, 10 miles from the Camelon end, is worth visiting, especially the ruined Palace. In the suburbs of Edinburgh are several rowing clubs and the Forth Canoe Club has a boathouse near Redhall, about a mile from the town.

Above Ratho (6 miles from Edinburgh) the water is dirty and smelly where it is polluted by industrial effluent. In summer it becomes almost overgrown with weed and swans may be troublesome. The canal is however, useful in giving access from the Forth and Clyde Canal to Edinburgh. It is controlled by British Waterways.

Road access is easy throughout and there is rail access at several places between Linlithgow and Falkirk ; camping should be possible in most parts. From Kingsknowe Bridge, 3 miles from the Edinburgh end, Hailes House Y.H. lies ½ mile south.

270. MONKLAND CANAL
O.S. 60 ; Barth. 44, 45

This canal, 13 miles long, led from the Forth and Clyde Canal, near Maryhill, through the centre of Glasgow, to Woodhall, near Airdrie, but is now closed.

INLAND LOCHS

There are many freshwater lochs in Scotland, of which a few are described elsewhere as forming part of coastal, canal or river systems. Loch Lomond, Loch Awe and the Trossachs Lochs, are described below. There are, of course, many other lochs which are worth exploring, but which, owing to the small size or inaccessibility from other waterways, do not merit description here.

Inland lochs are generally safe cruising grounds, as there are no currents and there is usually a shore within easy reach. It must, however, be remembered that strong winds and very violent squalls may often be met, especially where the shores are mountainous, and that a short, steep sea rises quickly. Fresh water not having the buoyancy of sea water, these waves often come aboard green, and accidents have occurred due to inexperienced canoeists driving an overloaded canoe without spray sheets into such a sea and being swamped. It is important, therefore, to take ordinary precaution and to fit good spray sheets. Nor must it be assumed that a loch is always a safe place for trying out fancy sailing rigs.

The fishing on most lochs is strictly preserved. Midges may be troublesome.

271. LOCH LOMOND
O.S. 53, 60 ; Barth. 44, 48

This famous and beautiful loch is a favourite with canoeists, and a week can easily be spent exploring it. It offers the largest single stretch of fresh water in Britain, and the many islands increase its attractiveness.

The loch is not dangerous, but quite heavy seas may be met in the more open parts, and waves rise quickly. If the canoe is not fitted for heavy weather the canoeist should find no difficulty in running for the shore or for the shelter of an island. There are no currents on the loch, in spite of many statements to the contrary, but some surface drift is noticeable after strong winds.

The loch is 23 miles long, 4 miles wide at the widest point, 23 feet above sea level, and over 600 feet deep in parts. There are 30 islands of various sizes, some with interesting and historic ruins.

No attempt is made here to describe an itinerary of the loch or to detail the many places of scenic and historic interest. The canoeist is advised to wander, with the aid of a map and perhaps a guide book, according as his inclination, time, and the weather, indicate.

Access. The best points of access are Balloch, Tarbet, Ardlui, Balmaha and Inversnaid.

Balloch (stores, hotel), at the S end of the loch, is the usual point of access. It is reached from Glasgow by bus or by train to Balloch or Balloch Pier Stations. There are some boathouses where canoes may be stored. Balloch is also connected, by the River Leven, with the upper Firth of Clyde (see below).

Tarbet (stores, hotel) near the middle of the W shore is on the main bus route, and Arrochar and Tarbet Station lies 1 mile from the loch. Tarbet is connected with Arrochar, Loch Long (Section 212) by a portage on 2 miles of good road, over which buses run.

Ardlui (hotel) at the N end of the loch, is on the main railway to Fort William, and on the bus route to Oban. This bus passes Dalmally (for Loch Awe, Section 272) and Taynuilt (for Loch Etive, Section 227), and also Crianlarich on the River Fillan (Section 276) whence a bus may be taken to Killin on Loch Tay (Section 277).

Balmaha (stores), in a bay on the E shore is reached by bus from Glasgow, and is the nearest accessible point to the Camping Club Permanent Sites.

Inversnaid (hotel), on the E shore 5 miles SE from Ardlui, is connected by a portage of $1\frac{1}{2}$ miles with Loch Arklet, the first of the Trossachs Lochs (Section 273).

Camping. Owing to the great popularity of the countryside, camping on the shores of the loch and on the islands is severely restricted. In fact, in most parts, it is prohibited except on authorised sites.

On the E shore there is Millarrochy Bay Permanent Site of the Camping Club of G.B. and I., N of Balmaha, and Inchcailleach Permanent Site on the island of that name lying 1 mile off. There is a small private site at Culness Cottage, almost opposite Tarbet.

On the W shore there is a public site at Inverbeg, beside the hotel, and also beside Inverbeg Y.H. There is another public site 1 mile N of Luss. Northward, camping is permitted at Ardlui Hotel.

Campers are often seen on some of the islands, and on deserted parts of the shore. These are generally unauthorised and are liable to be turned off if discovered.

Youth Hostels. Loch Lomond Y.H. lies at Auchendenan on the W shore, $1\frac{1}{2}$ miles from Balloch. It is very large and easily spotted from the water, lying $\frac{1}{4}$ mile inland. Canoes should land at the Lochside Tea-room.

Inverbeg Y.H. lies at the base of the point forming the mouth of the Douglas Water, on the W shore 10 miles N of Balloch. The best landing places are up the river or just S of the point.

Rowardennan Y.H. lies nearly opposite Inverbeg. The Scottish Hostellers' Canoe Club has its H.Q. and boathouse here.

The Clyde Canoe Club Clubhouse is at Millarrochy Bay.

General. The best way for a visiting canoeist to see Loch Lomond is by starting at Balloch, exploring the southern part of the loch while based either on the Camping Club Site or the Y.H., and finishing by travelling northwards, leaving the loch at Tarbet or Ardlui.

River Leven. This river, $7\frac{1}{2}$ miles long, leads from Loch Lomond at Balloch to the upper Firth of Clyde at Dumbarton (Section 209). It is generally easily navigable in both directions, though the current is strong enough to make travelling upstream very hard work.

272. LOCH AWE
O.S. 52, 53 ; Barth. 47

This beautiful and historic loch lies in the heart of the Campbell country, in Argyll. The loch is 23 miles long and a river flows in at each end, the outflow being westward by the River Awe, through the Pass of Brander near the N end of the loch. Points of scenic and historic interest are too numerous to be described in detail, but the following are worth visiting : Kilchurn Castle, Pass of Brander, Innis Chonain (ruined chapel), Innis Chonnel (ruined castle).

Access. The most convenient is Loch Awe Station (Oban line) on the loch side at the N end. The Oban bus route follows the shore of the loch at this part.

Dalmally (railway, bus, stores, hotel, Y.H.) lies 2 miles up the River Orchy at the N end of the loch. To reach the river from Dalmally Station, follow main road W and 200 yards past fork go R through farm by overgrown path to river bank.

Dalmally and Loch Awe Stations give access by rail, bus or road to other waterways as follows :

> River Fillan (Section 276) at Crianlarich (18 miles).
> Loch Tay (Section 277) at Killin (32 miles).
> Loch Lomond (Section 271) at Ardlui (28 miles).
> Loch Etive (Section 227) at Taynuilt (14 miles).
> Oban (Section 222, 225) (26 miles).
> Loch Fyne (Section 218) at Inveraray (16 miles) (no railway).

At the S end of the loch the village of Ford (hotel, bus) is connected by road with Loch Craignish (8 miles, Section 219) and the West Argyll Coast opposite Shuna (11 miles, Section 222). A car may be hired at Ford Hotel, and in summer a daily bus service, passing these points, runs from Ford to Oban (30 miles, Sections 222, 225). The Ederline Water flows into the loch at Ford, and is generally navigable to within 200 yards of the hotel.

From the arm of the loch which leads W through the Pass of Brander a portage of 4 miles on the main road (bus service) leads to Bonawe on Loch Etive (Section 227). The River Awe, which runs through this pass, has a fall of 35 ft./mile and is not navigable.

Camping. Sites are easy to obtain in all parts, though in places shores are steep. There is a Y.H. at Dalmally, 200 yards up the road to Monument Hill, and ¼ mile from the river.

Stores. Dalmally : good shops. Ford : Van calls occasionally. Kilchrennan (1 mile inland from N port, opposite Portsonachan): store.

The **River Orchy** above Dalmally is, in spate, mostly continuous Grade IV from Loch Tulla and Bridge of Orchy. Many falls requiring inspection, continuous fast water, landing often difficult.

273. THE TROSSACHS LOCHS
O.S. 53, 54 ; Barth. 44, 45

This is a chain of four lochs, noted for their scenic beauty. The through passage would make a good ending to the cruise on Loch Lomond, were it not that two of the lochs (Katrine and Arklet) are reservoirs, and Glasgow Corporation refuses permission for canoes to pass. Camping on the shores is also strictly prohibited.

The route comprises 13½ miles of loch, 1¾ miles of river, and 5½ miles of portage, as follows :

> Inversnaid (Section 271) to Loch Arklet : 1½ miles portage.
> Loch Arklet 2½ miles long.
> Loch Arklet to Stronaclachar on Loch Katrine : ¾ mile portage.
> Loch Katrine 6¼ miles long.

Loch Katrine to Loch Achray : 1 mile portage. Loch Achray 1¼ miles long.

Black Water River 1¾ miles long. Loch Venachar 3½ miles long. Loch Venachar to Callander 2¼ miles portage. Callander has railway, bus, stores, hotel. It is believed that the river (Eas Gobhain) from Loch Venachar to R. Teith at Callander is not generally navigable (see Section 275).

RIVERS

There are few rivers of any great length in Scotland, and none that are not liable to be shallow in summer. Spring is the best time for river canoeing in Scotland, and the most interesting rivers for the visiting fast water enthusiasts are the Spey, Tay and Tweed, which always give good sport except in dry summers.

Some smaller rivers are mentioned in the sections on canals and lochs, and there are, of course, a large number of short ones which can be run in one or two days, and which are chiefly of local interest.

Camp sites are usually easy to find on Scottish rivers. Midges may be troublesome to campers and precautions should be taken.

Fishing. During the season, which extends from January or February to September or October, salmon fishing is in progress (except on Sundays) on all Scottish rivers of importance, and canoeists should take care to disturb the anglers and the fish as little as possible as bad relations with these sportsmen might lead to a restriction of canoeing facilities. They will find fishermen friendly, and even interested, and often get useful information from them.

Canoeists should keep off the middle of big pools and avoid shouting and splashing in quiet reaches. When approaching an angler they should paddle quietly to the opposite bank and drift past if possible, greeting him with a wave rather than a shout. Fish are particularly sensitive to noises such as a paddle knocking against the gunwale, as these carry far through the water. If the angler is blocking the river it may be wise to walk up the bank and ask for room to pass.

TWEED AREA

The only navigable river in this area is Tweed. So far as is known the tributaries Gala Water, Leader Water, Leet Water, Yarrow Water, Ettrick Water and Teviot are not navigable for any distance.

274. River Tweed
O.S. 62, 63, 64 ; Barth. 41, 46
Grading : Rough Water I-III

Tweed is a good sporting river. In low water some parts are rather shallow but in high water plenty of excitement can be obtained. It is easily reached by road or rail. The country is rich in historical associations, too numerous to be described here. Good camp sites can generally be had for the asking and there are several accessible Youth Hostels.

A "cauld" is the term applied to a weir or similar structure on the Tweed. Care must be taken not to disturb salmon fishers.

Starting Points. Stobo in high water, e.g. in spring, gives 77 miles to Berwick. In summer Walkerburn, giving 61 miles, is probably better.

Fast water enthusiasts often leave the river at Coldstream or Cornhill, as the last 16 miles to Berwick are rather slow. Four to six days should be allowed from Stobo to Berwick.

Miles

0	*Stobo.* Bus. Launching place 50 yds. from disused stn. The river is small but there is usually sufficient water except in summer.
5	*Edston* L. Rapid 200 yds. above road bridge. S-bend, second corner runs close to cliff, but canoes kept straight will not touch the cliff. Barns Y.H. R.
6	*Neidpath Castle* L.
7	*Peebles.* Bus, stores, hotel. Cauld not runnable. Lift over R. Beware rocks in shallows. Landing L just below bridge.
14	*Innerleithin Bridge* and rapid.
15½	*Walkerburn Cauld.* Portage L. Shallows, lining down may be necessary.
16	*Walkerburn Bridge.* Bus, stores. Landing R 100 yds. below bridge.
21½	*Ashiestiel.* Tricky rapid just before single span road bridge. Keep as far R as depth will allow.
23½	*Yair Cauld.* Only to be shot in high spate ; portage or line down on R. Mill lade on L will take canoes past Yair Cauld and Fairnilee Rapid if desired.
24	*Fairnilee Bridge.* Bad rapids. Land L as soon as bridge is sighted and inspect. Above bridge keep L, and if possible use L arch ; below bridge use extreme L passage.
27	*Ettrick Water* joins L. Soon after the two bridges there is a broad, fast stretch of about ½ ml. A row of concrete blocks down the middle (to prevent netting of salmon) may be just above or just below the surface.
28	*Abbotsford.* Wire ferry. Landing L 150 yds. below. Bus.
30	*Gala Water* joins L. Rapid where river turns L. Keep R but watch for rock near bottom on R.
32	*Melrose Cauld.* Land and inspect L. Shoot near L bank when sufficient water. Melrose Abbey near bridge. Melrose Y.H. ¼ ml. L.
34½	*Leaderfoot Bridges.* River Leader joins L. Shallows.
36	*Old Melrose Rapid.*
37½	*Dryburgh Bridge.* Landing L below bridge. Rly., bus, hotel. Dryburgh Abbey (L) is worth visiting.
38	Island. Keep R. If the river is below normal the stretch below the island is obstructed by rock ledges. Rapid below, keep R, camp site L.

40 *Mertoun Cauld.* Shootable in normal water in centre ; beware strong drag to L ; approach by skirting edge of cauld from R. Portage R if necessary.

44 *Rutherford Cauld.* Land and inspect L. Run near L bank. Keep R at island below.

46 *Makerston House* L.

    Upper Makerston Rapid. Run on R. Inspect in low water. Beware half cauld on R below rapid.

47 *Middle Makerston Rapid.* Land and inspect R. Run to R of midstream.

    Lower Makerston Rapid. Most difficult rapid on Tweed. Usually portaged R. Though dangerous it is usually possible to run this rapid in a single seater near the R bank, where the passage consists of four heavy rips. The last between 2 rocks, has a bad drag to R which often turns canoes sideways. Approach close along the R bank. There is another passage near the L bank which may be possible in high water.

49½ *Floors Castle* L.

50 *Kelso Cauld.* May be run in high water, otherwise portage R or line down. River Teviot joins R.

50½ *Kelso Bridge.* Bus, stores, hotel.

53½ *Kelso Caulds.* Four caulds in succession, all shootable by salmon runs, though the water may be very heavy.

56 *Carham Cauld.* Usually shootable. R bank becomes English.

58 *Anna Side Island.* Keep R.

59½ *Cauld.* Shoot centre if water permits.

60½ *Cornhill* R. Hotel ½ ml. from river. Leet Water joins R.

61 *Coldstream.* Bus, stores, hotel.

61½ *Cauld.* Run on R.

72 River becomes tidal and slow.

77 *Berwick.* Rly., bus, stores, hotel. Land above new road bridge.

FORTH AREA

275. River Forth

O.S. 54 ; Barth. 44, 45

This is an easy, slow running river, falling only 80 feet in its course of 37 miles from Aberfoyle to Stirling, where it joins the Firth of Forth (Section 266). The river meanders considerably, the direct distance being only half that covered by the river, and in many parts there are high peaty banks which shut out the view, and make landing difficult.

The river should normally be navigable from Aberfoyle, and in high water from Loch Ard, two miles higher up. It has not been run in recent years, and little is known about its condition. There is a natural weir at Craigforth, 2½ miles above Stirling, which requires a portage, and to which the high tides reach.

Access. Aberfoyle, Stirling and a few places between.

Tributaries. The River Teith, with Eas Gobhain, runs from Loch Venachar (Section 273) through Callander, to R. Forth 3 miles above Stirling, a distance of 16 miles. It might be useful as a connecting river, but is probably only navigable in high water, and even then would be very difficult if not dangerous. There is a dam and a bad fall on Eas Gobhain between the loch and Callander.

The Goodie Water runs for 9 miles from the Lake of Menteith to R. Forth, about 22 miles below Aberfoyle, and might be useful as a connection. It is a small stream with a fall of 2-3 feet/mile.

TAY AREA

This area of Perthshire includes the important Rivers Tay, Tummel and Earn, with the lochs of the same names. It also includes the Rivers Fillan, Dochart, Lyon, Isla, Garry, Ericht, Almond and Bran.

The Rivers *Tummel, Fillan* and *Dochart* form approaches to the *Tay,* and the *Earn* flows into the Firth of Tay. These are described.

The *Lyon* is canoeable in high water from Fortingall, 5 miles above its junction with the Tay, and the *Isla* similarly from Rattray, 7 miles above its junction.

The *Garry, Ericht, Almond* and *Bran* are believed not to be canoeable.

RIVER TAY and LOCH TAY
(with tributaries)

276. Rivers Fillan and Dochart
O.S. 48, 53 ; Barth. 48
Grading : Rough Water I and II

These rivers, with Lochs Dochart and Iubhair, are only interesting as giving extra length to the Tay. They should not be attempted except in high water. Some wading may always be expected, and in any case there is a mile portage at Killin. Fall 64 feet in 10 miles.

Approach. Crianlarich (Y.H., rly., bus, stores, hotel) is on both Oban and Fort William lines.

Miles

0	*Crianlarich.* Launch below rly. bridge. No current.
1½	*Loch Dochart* (512 ft.) followed by Loch Iubhair.
3½	River Dochart begins.
4½	Stone bridge. Small weir below. If canoes cannot float over this when light, much wading will be necessary.
5½	Shallow rocky ledges. Later rocks and fall. Portage L in low water.
6¾	*Luib Station*, followed by wooden footbridge.
7½	Island. Channel R.
8	*Luib Hotel* R.
9	Stone bridge. Slow with shallows to Killin rapids.
13½	*Killin Rapids.* (Wood seen on L.) Portage ¼ ml., or continue portage to Killin.
14	*Killin Falls* begin. Impassable. Portage L to road when War Memorial comes in sight on R. Portage through town to River Lochay, where adjacent to road.

15 *Killin*. Rly., bus, stores, hotel, Y.H., short distance up R.
      Lochay (continue by road). Loch Tay (15 mls.—Section
      277) leads to R. Tay.

277. Loch Tay
O.S. 48 ; Barth. 48

This is a fine scenic loch, 15 miles long. Access at Killin (stores,
hotel, Y.H.) by River Dochart (Section 276), or by bus or rail to Killin
station. The Y.H. is reached by canoeing up the River Lochay to just
below the bridge. Some objection has been raised by Breadalbane
Estates to launching from their land at Killin, so launching from the
railway station at the loch side is probably best.

The loch connects the Rivers Dochart and Tay (Sections 276, 278).

278. River Tay
O.S. 48, 49, 55 ; Barth. 48
Grading : Rough Water I-III

The Tay is an easy river except for two stretches, the rapids at
Grandtully and the 3 miles of water starting at Campsie Linn. The
total length from Kenmore to Perth is 47 miles and the drop 348 feet.
Two or three days are required for the trip. During the season (Jan. 15th
to Oct. 15th) salmon fishing is carried on in all parts of the river, and
care should be taken not to disturb fishermen and to keep off the middle
of big pools. Fishermen will then be found to be friendly and even
interested. As bad relations might affect canoeing facilities this is
important. It is not necessary to ask permission to canoe the river.
Camp sites are available all the way down the river, farmers should be
asked and will generally give permission. Usual starting place is
Kenmore but other approaches are indicated.

Approaches :
1. Starting at Kenmore, reached by bus or car from Aberfeldy.
     Car or lorry may be hired at the Garage in Aberfeldy.
2. Starting at Aberfeldy, 6 miles lower down (rly., or bus).
3. By navigating Loch Tay from Killin (15 miles) (Section 277).
4. By navigating the Rivers Fillan and Dochart and Loch Tay,
     from Crianlarich (28 miles) (Sections 276, 277). Total 77 miles.
5. By navigating the River Tummel from Pitlochry (6 miles)
     (Section 281).
6. From Rannoch Station (Fort William line) by Loch Rannoch
     and River and Loch Tummel (Sections 280, 281). Total 70 miles.

Miles
0   *Outfall* from Loch Tay. 348 ft.
      Kenmore Bridge. Stores. Launch below bridge. Good camping
          L further down. Shallow.
½   Island. Main channel on L is overhung by trees.
1   *Taymouth Castle*. "Chinese Bridge." Inspect rapid from bridge.
          Use L arch. In low water turn sharp R and then L after
          bridge.
1½   Bridge. Islands below. Channel L of first R of second.

Miles

2¼ *River Lyon* (L) (300 ft.). Stream is greatly augmented.

2½ Island. Channel R round outside of bend.

3¼ Another island. Channel L.

6½ *Aberfeldy Bridge*. Centre arch. Hotel, rly., bus, stores. Landing ¼ ml. below on R bank.

9½ Rough rapid below fishing hut (L).

11¼ *Grandtully Rapids*. Difficult rapids starting ¼ ml. above bridge. Portage on R.

11½ *Grandtully Bridge*. Rly., bus, stores, hotel. Fall below bridge usually possible on R though tricky because of drag to R.

15½ *Logierait Rail Bridge*. Shallows in low water.

16½ *River Tummel* (L) (Section 281), (210 ft.). Camping R. Now begins 20 mls. with good current and no really rough water.

19¾ Rail bridge. The last 2½ mls. to Dunkeld are remarkable for beauty of beech woods.

20¾ *Dalguise Station* R.

23½ *Dunkeld Bridge*. Bus, stores, hotel, cathedral. Use L arch of bridge. Rapid below. Rather shallow.

24 *Birnam*. Town ¼ ml. from river (R). Dunkeld and Birnam Stn., bus, stores. Y.H. ½ ml. below bridge and ¼ ml. from river on R.

29 *Caputh*.

35 *Kinclaven Bridge*.

35¾ Rail bridge.

36½ *Mains of Stobhall* (L). Camp site below belt of trees. River now becomes more difficult with a series of small rocky rapids.

38½ *Campsie Linn*. River turns L, falling through a narrow channel into a pool. Keep R on approaching and land on largest island to inspect. The fall is heavy, and has a not very evident drag to R into the backlash, and the pool below is so full of currents and swirls as to make landing difficult. The Linn may be run (*a*) by starting close to the L bank and going with the current through the backlash, or (*b*) by using speed to cut across the current to L and avoid backlash. If in doubt, lift over to R of large island.

39 *Stanley Weir*. Land on L to inspect and lift over. Very difficult weir and has caused much trouble. Dangerous to attempt except in high water owing to iron spikes on weir. Anyone capsizing is in danger of being swept down the next ½ ml. of rocky water. The next 2 mls. are mostly rough water with rocks, and care is needed.

39½ *Hell Hole Corner*. River turns R. Keep to R shore. Heavy rapid below. Keep L.

40 *Stanley*. On R ¼ ml. from river. Bus. River turns L.

40½ *Thistlebrig Rapid*. Start on L and work over to R. The heaviest rapid of a heavy series. After this it is easy going to Perth.

43 *Hatton-Waukmill Ferry*.

45 *River Almond* (R).

45½ *Scone Palace*. Tides flow up to here.

47   *Perth*. Land on R on North Inch, just above first bridge. Rly.,
bus, hotels, stores. Y.H. at 107 Glasgow Road, ½ ml. from
river. Those who wish to continue down the Firth of Tay
to Newburgh or Dundee will find further information under
"Coastal Waters" (Section 252).

RIVER TUMMEL with LOCHS ERICHT and RANNOCH

The River Tummel joins River Tay 30 miles above Perth, and the
last 6 miles of it, from Pitlochry, make a good approach to the latter
(Section 278).

On the upper reaches of the Tummel three separate hydro-electric
schemes have been constructed, with the result that this waterway now
consists of three lochs connected by stretches of river which are in
general, too shallow for a canoe. However, a canoeist prepared for
some heavy portaging, can have one of the longest runs possible in
Scotland by making use of Lochs Ericht and Rannoch.

The longest run is from Dalwhinnie, and gives 54 miles to the Tay
(84 to Perth), made up of 35½ miles of loch, 6½ miles of river, and 12 miles
of portage. Another approach is from Rannoch Station, giving 41½ miles
to the Tay, i.e. 21½ miles of loch, 9 miles of river and 11 miles of portage.

The condition of certain parts of the river is liable to variation
according to the amount of water being let through the sluices, and in
good water conditions, an additional three or four miles of river may
be navigable, thus reducing the amount of portaging necessary.

Lochs Ericht and Rannoch

These lochs form an approach to the River Tummel (Section 281).

279. LOCH ERICHT (O.S. 48 ; Barth. 48) is 16 miles long. Its head
is ½ mile from Dalwhinnie (rly., stores, hotel). The shores are steep,
sparsely wooded and almost uninhabited, but camp sites are available.
Apart from hills there are few interesting features. Strong winds may
make the loch quite rough.

A portage of 4 miles by rough road from the foot of the loch leads to
Loch Rannoch near Bridge of Ericht. The best landing is to the west
of the dam.

280. LOCH RANNOCH (O.S. 48 ; Barth. 48) is 10 miles long. The
shores are heavily wooded but camp sites are available, and there are
some farms. The main road runs along the north shore and there is an
occasional bus service. It may be approached via Loch Ericht or from
Rannoch Station (Fort William line) by the River Gaur. This river is
controlled by hydro-electric schemes and is subject to sudden and
possibly dangerous variation. At usual level probably Grade III or a
little more. There are several rapids which require inspection. The
River Tummel (Section 281) flows out of Loch Rannoch at Kinloch
Rannoch.

281. River Tummel

(with Dunalistair Reservoir, Loch Tummel and Loch Faskally)

O.S. 48 ; Barth. 48

Grading : Rough Water II-III

See notes above. The river has not been run since the construction of the hydro-electric schemes was completed, and its condition is not accurately known. Access : Pitlochry (rly., bus), or from Loch Rannoch (Section 280).

Camping. Sites should not be difficult to find. Strathtummel Y.H. lies on Loch Tummel.

Tributary. River Garry, which flows into Clunie Reservoir is believed not to be navigable by canoe.

Miles

0	*Kinloch Rannoch Dam* (bus, stores). On coming from Loch Rannoch a portage round the dam will be necessary. The state of the water below varies according to the amount of water being allowed through the sluices, and, if they are closed, it will be necessary to portage 2 mls. to Dunalistair Reservoir. With the sluices open, a fast but straightforward run is to be expected.
2	*Dunalistair Reservoir,* 2 mls. long. Note Schichallion (3,547 ft.) on R.
4	*Dunalistair Dam.* The next 2½ mls. of river appear to be impossible, as the greater part of the water runs through the aqueduct. Canoeing in the aqueduct is not permitted, as it normally flows much too fast for safety, and is liable to sudden fluctuations in flow which would be very dangerous and landing is extremely difficult at the other end. A portage is, therefore, necessary, probably as far as Tummel Bridge, and is best done along the road on the L bank.
	When there is enough water in the old river the stretch from Dunalistair Dam to Tummel Bridge is exciting, much of it Grade IV with two impossible falls where it would be difficult to stop and portage. Real risk of being carried down the falls.
7½	*Tummel Bridge.* Rapid : Grade III-IV. Inspect.
7½	*Tummel Bridge.* Launch below bridge if there is sufficient water. Otherwise portage ½ ml. to head of Loch Tummel.
8	*Croy.* Portage R round weir. From below the weir Loch Tummel extends 7 mls. Both shores are wooded and the main road runs near the northern shore. Strathtummel Y.H. (L) 1 ml. before dam.
15	*Loch Tummel Dam.* Land on R. For the next 2 mls. the river runs through the Pass of Tummel which contains Cammoch Falls and Tummel Falls, both of which are quite unshootable. A road portage of 2 mls. from near the dam leads to the head of Clunie Reservoir. Those who do not mind arduous portages through rocks and undergrowth can run the mile or so of river between the two falls, but must inspect this part of the river carefully as there are many dangerous rapids. The best portage round Cammoch Falls is on the R,

Miles	
	and that round Tummel Falls on the L just below the footbridge.
17	*Loch Faskally*, is 2½ mls. long, and the road runs along its W shore.
19½	*Pitlochry Dam.* Portage. The river from here is easy but has sufficient rapids to provide interest without being dangerous, but the water level can vary suddenly according to the sluice setting.
	As far as Ballinluig there are three minor rapids and one heavy one just above the bridge.
19¾	*Pitlochry Suspension Bridge.* Land R. Town ½ ml. L over bridge. Rly., bus, stores, hotel. Pitlochry makes a good starting place for a run down the River Tay.
24¾	*Ballinluig Bridges.*
25½	*Junction* with River Tay (Section 278).

LOCH EARN and RIVER EARN
282. Loch Earn
O.S. 54 ; Barth. 48

This pretty loch is 6½ miles long, and lies in a fine mountain setting. Access at Lochearnhead (rly., bus, stores, hotel).

283. River Earn
O.S. 54, 55 ; Barth. 48
Grading : Rough Water II-III

Has been canoed from Loch Earn to Comrie, though found to be shallow. Several weirs and a 300 yard gorge, "not too difficult".

From Crieff, 5 miles below Comrie, the river is 30 miles long to its mouth in the Firth of Tay (Section 252) but the last 10 miles are tidal. It is a sporting river, flowing through pleasant scenery.

Miles	
0	*Crieff.* Bus, stores, hotel. Launch below bridge R at Bridge End. Several small rapids in next few mls. 1 ml. down where river divides take R channel. Shortly after at a gravel bank L channel.
2½	Rly. bridge.
3	*Dornoch Weir.* Long stretch of broken water, difficult. Portage usually advisable. Shallow stretches below.
5	Ruins of Innerpeffray Castle L.
5½	*Colquhalzie Weir.* May be shootable on L.
6	*Mills of Earn*—1st weir. Inspect. Shootable through gap on L of rock. Fair drop. Fast shallow stretch below. Tricky.
6¼	2nd weir. Portage on small rocky island on R of gap.
6½	*Kinkell Bridge.* Fair current below here but few excitements.
12½	*Dalreoch Bridges.* Buses Perth-Stirling.
16½	*Forteviot Bridge.* Village ½ ml. S.
17½	*Dupplin Weir.*
20	*Forgandenny Rly. Bridge.* Tides flow to here (*Const.* + 5 hrs. 50 min. Dover). River starts to wind much more.
23	*Dunbarney Rly. Bridge.*
25	*Bridge of Earn.* Village and stn. R. Bus.
30	*Ferryfield.* Ferry landing R.
30¼	*Confl.* with Firth of Tay. (*Const.* + 4 hrs. 19 min. Dover).

THE ABERDEEN RIVERS

284. River Dee
O.S. 40 ; Barth. 52

The river offers little to the canoeist. The upper reaches, from Braemar to Banchory (45 miles) are probably only possible in a spate so high as to be really dangerous. At most times it is a continuous series of shallows and boulder-strewn rapids, and quite impossible.

Below Banchory the river runs 18 miles to Aberdeen. This part is easily navigable, with only one bad rapid just below Banchory, and is on the whole rather dull, the last 12 miles being slow, and the last 3 miles tidal.

285. River Don
O.S. 40 ; Barth. 52, 56

This river is not favoured by canoeists as it is badly polluted by industrial effluent. It is probably navigable from Kemnay to the sea (25 miles), and the fastest part is probably the last 5 miles, but as there is no record of the river having been canoed, accurate information is not available.

SPEY AREA

286. River Spey
O.S. 29, 37, 38 ; Barth. 51, 55, 56
Grading : Rough Water I-III

The Spey is probably the fastest of the major rivers in Britain, and carries a fair volume of water even in summer. It can be relied on to give good sport at all seasons, and gives a run of 73 miles.

The first 30 miles are moderately easy, but below Grantown it must be classed as difficult. Apart from those at Grantown and Knockando, which are tricky, the rapids are fairly straightforward, but give rise to heavy water, throwing waves well over the deck.

Starting Points. Newtonmore is the highest point possible in normal water, but Kingussie is better as the intervening 4½ miles of river are slow and may be shallow. It is said to be navigable in spate from the junction of the Mashie Water, 10 miles above Newtonmore.

Access. Road and rail follow the river throughout most of its length.

Tributaries. So far as is known none of the tributaries is navigable.

Miles

0	*Spey Bridge, Newtonmore.* Public camp site.
¼	*Rail Bridge.* Shallows for first mile, then deep and slow with sandy beds.
1½	Islands.
4½	*Kingussie* (*Bridge*). Several minor rapids.
6	*River Tromie* (R). Scour to L. Then little current and marshy banks.

Miles

10   *Loch Insh*. Camp site at near end 200 yds. R.

11   *Kincraig*. Bridge at end of loch. Good store 100 yds. up road, L.

11¼ *Island*. Channel either side. River current restarts.

11½ *River Feshie* (R). No major difficulties for next few miles but
       several small rapids and scours.

12   *Broken Footbridge*.

13   *Duchess of Gordon's Monument*.

15   *Duke of Gordon's Monument*.

17   *Aviemore Bridge*. River Druie (R). Small rapids for 1 ml. below
       Aviemore. 3 mls. below Aviemore start of change of river
       bed to rocky boulders but no difficulty as far as 1 ml. above
       Boat of Garten. First heavy rapid just above green fishing
       hut on R bank.

24   *Boat of Garten Bridge*. Rocky rapid above, another ¼ ml. below.

26½ *Cullachie*. Small canal on R. Camp site.

27½ *Railway Bridge*.

28½ *River Nethy* (R).

28¾ *Broomhill Bridge*. River runs diagonally into piers. Take minor
       channel on R; main channel is fast and runs into fence
       projecting some way into water. Awkward stakes and scour
       just below.

29¾ *River Dulnan* (L).

32   *Inverallan Churchyard* (L). Valley narrows. Rocks—keep R.

33   *New Bridge, Grantown*. Broken water between bridges. May
       require some wading in low water. Land L and inspect.
       Tricky. Pass under bridge L, and head diagonally for
       midstream; then turn L, and keep near to L bank.

33½ *Old Bridge*. Approaching this bridge rapids become heavier with
       a more defined channel, going diagonally L to R.

34   *Congash Farm*. Suitable for camp.

36   *Cromdale Bridge*. The farm here might also prove a good camp
       site.

37¼ *Islands*. Rapids both sides. L best.

38¼ Another rapid at sharp bend where railway meets river.

42   *Duiar*. Islands. Shallow rapids.

43½ *Advie Bridge*.

44¼ *Islands*. Shallow rapids.

47¼ *Ballindalloch Rail Bridge*. On sighting this, look out for metal
       posts across river, almost 15 ft. apart.

47¾ *River Avon* (R). Heavy rapid on double bend for almost 100 yds.

48   *River Gheallaich* (L).

49   *Blacksboat Bridge*. Rapid at Island of Weiroch just below.

50½ *River Arder* (L). Soon after this is an island. R channel best.
       River swings L and one catches view of distillery chimney
       stack which serves as a warning of the approach to Knockan-
       do rapid. Land here. Camp site on L.

51   *Knockando*. Heavy rapid with large rock in channel. Inspect.
       Start R of centre and head diagonally L.

51½ Another rapid at sharp bend. Keep L and then in midstream
       round corner.

52   *Island*. Channel R. Rapid.

52¼   Rapid at another sharp bend.

53¼   *Dalmunach.* Very heavy rapid. Straight run through.

54¼   *Carron Bridge.* Rapids continue to 1 ml. above Aberlour.

57¼   *Aberlour.* Suspension footbridge.

59   *Easter Elchies.* Keep L.

59½   *Craigellachie Bridge.* Heavy rapid just below.

59¾   *Rail Bridge.* River leaves hill country. Shingle rapids.

64   *Rothes Burn* (L). Rothes ¾ ml. L.

67   Heavy rapid. Awkward rock in mid-channel.

67½   *Boat o' Brig Rail and Road Bridges.* Camp site on L between
       bridges.

72½   *Fochabers Bridge.* Current maintained but river splits into
       several channels. Shingle rapids.

75½   *Spey Bay Rail Bridge.* Normal tides only come a short distance
       below here.

76½   *Tugnet.* Landing may be made here.

GALLOWAY AREA

287. Ken and Dee

Although there are no difficulties below Allangibbon Bridge, just
above St. John's Town of Dalry, other than minor rapids, the river is
well worth doing for the sake of the beautiful and interesting country
through which it passes. It is virtually an unknown corner of the
country and is teeming with wild-fowl. Greylag and Greenland white
front geese are comparatively common besides many other species too
numerous to mention here. For most of the way there is a series of
lakes with artificial dams for hydro-electric generating stations. Elsewhere, Grade II-III in the river sections above Allangibbon Bridge,
which are suitable only for experts. From the bridge Grade I-II.

O.S. 73, 74 ; Barth. 37

Miles

0   *Carsphairn.* Bridge (A.713) over Water of Deugh. Possible to
       start here, or even higher, except in low water conditions.

1¾   *Kendoon Loch.*

3   Bridge over loch, halfway down its length : there is a dam on R,
       just beyond. Portage here to river below. Another dam at
       S end ; but river below may be nearly dry.

5½   *Garsfad Loch.*

6½   Dam at S end of loch. Portage R into river (Water of Ken).
       Rapids. Shortly before the river enters Earlston Loch there
       is an innocent-looking small fall followed by fast water
       leading to an impossible 12 ft. drop to the loch when the
       loch water level is very low. Portage on R. *This stretch
       should all be reconnoitred* as conditions vary according to the
       water level in the loch.

7½   *Earlston Loch.*

8½   Dam at S end of loch. Long portage R ; re-embark downstream
      of—

8¾   *Allangibbon Bridge,* near bungalow by the power station (A.**713**).
      This is the best starting point for those wanting an easier
      trip. Good water when turbines are *all* working—no water
      otherwise, as it will be held up. Best time is probably
      between 11 a.m. and 5 p.m.

9   *St. John's Town of Dalry* L.

12½ *Ken Bridge* (A.**712**). Easy starting point at all times. New
      Galloway ¼ ml. R.

13   *Loch Ken.* New Galloway on R.

13½ *Kenmure Castle* on R.

18½ Rly. Viaduct over loch. End of Loch Ken, but the next 5½ mls.
      is lake, though rather like a swollen river.

19   *Boat of Rhone.* Blackwater of Dee enters on R.

23   *Crossmichael.* Shops.

24½ *Glenlochar Dam.* Portage L. River now called Dee. Wide, deep
      water, no rapids but good scenery.

27   *Threave Island.* Main channel L, but R channel advised as it
      passes Threave Castle. Shallows where it rejoins main
      channel.

27½ *Lodge Island.*

28   Railway bridge.

29½ *Threave Bridge.* Rapid 100 yds., beginning under R arch. Castle
      Douglas 3 mls. L.

30   *Bridge of Dee* followed by some shallows. Quieter water, gradu-
      ally widening into reservoir.

33   *Tongland* at S end. High dam. Land on R and finish here as
      water is now piped about 1 ml. to power station. It is then
      tidal to and through Kirkcudbright.

288. Nith

The Nith rises in the Galloway hills and flows E and then S through
New Cumnock, Thornhill and Dumfries to the Solway Firth.

It has been canoed in medium water from Sanquhar but there are
many hazards in the beautiful stretch between there and Drumlanrig,
particularly in the stretch below Enterkinfoot, where the river flows
through a "strid" and then a gorge ("Jaws of Nith") which is easily
blocked by trees. The river is liable to sudden spates. Permission
required to pass through the Buccleugh estate between Enterkinfoot
and Thornhill. Sanquhar to Ardoch Bridge Grade II. Ardoch to
Drumlanrig III-IV (gorge IV), probably more difficult in spate. The
fall varies between 13 and 36 feet per mile, and the whole of this stretch
is best left for experts. Sanquhar to Thornhill 13½ miles. Below Thornhill relatively straightforward, Grade I (II in a few places), and makes
an interesting short cruise through a pleasant countryside. Regular
bus service along the valley road (A.**76**).

O.S. 68, 75 ; Barth. 37, 40

Miles
- 0   *Thornhill.* Stn. 2 mls. from river.
- 2½   *Mouth of Scar Water* R. A vicious eddy : keep L of the rapid leading to it. Lively current with minor rapids to—
- 6   *Barburgh (or Burbrough) Mill* (L).
- 7½   *Auldgirth Bridge.*
- 10½   Rly. bridge. Weir—portage L.
- 15¾   Rly. bridge. Weir : beware of iron spikes.
- 16   *Mouth of Cluden Water* R.
- 16½   Rly. bridge.
- 17½   *Dumfries.* Weir, then tidal. Stn.
- 19   *Kingholm Quay* L.
- 23   *Glencaple* L. The estuary widens out considerably into the Solway Firth.

IRELAND

Ireland offers attractive canoeable waterways in plenty ; the sections that follow by no means exhaust the possibilities and do no more than give particulars of the principal rivers and loughs.

Transport. On a number of railway branch lines shown on the O.S. maps passenger train services have been withdrawn and replaced by buses, and on those that remain there are often only one or two trains each way on weekdays. This process may be extended. Even where there are rail services, there are parallel long-distance bus services from Dublin, which may be more convenient. Transport services should accordingly be verified beforehand. The Ulster Transport Authority, Belfast, Coras Iompair Eireann, Dublin, the Ulster Tourist Board, 13 Regent Street, London, S.W.1, or the Irish Tourist Information Bureau, 71, Regent Street, London, W.1, will give rail and bus times.

No difficulties in taking folding canoes into Ireland by the usual steamer routes have been heard of ; they should be declared at the Customs as personal luggage. On trains the official recognition by the Railway Executive of collapsible canoes as within the free personal luggage allowance does not, of course, apply, but they are as a rule accepted as such. The long-distance buses will take folding canoes. The Erne route into Ulster is an "unauthorised route"—see Section 304.

Camp Sites. Usually easy to find.

Maps. The Ordnance Survey maps do not appear to have been corrected much since 1914 ; the 1-inch sheets are very small, and contain little that is not on the ½-inch layered edition. References throughout are to the ½-inch O.S. map unless otherwise stated.

Note. Where up-to-date information on the waterways is incomplete, it has been supplemented from maps and other works of reference and is thought to give a reasonably good indication of the conditions. The chief examples of this are the following : Bann, Foyle, Inny, the higher parts of the Suir, the Liffey, Boyne and the Meath Blackwater. The condition of the canals is not known for certain and information on these has been kept to the minimum.

Arrangement of the Sections

These are grouped by river basins under Ulster, Central and West Ireland, South and East Ireland.

ULSTER

301. BANN AND LOUGH NEAGH

The *Bann* draws its headstreams from the Mountains of Mourne and flows NW through Lough Neagh to the sea near Coleraine. The river is navigable all the way from Portadown (stn.); 5 locks on the lower river between Lough Neagh and the sea. The scenery is not striking, but improves a little just before Coleraine is reached.

Lough Neagh has the largest area of any lake in the British Isles, being 20 miles long and 12 miles across at the widest point. The surroundings are flat ; it is subject to high winds and should be treated with respect.

O.S. 2, 5 and 8 or 9

Miles

0	*Portadown* (stn.). Formerly connected by the *Newry Canal* with *Carlingford Lough* on the E coast, under the Mountains of Mourne.
9	*Bann Foot Ferry*. Outlet into *Lough Neagh*. The *Lagan Navigation* from Belfast (29 miles, 26 locks) enters at Morrows Point, 10 mls. E of Bann Foot Ferry.
11¼	*Maghery Ferry*, along shore to W of mouth of the Upper Bann, is the mouth of the *Armagh Blackwater*, which formerly connected with *Upper Lough Erne* via the Ulster Canal.
15¼	*Kells Point*, on the W shore of the lough.
25	*Ballyronan* (L).
29	*Toome*. The river flows out of the lough over a wide weir, lock cut on R.
29¾	*Toome Bridge*. Eel weirs on this stretch, but they do not stretch all the way across.
31	*Lough Beg*, 3½ mls. long.
39	*Portglenone Bridge*.
46	*Portna Bridge*, ½ ml. below Portna Lock. Kilrea, on hill ¾ ml. L. 2 locks in the next 7 mls.
53½	Road bridge ; railway bridge 2 mls. below.
59½	*Castleroe Lock*. Tidal below here.
61	*Coleraine Bridge* (stn. R). From here Portrush and the Giant's Causeway can be reached. H.W. Dover — 4 hrs. 11 min.
65	*Castlerock*. Mouth of the Bann. Londonderry can be reached in good weather (19½ mls.) by rounding Magilligan Point and going up Lough Foyle (see Section 303).

302. STRANGFORD LOUGH

To the E and SE of Belfast, a long inlet from the sea some 2-3 miles wide and 10 miles long with a narrow entrance. Can be reached by rail from Belfast at Comber or Newtownards. The W shore is more interesting because of the islands along it. Landing in the narrow part at Portaferry or Strangford. The tide is very fast through here.

O.S. 5 and 9

303. FOYLE

From the confluence of the Mourne and the Finn at Lifford the *Foyle*, tidal throughout, runs for 20 miles past Londonderry to Culmore where it widens into Lough Foyle. The run through Londonderry is worth doing, but the continuation from Culmore round Magilligan Point to Castlerock, at the mouth of the Bann is very dependent on the weather conditions.

245

Distances from Strabane (stn.), on the Mourne, just above the confluence :

to   Montgevlin Castle, 7¼ miles.
      Londonderry, 15 miles. H.W. Dover — 2½ hrs.
      Culmore, 20 miles.
      Magilligan Point, 36 miles. H.W. Dover — 4 hrs. 10 min.
      Castlerock, 44½ miles. H.W. Dover — 4 hrs. 50 min.

From Lifford to Carrigan the Foyle forms the boundary between Ulster and the Republic of Ireland.

O.S. 1, 2 and 4

304. ERNE AND ITS LOUGHS

The Erne retains its name all the way to the sea at Ballyshannon, but the greater part of its course runs through lakes. The distances given are the shortest routes through these lakes, and a moderate degree of exploration will extend the total distance to between 200 and 300 miles.

Access. (a) At Drumhawnagh, where the river is very narrow but will normally have sufficient water to float a canoe.

(b) At Scrabby, a village on Lough Gowna.

(c) At Killashandra on Lough Oughter.

There is no rail access to any of these. Buses run to Cavan and Killashandra from Dublin and will take folding canoes on roof.

Though Lough Gowna is 214 feet above sea level, at no point on the river is there any appreciable stream, the fall being taken up mainly in the last 6 miles between Belleek and the sea, and partly in the connection between Lough Gowna and Lough Oughter. The voyage is therefore a purely paddling one, though there is plenty of scope for sailing, particularly on the lower loughs. Shopping facilities are rare except at Killashandra, Belturbet and Enniskillen. The river and lakes are little frequented, and the channel is not always easily found, being often obscured by rushes and extensive beds of water-lilies and weeds. A good map and compass are essential to steer a course through the labyrinth of Lough Oughter, and the many islands of Upper and Lower Loughs Erne. The scenery is first-class for the greater part of its length, and nowhere, apart from a few short stretches on the connecting portions of the river, is there any feeling of being shut in. The views are wide and open and the country hilly, becoming mountainous as the lower loughs are reached. Camping sites will be found without difficulty.

O.S. ½-in. 3, 7, 8, 12 ; the 1-in. 45, 57, 68 are easier to follow for the lakes than ½-in. No. 8.

Note. Entrance into Ulster from Eire by the River Erne is an "unauthorised route," and permission should be obtained beforehand from the Collector of Customs at Belfast to use it ; any question of a deposit for the temporary importation of a non-British boat on which British customs duty has not been paid, must be taken up with the Customs Officer at Enniskillen.

Miles

0   *Drumhawnagh.* Stn. closed.

1   *Kilsaran Bridge.*

3½ Entrance to *Lough Gowna.* The entrance lies to the L ; most of the lough is off the direct course down the Erne. It is very fine and should not be missed. Both the N and S parts are well worth exploration. A narrow passage at Dernaferst Bridge connects them. Ruined abbey on Inchmore. Shops at Scrabby.

6½ *Sallaghan Bridge.* 100 yds. below the bridge is a small weir with passage to the L, one of a number of similar weirs and stepping stones between here and Lough Oughter. These small weirs do not hold up the water to any appreciable extent, and there is practically no fall. The canoe may usually be eased through the widest opening.

7   *Dingins Bridge.*

8   *Carrickclevan Bridge and Mill.* Weir beneath bridge followed by rough, rocky stretch of 300 yds. Canoe must be floated down, as a portage would be extremely difficult. At the end of this stretch a mill-feeder goes off to L, but to join the river the canoe will have to be lifted over the retaining wall to the R, or may be slipped through a narrow opening by partly lifting and turning on its side.

10 *Lackan Mill.* If water allows, the canoe may be passed through the sluice on L, otherwise it will have to be lifted over the retaining wall. The sluice is 300 yds above the mill, the feeder to which is apparently the main stream. A portage at the mill is impracticable. If the feeder is inadvertently taken, a return to the sluice is advisable.

10¼ *Lackan Bridge.*

11¼ *Drumcrow Mill.* A portage here is unavoidable, and should be made on the L bank to just above Cloghy Bridge, about 200 yds. on. Occasional shallows to—

14 *Bellahillan Bridge.*

15 Rly. bridge.

16 Entrance to *Carr's Lough.* A narrow opening in reeds to L. A cul-de-sac.

16½ *Lough Oughter.* A good map is necessary to steer a direct course through this labyrinth, but the whole lake repays exploration, particularly the passage via Lough Tullyguide, and Town Lough to Killashandra (stn. closed). The channel between Trinity Island and Tawlaght is blocked when the lake is low. There is a causeway to the W of Eonish, and a cut across the neck of land between Inch Island and Eonish.

Shortly after passing Killykeen Cottage the romantic ruins of Cloghoughter Castle are seen on a small island. There is a good camping place on the headland on the L side of the narrow channel as the castle is approached.

2¼ mls. beyond the castle Inishmore is reached, and may be circumnavigated either to E or W. The western route is best in low water. Inishmuck, to N of Inishmore, is connected to the mainland by a causeway with no opening for boats.

247

25¾   *Bakers Bridge.* Watch for sharp piece of rail in L arch.

29½   *Belturbet Railway Bridge.* (Stn. closed.)

30   *Belturbet Bridge.* Ledge below may necessitate a portage across the bridge. About 2½ mls. beyond Belturbet there are two alternative routes into Upper Lough Erne, both attractive— (i) under a road bridge to L past the mouth of the *Woodford River* ; (ii) 1 ml. further on at Bunamunery to R via *Quivvy Lough.* The Erne itself continues to—

35   *Bloody Pass.* Here there is a narrow opening to L, but it involves a portage over a causeway to reach Upper Lough Erne and route (i) above. The Erne continues beyond Bloody Pass and after being joined by route (ii) enters—

36¼   *Upper Lough Erne* near ruins of Crom Castle. Between Bunamunery and Bloody Pass the boundary is crossed into Ulster.

     Quivvy Lough is joined by the *River Finn* which formerly connected via the Ulster Canal and the *Armagh Blackwater* with *Lough Neagh* at Maghery Ferry.

     The *Woodford River* enters Upper Lough Erne to the SE of Crom Castle. It can be followed for some 20 mls. upstream past Ballyconnell to Garadice Lough which is some 15 mls. by road from the *Shannon* at Drumshanbo. The lough is only 20 ft. higher than Lough Erne. The *Dale* and *Yellow Rivers* beyond Garadice Lough were formerly canalised and it may still be possible to reach St. John's Lough or Lough Scur, which is only 5 mls. by road from Drumshanbo.

36¾   *Crom Church.* Opposite tower on small island.

39¼   *Ross Ferry.*

41   *Trasna Island.* Bridges connecting with mainland, not marked on map.

48   Outfall from Upper Lough Erne behind Killygowan Island to the W of "Bellisle," which reunites in a mile or so with the eastern passage. There is another outlet at the extreme NW corner of the lough.

50½   *Carry Bridge.*

54   *Tamlaght Bay.* Opens to R.

55½   Junction of western outlet on L.

57   Keep L of island.

58   *Lisgoole Abbey.* On L.

59   Rly. bridge, removed.

59½   Junction of Scilier River L.

61   *Enniskillen.* Built on an island, but channel (R) going round town is impracticable. Keep straight on under bridge. Boathouse L above bridge, suitable for landing. Half a mile below bridge is a barrier with a lock on the L. If the barrier is closed, portage round lock on L, otherwise carry on through the arches.

62   Entrance to *Lower Lough Erne.* The distance of 20½ mls. from Enniskillen given below is the shortest through the lough, but this extremely beautiful lake is worth greater exploration. Whether a direct route is possible or not will depend on the wind. The lake is so large that a fresh breeze will

raise a considerable sea, even in the thickly islanded southern part. The wide, open, northern part (up to 6 mls. wide) should be avoided. Sudden storms can raise a terrible sea in a very short time. In strong winds advantage should be taken of the islands and headlands to obtain shelter and rest between bouts of paddling, and the windward shore followed round. With strong northerly winds the distance from Enniskillen to Rosscor may easily be doubled of necessity.

63　*Devenish Island.* A holy island. Ruined churches and very fine round tower. Good camping on S shore.

70　*Inchmacsaint.* Another holy island.

81½　*Rosscor.* River leaves the lake.

85　*Belleek.* If the sluice gates are open there may be a good stream between Rosscor and Belleek. Just before Belleek the river divides, the R branch leading to a large sluice, the L branch leading past the boat landing on the R bank steeply to join the R branch below the sluice just above the road bridge. Land at boat landing—the road is reached by a small bridge near a creamery. Stn. closed. Bus from Belleek or Ballyshannon to Armagh then rail to Belfast.

The Erne crosses the border into the Republic and continues for another 6 miles through two hydro-electric impounding reservoirs to Ballyshannon. Reports conflict as to whether this stretch is worth attempting.

CENTRAL AND WEST

305. SHANNON

The Shannon is the largest, though not the longest, river in the British Isles, much of it being lake. It is a navigable river for about 135 miles between Lough Allen and Limerick. As such it offers little in the way of rapids, but the lakes offer good sport in a strong wind, especially if sail is carried. The current is so slight on the navigable stretches that it is not hard to go upstream, and with the prevailing wind in the SW, it may be easier to do so, especially with a sail. The scenery, whilst not being spectacular, has a quiet charm unspoiled by vulgarity. Reed-fringed callows (water meadows) running to the water's edge leave the views of the surrounding country unimpeded. Parts of the lakes are extremely beautiful, and abound in deserted ruins where many pleasant hours may be spent. The river falls only 35 feet between Lough Allen and Killaloe (121 miles), then 100 feet in the 14 miles to the tidal river at Limerick. There are 5 locks between Battlebridge and Killaloe for which a fee of 1s. is charged per lock, but a fee of 9s. covers these and the use of the locks and headrace between Killaloe and Limerick (Shannon Navigation, Limerick). Locks not worked on Sundays. But a canoeist, who does not use the locks is not likely to be questioned. Drumshanbo, at the S end of Lough Allen, is now some distance from the lake. Drumshanbo stn. is closed, but there are bus connections from Carrick on Shannon (stn.). Alternative approaches at Carrick (stn.) and Boyle (stn.) (see below). Bus service from Dublin to both. The last is extremely attractive as it includes Lough Key, a very lovely lake.

Camp sites are plentiful and are rarely charged for. If near a farm it is a matter of courtesy to ask before pitching the tent, but in the more remote parts no exception is taken to camping on the river bank or islands.

Ten to twelve days should be allowed for the full distance from Drumshanbo or Boyle to Limerick.

O.S. 7, 12, 15, 18

Miles

Lough Allen—a pear-shaped sheet of water about 8 mls. long lying between Slieve Anierin and the Arigna Mountains and is the most mountainous lough on the Shannon. It has fine sandy beaches on N and E shores. The S end is rather muddy.

0   *Bellantra Bridge*, *Drumshanbo*—at the S end of Lough Allen. The canal from Drumshanbo to Battlebridge is disused and dry. The river leaves the lake through sluices at the S end at Bellantra Bridge where a portage will be necessary in low water or if the sluice gates are shut. There are several short rapids in the next 6 mls. which offer little difficulty.

6   *Battlebridge*. Before the bridge care should be taken, as there are stones in the arches. If necessary the canoe may be waded down on the R bank to below bridge. Immediately after the bridge, a shallow rapid where a portage will be necessary in low water. From here onwards the river is wide and deep, and is navigable by barges. Posts mark the river bank which may be submerged in times of flood.

6½   *Leitrim* (L).

10   *Lough Drumharlow* (R). Do not miss turning NW through this Lough and continuing by the *Boyle River* to *Lough Key*, one of the most beautiful lakes in Ireland. Boyle has rail and long-distance bus services and is probably the best starting point for a Shannon cruise. Start at Wooden Bridge, now made of concrete, 2 mls. from stn. From here to the Shannon is about 10 mls. with 1 lock. The Shannon runs to—

11½   *Carrick on Shannon Bridge*. Stn. 1½ mls. on the river broadens into Lough Corry.

18½   *Albert Lock*. A short canal through solid rock entered on the R, cutting out loop and weir. Canoe portage round lock on either side but bank is steep. The river continues past Jamestown and Drumsna, in a big loop. It is to be preferred to the canal as it is one of the prettiest parts on the river. Portage L at Jamestown Weir.

20¼   End of canal. After leaving the canal the river opens out into Loughs Tap, Boderg and Boffin, the last two being very pretty.

250

Kilglass Lough and the *small lakes around Grange* can be explored by following the channel under Carnadoe Bridge on the W side of Lough Boderg through beds of reeds into another part of the lough and Kilglass Lough. Some navigation markers have rotted away. At the SW end ("Grange" on O.S. map) a little river runs in from the W beside the ruins of the old quay. It becomes shallow under the bridge and remains rapid and shallow for nearly a mile ; wading may even be necessary at low water, but soon after the second bridge (look out for wire) it becomes deeper and quiet passing through fields into Lough Nablahy (1½ mls. long), a pleasant little lake with much sand at its upper end.

From here there is a chain of little lakes connected by stretches of river to be explored. Small hills and woods make the journey interesting as the loughs Clooncraff, Dooneen, Cloonahee and Nahincha and others, unnamed on the maps, can be reached.

Note. There is a shop at the Carnadoe creamery, but none at the quay at Grange so that supplies may have to be obtained from Strokestown. A travelling shop passes over Grange Bridge each afternoon (except Friday).

At the S end of Lough Boffin a tower is seen. Keep to the L of this to enter the river.

25½   *Roosky.* Weir and lock on main river below bridge.

29½   *Lough Forbes.* The *River Rinn* flows into the northern end of Lough Forbes. It flows through bog for most of its 7 mls. from *Lough Rinn*, which is reached by a short carry. The lake is well wooded and is about half a mile wide by almost 3 mls. long. Supplies at Johnston's Bridge. The N end of the lake is only 2 mls. from Mohill by road. The river and lake are most conveniently explored by a return trip from Lough Forbes up to Lough Rinn and back the same day.

33½   *Termonbarry.* Weir and lock below bridge. Portage round on L bank. Boathouse R.

41   *Lanesborough Bridge.*

42   *Lough Ree.* This lough stretches 19 mls. to Athlone. Many pretty islands. There are submerged rocks between the islands and shore in many places out of the navigable channel. Antiquities of interest are on Quaker Island, Inchboffin, and Saints Island, also Galey and Rindown Castles on W shore. Several side bays to E are worth exploring especially Killimure Lough.

45½   *Inchenagh.*

48¼   *Inchcloitrin* (ruined churches).

52¼   *Rindown Castle* (R).

     Black Islands. The bay to the E runs for about 5 mls. In it is Inchboffin. It receives the waters of the *Inny River.*

54½   *Inchmore* L.

55¾   *Yew Point* R.

56¾   *Hare Island.*

59½   *Outfall of Lough Ree.*

60½   *Athlone.* Stn., weir and lock below bridge. Portage over in low water. Except for Clonmacnoise the next 20 mls. are rather uninteresting.

64   *Long Island.*

70   *Clonmacnoise.* Also known as Seven Churches, as there are ruins on the L bank dating from the 6th century. Also a castle.

75   *Shannon Bridge.* Junction of *River Suck,* a slow, deep river, navigable from Ballinasloe and higher, but uninteresting.

81½   *Shannon Harbour.* Junction with Grand Canal from Dublin (82 mls., 44 locks).

83½   *Banagher Bridge.* Scenery begins to get more interesting.

88¼   *Meelick.* Weir, lock and short canal. A little to the L of the weir is a hinged plank in footbridge to facilitate lifting boats up or down. A rapid commences here. Channel runs to R side then crosses over to L before shallows at foot of rapid are reached. Or take arm to L 2½ mls. above Meelick, portage at the mill and rejoin main river below lock.

96¼   *Portumna Bridge.*

97   *Lough Derg.* 25 mls. long. A look out should be kept for submerged rocks. Some time will probably be spent exploring the islands and bays. Fine mountain scenery at lower end. Do not mistake Youghal Bay for the exit.

121½   *Killaloe.* The river is entered above the town. Bridge—good landing L above it. Bus to Limerick.

       Below the town the water level has been raised by a dam near O'Brien's Bridge, and the scenery is rather desolate with dead or dying trees sticking out of the water. The headrace to the power station at Ardnacrusha, which also serves as a canal starts at the dam. To enter the headrace without a permit a portage on the R bank will be necessary. The headrace is about 8 mls. long and is deadly monotonous, the view being shut out by high concrete walls. At the power station the canoe may be lifted out at a landing stage on the L bank and carried round to the tail race which shortly joins the tidal river at Limerick.

       It is suggested that the river be tried between the dam and Limerick. In this case the portage will be on the L side of the dam. At least one portage will be necessary at Castleconnell where the river falls over limestone ledges, and trouble may be experienced with the fishing interests.

135¼   *Limerick.* Long, handsome street, castle, cathedral. Stn. Below here the river widens out into an estuary, which extends for 50 mls. to the sea past Foynes and Shannon Airport. H.W. Limerick : Dover — 5 hrs.

306. Inny

The Inny, a tributary of the Shannon, flows from Lough Sheelin on the borders of Co. Cavan, Co. Meath, and Co. Westmeath, quite close to Lough Gowna and the source of the Erne. It runs S through Lough

Derravaragh into the big eastern bay of Lough Ree. As far as Lough Ivon there is practically no loss in height ; from there the fall is some 75 feet in 23 miles.

O.S. 12

Miles

0	*Lough Sheelin* (Mount Nugent). Some 7 or 8 mls. from Lough Ramor, from which the *Meath Blackwater* flows E to the *Boyne* (see Section 22).
4¾	*Finnea Bridge* just beyond the outfall.
5¼	*Lough Kinale*, ½ ml. long. Ballywillin Stn. is closed.
14½	*Coole Bridge*.
17¾	*Lough Derravaragh*, 6 mls. long, pretty at S end. The Inny leaves it 1½ mls. along W shore.
23½	*Ballinalack Bridge*.
25	*Lough Iron*. Outfall at Baronstown ½ ml. W.
36	Aqueduct of *Royal Canal*. Several weirs and falls—at Clynan, Newcastle, Ballymulvey and near Ballymahon.
43¼	*Ballymahon Bridge*.
45¼	*Shrule Bridge*. Mill above. Take R channel where river divides.
48¾	*Mouth of Inny into Lough Ree*. River divides just above.
62¾	*Athlone* on the Shannon.

THE LAKES OF THE WEST

307. Lough Gill

O.S. 7

Though not so well known, Lough Gill is judged by many to be the equal of Killarney. Apart from its scenery its chief interest to canoeists lies in its relation to both the Erne and the Shannon. It is readily accessible by bus from Belleek or Ballyshannon, and is only 10 miles by road from Lough Allen, at the head of the Shannon.

Access to Lough Gill is from Sligo (near the weir) by the River Garavogue, a charming run of 3 miles to the lake past the "Irish Stonehenge." There is a fine ruined abbey at Sligo, which has rail and long-distance bus services. The lough is well wooded and is surrounded by mountains and has several islands at the W end. At the E end the River Bonet can be taken to within 1½ miles of Dromahaire, the nearest point to Lough Allen. Lough Gill is 5½ miles long and nowhere exceeds 2 miles in width.

308. Loughs Conn and Cullin

O.S. 6

In Co. Mayo. Many islands and ruins ; overlooked by Nephin, 2,600 feet high. Lough Conn is about 11 miles long and 3 miles wide with fine sandy beaches. The outflow from Lough Cullin is into the *River Moy* which flows N to Ballina (stn.) with a tidal stretch to Killala. It is not known if it is feasible between the lake and tidal portion.

253

309. Loughs Carra, Mask and Corrib
O.S. 11 and 14

Lough Carra, in Co. Mayo, is a pretty lough about 7 miles long and 3 wide, connected with Lough Mask by a short river. Access at Partry by bus from Claremorris (stn.). Ballinrobe Stn. is closed. *Lough Mask*, also in Co. Mayo, is about 10 miles long and about 4 miles wide with two arms leading into Joyce's Country. There is a fine mountain range to the W. The whole district is very isolated. *Lough Corrib* is about 4 miles S of Lough Mask and mostly in Co. Galway. Portage is necessary as the river runs underground (sink-holes near Cong). It is about 20 miles long followed by 6 miles of river to Galway (stn.). Market cross and abbey at Cong. Ruins on various islands and at various points on the shores of the lough.

All three loughs are well worth a visit.

Weather. The loughs should be treated as the sea. Dead calm water to white horse waves within ¼ hour is a common occurrence, and the water can be unsafe for canoeing for days on end. Choppy seas are more common than a swell and, unlike the sea, the water calms down almost immediately the wind drops. There are no currents. A fair amount of rain is to be expected in most summers.

The water in Lough Carra, which is entirely on limestone, is an exceptionally clear, pale green colour, while Lough Mask and Lough Corrib, although clear, are a dark, peaty brown, as they are bordered by the mountains on the west. All the water is fit for drinking.

The chief navigational hazards are rocks. Not only near islands, but also in deep, open water, rocks an inch or two below the surface are liable to be encountered without notice. On Carra the rocks are of rotten limestone which crumbles at a touch, but on Mask and Corrib they are mostly of hard, jagged limestone. The southern half of Lough Corrib needs special care in this respect, but there is a well-marked navigation channel the whole length of this lough from Cong to Galway.

The O.S. maps of the area are of varying dates. Since they were drawn the level of the lakes has dropped, consequently there are numerous rocks and small islands not shown on the maps. Further work being carried out in Galway will soon drop the levels even more.

Camp sites can be found anywhere. Milk is readily available at farms, but meat is only obtainable in the larger villages. All the islands are believed to be uninhabited.

Access from Carra to Mask is down the "Keel Canal" (1 mile). Only the first ¼ mile is canal, then there is a weir (easy portage), the rest being a narrow river with shallow and rocks.

Access from Mask to Corrib involves a long portage as the water flows underground. The shortest way to do this seems to be from Ferry Bridge to Coalpark Quay, near Clonbur (4 miles); farm transport may be obtainable at Ferry Bridge.

The SE corner of Lough Mask (on which Lough Mask Castle stands) is at a lower level than the lough and is reached down the approach channel of the canal, which is swift-flowing between walls and ends in an unshootable rapid. The alterations in water levels make the O.S. maps particularly misleading in this area. The final outflow from Mask is through sinks near the canal entrance and the water rises again at several points near Cong to form the Cong River into Lough Corrib (1 mile with one weir). Cong village is a suitable launching point. (Bus from Galway.)

Of the "365 islands" in Lough Corrib the fourth longest, Inchagoill, is worth special mention. One mile long with sandy and rocky beaches and mostly wooded, it contains two fine ruined Romanesque churches and the burial place of St. Patrick's nephew.

The anglers' village of Oughterard can be reached up the Owenriff River which has a dredged channel for $\frac{1}{2}$ mile almost into the village.

Galway is approached by $4\frac{1}{2}$ miles of the Corrib River ; there are also two canals direct from the lough into the river affording slightly shorter routes.

At Galway there is a weir with drainage excavation work being carried out below (1959), but the right-hand channel above the weir leads to the canal. After $\frac{1}{2}$ mile there is a disused lock and a portage of over $\frac{1}{4}$ mile must be made to reach the sea in Claddagh Basin.

Galway Station is $\frac{1}{2}$ mile from the weir. The city is interesting for its past connections with Spain.

SOUTH AND EAST

310. KERRY COAST

The Kerry Coast is divided roughly into three great inlets, *Bantry Bay*, *Kenmare River* and *Dingle Bay*, although *Baltimore* and *Roaringwater Bays* well repay a visit. The journey is best commenced at Bantry, which is accessible from Cork.

General remarks. The tides along the coast are not, generally speaking, fierce, but local inquiries should be made about currents, at various points, e.g. Berehaven. There is always a long swell coming in from the W and SW, the motion of which is pleasant so long as it does not become a breaking sea. There is usually a short steep chop with the afternoon breeze on a hot day. Be prepared to be weatherbound for several days if conditions are not favourable.

Bantry Bay (O.S. 24). Leaving Bantry harbour, go to the northward of Whiddy Island and take a course for Glengarriff, taking care, once Whiddy Island is left astern, to bear away from the mainland again as there is a long reef about a $\frac{1}{4}$ mile off-shore. This is buoyed naturally because the swell is always breaking on it. Bantry Bay is exposed to the SW and there is always a swell. H.W. Bantry Harbour : Dover + 5 hours 6 min.

At Glengarriff do not fail to visit Garnish Island, which is a wonderful garden containing nearly every type of flora known to natural history.

After leaving Glengarriff make along the N shore for Adrigole Harbour, passing Shot Head en route. Along this stretch of coast keep well into the shore as it is generally a weather shore. From Adrigole to Berehaven will be a quiet trip, once the shelter of Bere Island is reached. Land at Castletown ; it is advisable to portage to Ardgroom on the *Kenmare River* (bus).

Kenmare River, a very beautiful inlet (O.S. 24 and 20). With good weather cross direct to Parknasilla and up the delightful river to Sneem, but if doubtful keep to the SE shore until sheltered waters are reached before trying to cross. Dangerous seas can get up in a very short time, though it is not as exposed as Bantry Bay. The mountains inland stand up well behind the blue waters of the inlet. At Kenmare at the head of the inlet the canoe can be packed for transport to the Lakes of Killarney some 10 miles by road.

Dingle Bay (O.S. 20), the largest and most exposed inlet of the Kerry Coast, should only be attempted in settled weather and then the E shore should be avoided. Ventry and Dingle Harbours offer good shelter and are worth a short stay, but the coast between there and Castlemaine is very inhospitable if it begins to blow.

311. LAKES OF KILLARNEY

(1-in. Special Map "Killarney")

Away from the tourist routes are long expanses of shore that are as lonely as anywhere in Ireland. Camping rather difficult. The best centre is St. Brendan's Club boathouse (write in advance to Secretary for permission). The Upper Lake is very fine and connected by the Long Range, which has a short rapid at Old Weir Bridge (towpath), with Muckross Lake and Lough Leane, near which stands Killarney (stn.). About 12 miles from the head of the Upper Lake to the foot of Lough Leane by the shortest route. From here the *River Laune* runs in about 12 miles to Killorglin, from which it is tidal into Castlemaine Harbour and Dingle Bays (difference in water level about 75 feet). Navigation difficult owing to shallowness.

312. LEE (CO. CORK)

The source of the River Lee is near Gouganebarra Lough, not far from Kenmare or Bantry. It flows east, through some lovely, semi-mountainous country, full of old, ruined castles, until it reaches Cork and Cork Harbour.

Formerly the river ran fast (though shallow in places) with one or two gorges that call for prior inspection. Now, however, two hydro-electric dams hold up the river over most of the distance between Macroom and Cork City. At present (1960) no canoeing is permitted on the reservoirs by the Electricity Board.

At Cork City the tidal portion starts and a trip can be made through the famous Cork Harbour and its various inlets to Cobh (Queenstown) and Crosshaven. Rail connection back to Cork from Cobh. H.W. Cork and Cobh approx.: Dover — 5¾ hours.

313. CORK BLACKWATER

The Blackwater is one of the loveliest and most varied rivers in the British Isles, with a good current, clear navigation, many small rapids, mostly easy, and only two portages between Mallow and the sea.

Access by rail to Mallow is very easy, as Mallow is on the main line, Dublin-Cork, and also on the Rosslare-Waterford-Killarney line. The latter follows the river valley for the greater part of its length.

The Blackwater can be made a part of a very fine extended cruise in South Ireland, starting with the Kerry Coast and Killarney, and followed by the Suir, the Nore and the Barrow—a cruise that can be thoroughly recommended.

The source of the Blackwater is in the hills to the NW of Killarney and its tributaries rise in the mountains to the S and SW where the rainfall is heavy. Its headwaters being entirely unregulated it is subject to a sharp rise and fall in level, after storms in the hills. Camp sites should therefore be chosen on raised ground. Tidal influence starts just below Lismore, but the tides are rarely strong. Unlike most tidal sections, however, the tidal part of the Blackwater between Cappoquin and the sea is very fine.

For most of its course the Blackwater flows along a charming valley, well wooded, between parallel ranges of heather-clad hills, turning abruptly from E to S at Cappoquin and then cutting through three or four ranges of hills at right-angles.

To link up with the Suir at Caher or Newcastle, a lorry may be hired in Youghal, or if a return trip is made on the flood, at Cappoquin, which is only 11 miles from the Suir. The road climbs right over the Knockmealdown Mountains, with striking views.

The Blackwater has been canoed from Rathmore (stn.), but Banteer (stn.) or Mallow (stn.) is more usual.

O.S. 21, 22

Grading : Rathmore - Mallow Grade II (III in spate)
Mallow - Lismore Grade I - II

Below Lismore : tidal.

High Water—Youghal : Dover — 5 hours 30 min.

Miles

0	*Rathmore* (stn.).
5	Road bridge.
9	*Keale Bridge*—many small rapids.
13	*Colthurst Bridge*.
13½	*Rathcool*—weir under bridge—shoot R or portage L.
17	Large weir—portage L.
18	*Ballymaquirk Bridge, Banteer*. Banteer stn. (Mallow-Killarney line) ½ ml.
22¼	Rapid on L, with 5 shoots. Take second from R or extreme L. Long running rapids to Lombardstown Bridge.
22½	*Roskeen Bridge*. Broken water, then weir under bridge (second arch from R).
25½	*Lombardstown Bridge*. Several heavy rapids.
28	Limestone cliff with ruined castle R, and weir—shoot L.
28½	*Longfield's Bridge*. Rapid, difficult in flood with high waves and bushes and overhanging trees.

257

Miles

31   *Mallow Railway Viaduct.* Mallow stn. ½ ml. From Mallow stn. turn R under bridge, and through a gate L beside the embankment. This is a more convenient starting point than the town bridge.

31½   *Mallow Bridge.* A fairly busy market town ; shops, hotels, castle. Caution at the step under the bridge.

36   *Carrig Island.* Castle L.

37½   *Killavullen Bridge.* Castletownroche stn. ½ ml. NE.

39   *Carrigacunna Castle* R. River bends sharp L to a fishing weir—shootable in good water.

41¾   *Bridgetown Abbey* L. Fine ruins on a picturesque site.

43½   *Convamore.* Burnt out mansion on the hill L. Scenery good.

44½   *Ballyhooley Bridge.* Stn. ¾ ml. N. Look out for step at the bridge.

47½   *Cregg Castle* L.

49   *Castle Hyde* L.

51   *Fermoy.* Shops, inns, etc. High weir running obliquely across the river, under the bridge. Keep R, and carry over dry part of weir ; or land L just above weir, cross small meadow and road ; or land at boat landing on R above weir and trolley across the bridge to L bank. Stn. 1 ml. L.

52   *Railway Bridge.*

54½   *Clondulane Weir.* Portage L close to weir unless water high, in which case land well back and inspect. Fish pass may be shootable.

60   *Mocollop Castle and House* L.

62¼   *Ballyduff Bridge.* Fine parklands between here and Lismore.

67½   *Lismore Weir.* There is a large, shootable gap in the weir. Portage R if preferred.

68   *Lismore Castle and Bridge.* Strong resemblance to Warwick Castle. Town and cathedrals R up the hill. Stn. 1 ml. S.

70¼   *Kilbree Castle* R.

71½   *Cappoquin Bridge.* Village and stn. L. Land at steps L to inspect tide-tables by the road. Railway to Waterford and Rosslare leaves the river at this point. River turns sharply to S. At low tide shingle bank exposed on L : channel swings to R. Fine views of Knockmealdown Mountains. Tidal.

75½   *Dromana House* L.

76½   *Villierstown* L. Ferry.

77½   Confl. of *Bride* L. Navigable about 7 mls. at high tide. Quays on either side at intervals from here on. Strancally Castles and Molana Abbey are passed on the R.

85¼   *Rincrew Castle* R. The estuary becomes very broad.

85¾   *Youghal Bridge.* Long girder bridge with swing span.

87¾   *Youghal Ferry.* Town R. Interesting. Shops, hotels, etc. Sir Walter Raleigh was once mayor of Youghal. His manor house can be seen. Landing at fishing quay, but it is better, unless the weather is rough, to continue beyond the town to the open sea and round to the R and land on sandy beach at—

88¾   *Youghal Beach.* Bus to Cork.

314. SUIR

The Suir (pronounced "shoor") rises to the NW of Templemore in Co. Tipperary and flows S through Thurles and Caher, turning N and then E when it comes up against the mountains to the N of the Black-water Valley. It continues through Clonmel and Carrick on Suir becoming broad and tidal and finally opening out into Waterford Harbour.

The fall in the river between Thurles and Caher is about 5 feet to the mile and there are some dozen or so weirs of various kinds. The scenery is fair but not remarkable. No recent reports of this upper part have been received. Beyond Caher the scenery is delightful to Clonmel and thereafter pleasant enough. From Caher to Clonmel the current is fast and the few weirs cause little trouble. After Clonmel the river becomes broader and deeper and beyond Carrick it is tidal and majestic.

O.S. 18, 22, 23

Grading : Caher-Clonmel : Rough Water I

Miles

0	*Thurles Bridge.* Stn. on Dublin-Cork main line. Shops, cathedral, etc. River deep, quiet and clear at Thurles, about as wide as a canal.
1¼	*Turtulla Bridge.* Two weirs, the lower of which may be shootable.
2½	*Cabragh Mill.* Portage.
3½	*Beakstown.* Two weirs and a fast, rocky stretch.
4½	*Holy Cross Abbey.* A weir above and below the bridge with fast water between.
6½	*Glenbane Bridge* across an island. Weir. Prospect before choosing which arm of the river to take.
11½	*Ardmayle Bridge.*
13½	*Camus Bridge.* Small falls above and under.
15	*Kilbriston Weir.*
18¼	*Golden Bridge.* Small falls above and under.
19¼	*Athassel Weir.* Abbey ½ ml. below R. Another weir about ½ ml. further on.
21	*Suir Castle Weir.* Fish ladder under castle ruins L.
21½	Bridge, fall under.
29¼	*Killemly Mill.* Portage R.
29¾	*Suir Mill and Weir.* Reported to be very awkward to pass.
30¾	*Caher Weir and Bridge* below. Awkward to pass. Castle. Stn., shops, etc. (pronounced "Care"). Delightful park scenery for 3 mls. or so followed by good views of the Knockmeal-down Mountains.
36¼	*Ardfinnan Weir and Bridge.* Weir only a foot or so high and can be passed at extreme top right hand side. Rough fall (shootable) under bridge.
41	*Newcastle Bridge.*
42½	*Confl. of Nier.* The Suir turns N.
47	*Knocklofty Bridge.* Charming scenery.

 51   *Clonmel*. Three bridges. Awkward portage at the weir, near the middle bridge. Land R above bridge and carry round through houses. Good shopping in town. Stn.
 53   *Twomilebridge*.
 56¼   *Kilsheelan Bridge*. Stn. L.
 63½   *Carrick on Suir*. Shops, etc. Castle. Stn. Weir above bridge, channel on R, covered at high water. Tidal from now on and a head-wind can be very much of a nuisance. The tidal stretch on the Suir is fine but not so good as those on the Blackwater or the Nore.
 68½   *Fiddown Bridge*. Stn. L. Either arm navigable.
 76   *Mount Congreve*. River turns NE.
 80   Railway bridge.
 81½   *Waterford Bridge*. Carry on beyond bridge to rowing club house ½ ml. further on, on the L. Stn. adjoins the bridge.
 84½   *Little Island*. King's Channel to the S round the island, 2 mls.
 87½   *Cheekpoint*. Junction with Barrow Estuary. 9 mls. more to the mouth of Waterford Harbour at Dunmore.
        High Water—Waterford : Dover — 5 hours.

315. NORE

The Nore rises in Co. Tipperary near the source of the Suir, and flows E and then S through Abbeyleix and Kilkenny to join the Barrow near New Ross.

From Abbeyleix the river is very narrow, and although it carries enough water it is often blocked by fallen trees. Woodland scenery. Five miles below is Castlewood Weir and a fish weir 2 miles further on. After another 1½ miles comes Archer Weir (several ledges close together), and another weir just above Ballyragget Bridge, 10½ miles from Abbeyleix. This is a better starting point.

From Abbeyleix to Inistiogue the fall is about 5 feet per mile, and there are numerous mills, weirs and rapids above Thomastown. From Thomastown where it plunges into a deep, winding valley, with fine wooded sides to Inistiogue is an almost continuous series of medium to heavy rapids, very enjoyable.

> *Grading* : Above Thomastown—not known.
> Thomastown-Inistiogue : Rough Water II.
> Inistiogue-New Ross : tidal.

O.S. 18, 19

Miles
 0   *Ballyragget Bridge*.
 ¼   Weir. Two bridges before—
 7¼   *Junction of Dineen* L. Heavy rapid, two channels. Mount Eagle Weir beyond. Two more weirs before—
 12¼   *Kilkenny*. At the weir above the bridge land on L. 2 weirs ½ ml. below St. John's Bridge. Then 6 weirs, one of them a fish weir, to—
 18½   *Bennettsbridge*. Weir. Rapids now more numerous.

21½   *Annamult Weir.* Two bridges between which is a series of rapids, the first—between an island and a wall overhung with high trees being taken on the L.

23½   Broken weir—shoot L ; followed by heavy rapid. ½ ml. further on a small broken weir with floodgate grill in centre—shoot L.

25   Viaduct.

25½   *Thomastown Weir.* Portage L. Thomastown Stn. ½ ml. up the hill to L. From here a continuous series of rapids through a lovely valley. Dysart Castle on R.

30¼   *Kilmacshane Bridge.*

32¼   *Inistioque Bridge.* Village R. Tidal influence starts just below. The scenery remains fine most of the way to the Barrow.

41   Junction with Barrow.

44½   *New Ross Bridge.* Land L at slope below bridge (buses and shops) or R at boathouse. Stn. closed. Bus service to Waterford and Rosslare.

High Water—New Ross : Dover — 5 hours (est.).

316. BARROW

The Barrow has been canoed from Mountmellick, but as Portarlington is on the main railway from Dublin to the SW, details are given from there. Between Mountmellick and Athy (pronounced "a-thigh") the Grand Canal roughly follows the line of the river. From Athy the Barrow is a navigation. From Portarlington to Monasterevan the width of the river varies very much, the banks are low and the countryside flat. Thereafter the river is large ; the scenery good just after Monasterevan and again before Athy. Below Athy the river is pretty, with a good stream, though it is possible to paddle upstream as well as down. The locks are operated by the Grand Canal and canoes are not officially allowed in the locks. It is, of course, possible to portage at the weirs. The Barrow makes a good cruise. Between St. Mullins, where the tidal part begins, and Mountgarrett the scenery is very fine. Here the river is wide, and after being joined by the tidal Nore and the Suir it broadens into Waterford Harbour.

High Water—New Ross : Dover — 5 hours (est.)
O.S. 16, 19, 23

0   *Portarlington.* Stn. Lea Castle 3 mls. or so beyond. No portages before Athy, except such as may be required for fallen trees, wire, etc.

7   *Monasterevan Bridge.* ¼ ml. above, Grand Canal aqueduct. Stn. Banks rather low and flat for the greater part of the way to Athy.

21   *Athy Weir.* Portage easy. Bridge just below. Stn. The Canal joins the river below the bridge, and it is now a navigation. Four locks—at Ardree, Levitstown, Newtown and Bestfield.

33   *Carlow*. Shops, castle, stn. Carlow Lock below bridge. At
         Clogrenan lock cut 1½ mls. further on, take weir stream to L.
         The fall is slight, over a ledge halfway down. Locks at
         Milford Mills and Rathvinden.
40¾ *Leighlinbridge*. Lock at Rathellin.
44   *Bagenalstown* L. Lock.
45½ Railway bridge. 3 locks follow.
50   *Goresbridge* R. (Stn. closed.) Lock. From here to St. Mullins is
         one of the finest stretches of the river. Locks at Ballyteige,
         Borris, Ballynagraigue, Clashgruny, and Ballykeenan.
59¼ *Graiguenamanagh Bridge*. The river flows alongside Brandon Hill.
         Locks at Tinnahinch, Knockeen and Carriglead.
62¼ *St. Mullin's Lock*. The river is tidal below here and the scenery
         is very fine.
70¼ *Mountgarrett Bridge*.
71½ *Ringwood*—Junction of Nore.
74¼ *New Ross Bridge*. Land at slope below bridge L (buses and
         shops) or at boathouse R. Stn. closed. Bus service to
         Waterford and Rosslare). Shops, etc., L.
83   *Ballinlaw Ferry*.
85½ *Cheekpoint*. Junction of Suir. Waterford 5½ mls. up the Suir.
         Dunbrody Creek L (abbey ruins).
87½ *Passage East* R.
         Ballyhack L. The estuary becomes very wide.
90¼ *Duncannon* on E shore.
93¼ *Dunmore East* on W shore.
         High Water : Dover — 5 hours 25 min.

317. SLANEY

The Slaney rises in the mountains of Co. Wicklow and flows S through
a charming valley into Wexford Harbour. Above Enniscorthy it is a
fast, clear, shallow stream, with rocky cataracts from time to time.
Few recent trips on this river have been reported, and the information
given below indicates the type of difficulty to be met with rather than
a detailed description. The chief rapids should be inspected to see
whether they are shootable.

The Slaney is canoeable from Stratford 4 miles above Baltinglass
when the river is fairly full. Narrow and rocky. Weir just before
Baltinglass—portage L. From there to Tullow (approx. 17 miles) there
are many boulders. About 3 miles before Tullow an unshootable mill
cataract.

O.S. 19, 23

0   *Tullow Bridge*. Preferable to start below mill weir a few hundred
         yards lower down, L bank. Shallow stretches. Two mills in
         the first 3 mls.

Miles

3   *Junction of River Derreen* (L).

3¼ *Aghada Weir* followed by some shallows and a ¼ ml. of cataract between rocks. Possibly the mill leat would enable this to be avoided.

4   *Aghada Bridge.* After a stretch of quieter water, a similar cataract occurs near Ballintemple House at the head of—

6   *Monaughrim Glen,* a fine wooded ravine.

8¼ *Kilcarry Bridge.* Deep rapid under R of bridge.

8½ *Kilcarry Mill.* Three ledges and a long cataract after. From this point rapids are frequent, some boisterous, but mostly shootable.

10½ *Junction of River Derry* (L) and *Kildavin Bridge.*

13½ *Newtownbarry (Bunclody) Bridge.*

15½ *Clohamon Bridge.* Mill weir below.

20½ *Ballycarney Bridge.* Fall underneath.

22½ *Farmley Weir,* a deep broken weir. Let down near R bank.

23¼ *Scarawalsh Bridge.* Small fall underneath.

28   *Enniscorthy Bridge.* Stn. Abrupt change to a deep, tidal stream.

31½ *Edermine Ferry Bridge.* Stn.

33¾ *Macmine Junction Station* (R).

37   *Killurin Bridge.* Stn.

41   *Ferrycarrig Bridge.*

43   *Wexford Bridge.* Boathouse above bridge. Stns., hotels, etc. Wexford Harbour widens out considerably and opens into the sea at Rosslare Point.

High Water—Wexford : Dover — 3½ hours.

318. GRAND CANAL

The Grand Canal (controlled by C.I.E., Canal Section, James' Street, Dublin) connects Dublin with the Shannon at Shannon Harbour, and the Barrow at Athy.

Dublin (Ringsend)-Shannon Harbour : 83 miles ; 44 locks.

Dublin-Athy : 54¼ miles ; 29 locks.

319. ROYAL CANAL

The Royal Canal connects Dublin with the Shannon at Parmonbarry (90½ miles, 47 locks). The scenery is not of a high order. The canal crosses the Inny (see Section 306) which leads into Lough Ree and the Shannon, and the Boyne at Clonard (see Section 311). Particulars of charges, permits, etc.—apply to C.I.E., Traffic Department, Canal Section, James' Street Harbour, Dublin, for information.

320. LIFFEY

This is canoeable but may be very laborious owing to portages. It rises in the hills to the S of Dublin and flows in a semi-circular course to the sea at Dublin. There is a big hydro-electric reservoir at Poulaphouca 6½ miles long. The tail race returns to the river near Ballymore Eustace, below which the river is subject to sharp rises when the power stations starts up. Between Cellbridge and Leixlip is another reservoir 2 miles long but not more than 100 yards wide.

Miles
0	*Poulaphouca Dam.*
¼	At the power station below Poulaphouca Dam the water returns to river.
1¼	*Golden Falls Dam* and equalising reservoir. Long portage either side.
1¾	*Ballymore Eustace.*
7¾	*Kilcullen.*
12¾	*Newbridge* L.
18¾	Road bridge—Naas 3 miles R.
20¾	*Grand Canal aqueduct.*
23	Road bridge.
27	*Straffen* L.
32	*Cellbridge*—beginning of Leixlip reservoir.
35½	*Leixlip power station.* Portage R. Leixlip Town L.
46	*Dublin.*

The grading of difficulty varies greatly according to water level. If water low, many awkward portages.

321. BOYNE

This is reported to be canoeable from above the Royal Canal Aqueduct at Clonard : the scenery is reported to be good most of the way. The upper parts are apt to be weedy. No recent reports have been received of this river and a detailed description cannot therefore be given.

Miles
0	*Clonard, Canal Aqueduct.* River narrow in places, and fast. Several weirs on approaching—
15¼	*Trim.* About 6 weirs between here and—
27¾	*Navan.* From here the Boyne was a navigation, partly by canal cut and partly using the river itself. On the old river there are about 13 weirs before Slane. Scenery good.
35½	*Slane.* About 4 weirs before Drogheda.
47½	*Drogheda.* Boathouse below rly. bridge.
	High Water : Dover + 12 min.

322. Meath Blackwater

A tributary of the *Boyne*, which it joins at Navan. This is a slow river, which is fairly easy to ascend, with 5 or 6 weirs, and it can be used as a canoe route from the Boyne to the Shannon, by way of Lough Ramor and Lough Sheelin on the *Inny* (see Section 306). The distance from Navan to Lough Ramor is 27 miles, and there would be a road portage of about 8 miles to Lough Sheelin.

INDEX

*Note.   The above are **not** page numbers*

*Note. The above are **not** page numbers*

*Note. The above are **not** page numbers*

*Note. The above are **not** page numbers*

*Note. The above are **not** page numbers*

Note. *The above are* **not** *page numbers*

ENQUIRY FORM

FOR INDIVIDUAL MEMBERSHIP

To THE MEMBERSHIP SECRETARY
British Canoe Union
26-29 Park Crescent
London, W.1

Please send details about Individual Membership of the Union

FULL NAME (Mr./Mrs./Miss)...
(*block capitals*)

ADDRESS...

....

Date of Birth (*if under* 19)..

Interests :
        Touring/Racing/Canoe Slalom/Sailing/Teaching/Armchair

Canoe Clubs (if any)................................ Can you swim?................................

DATE..   SIGNED..

[P.T.O.

To THE GENERAL SECRETARY

British Canoe Union
26-29 Park Crescent
London, W.1

Please send me the current list of canoe clubs in my area affiliated to the Union. I enclose 4d. stamp for reply.

NAME ....

ADDRESS ....

....

To THE GENERAL SECRETARY

British Canoe Union
26-29 Park Crescent
London, W.1

Please send me the Book and Map List. I enclosed 4d. stamp for reply.

NAME ....

ADDRESS ....

....